SOUND SALISH STRAITS

Central Salish Sea Cultures

Jay Miller, PhD

Please Report Typo Gnomes!

© 2019

contents

SOUND SALISH STRAITS

1 Intro Coast Salish Family

7 ~ PANORAMIC SENSE OF PLACE

8   Stockaders
9   Duhlelip
12   Spirit Bonds
15   Sharing Strategies
17   Feast Flee Fight Fidget
19   Culture & Survival
20   Shamans
21   Shakers
22   Attacks

26 ~ PLACES ALONG THE SKAGIT DRAINAGE SYSTEM

26   codes   26 Map
26   Skagit Mouths
27   Burlington
30   Mt Vernon
31   Sedro Woolley
33   Lyman Hamilton
34   Baker Concrete 34
35   Birdsview
36   Rockport
38   Marblemount
38   Newhalem, Ross Lake
39   Tributaries 39 Nookachamps 40 Illabot 40 Cascade
42   Stillaguamish 41

45 ~ ANCESTRAL TRIBES

46 Rituals Growlers Ghost Feedings Redeemng
47 Shields sgʷədiləč
48 Legendary Beginnings
49 Public Privileged
50 Robe Boy ~ x̣uyaliċa
51   Starchild
52 Renowned Names
53   ləx̣albid kʷəskadəb
54   petiyus sx̣ʼəbibtəkəd
55   ẏagʷało
56 Portage
57 Duhkwautsub War
59 paqʼ̇ʷ

61 ~ REDEEMING

contents
67 ROCK & LOGJAM

67 Intro
67   Ancestors kʷəskadəb
71   ləx̣albid
72 Drainages
73 Nets
73 Beliefs
74 Katzie
75 Nuuxalk
77 Lushootseed Chronologies
79 Finale

80 NAMING CULTURE

81 Institutions
82   Person ~ Blood Place ~ Mud
83   Kin
84   House
85 Resources Kʷaskadub
89 Conclusions

90 SAANICH 1935

93   Economic Cycle
95   Hunting
100   Fishing
105 Dwellings
112 Clothing
114 Adornment
115 Social Organization
120 Warfare
125 Childhood
127 Adolescence
132 Marriage
135 Childbirth
136 Funerals
139 Potlatches
143 Games
145 Nature & Man
148 Appendices A ~ Willow Net B ~ 1st Salmon 151 C ~ puberty D ~ Songhees puberty
        E ~ funerals F ~ funeral feasts 156 G ~ kin terms
157 Diamond Jenness (1886 – 1969)
160 Lushootseed & Northern Straits Languages
162 Contrasts (55) of Northern (NL) and Southern (SL) Lushootseed
164 Saanich ~ SENĆOŦEN ~ sənčaθən

165 FINALE

166 Censuses 166 Swinomish 168 Snoqualmie 171

172 Salishan Toponymy
177 Bibliography 185
190 Amazon

Notes #1-124
Index 186-189

SOUND SALISH STRAITS

Introduction

The European unsettling of the Salish Sea gave rise to famed Indien[1] war lords whose names are still passed down through native families. Pandemics killed off thousands and, in their aftermath, upriver survivors moved down to depleted shorelines while strong leaders claimed and fortified rich resource locations.

One such is the innocuously named Granny's Hill, once with a native fort at its summit, at the elbow of the Samish River where a shift in language speakers replaced devastated Lushootseed Skagit speakers with Straits Samish under the leadership of a line of war lords ~ warriors, fathers to sons, named čədəsqidəb among Lushootseeds and čənəsqinəm among Samish, showing the regular shift of older B > M and older D > N in this region. Both languages belong to the Coast Salish family (below), with related Interior Salish languages across the Cascade Mountains to the east.

Samish brought with them a conflict with other Northern Straits speakers of WSANEC ~ Saanich, who took the trophy head of at least one čədəsqidəb back to the Saanich Peninsula. More than martial trophies, raiders sought slaves to sell, loot to trade, and deeds of glory for their names and titles. Thus to explore the culture, heritage, and tradition of northern Puget Sound, cross-water natives on Straits of Georgia and Juan de Fuca along the angle of southern Vancouver Island are included herein, as they have been historically interlinked via intermarriage, native religion, and conflicts, of amity and enmity. In 1860, US Indien agent Robert Fay ransomed two Skykomish women and a boy enslaved by Vancouver Island raiders.

These residents spoke Coast Salish languages, as charted here:

COAST SALISHAN FAMILY

Nuxalk ~ Bella Coola

Central
  Comox
  Pentlatch
  Sechelt
  Squamish
  Halkomelem
  Cowichan
  Musqueam
  Chilliwack

Straits* {of Georgia, of Juan de Fuca}
  Northern
  Southern

---

[1] Indien, from the Indies not India, refers to the natives of the Americas. A tilde ~ marks equivalents, {curved brackets} adds commentary.

Nooksak

Lushootseed* ~ Puget Sound Salish
  Northern ~ Skagit
  Southern ~ Nisqually ~ tx^{w}lshootseed

Twana ~ Skokomish
Tsamosan
  Quinault ~ Queets
  Upper Chehalis
  Upper Cowlitz[2]

Tillamook

More specifically, these are adjoining branches of Straits, distinguished by /l/ or /y/ phonemes, and Lushootseed:

Straits

Northern {/l/}
  Semiahmoo
  Lummi ~ Klalakamish ~ Swallah
  Samish
  Saanich ~x^{w}sanəč
  Songhees ~ Songish ~ Lkungen
  Sooke {/y/}
Southern {/y/}
  Klallam ~ S'kallam

Lushootseed ~ Puget Salish

Northern
  Skagit ~ Sauk-Suiattle
  Swinomish
  Snohomish ~ Skykomish
Southern ~ Whulshootseed
  Suquamish
  Snoqualmi
  Duwamish ~ Muckleshoot
  Puyallup
  Nisqually
  Steilacoom
  Sahewamish ~ Squaxin

---

[2] Cowlitz spoke seven languages: Salishan Upper Cowlitz, Sahaptin Taitnapam, Chinookan Lower Chehalis, Athapaskan Swaal, and Chinuk WaWa, in addition to Metis French, English, and other native languages.

Lushootseed has obvious northern and southern dialect chains, with suggestions of five internal dialects. Those of the north, with the larger population and proximity to the Coast Salish heartland on Boundary Bay and the Lower Fraser River, were Skagit (including the Sauk-Suiattle), Swinomish, and the Snohomish (including the Skykomish); while south of Whidbey Island, Whulshootseed dialects were Suquamish, Snoqualmi, Duwamish (including Muckleshoot), Puyallup, Nisqually, Steilacoom, and Sahewamish at the south, together with Suquamish on the west side. Important linguistic distinctions are respective accents on the first or second vowel of the basic root of a word, separate names for salmon species, some body parts, and some artifacts.

Culturally, the pattern number 4 (repetitions done four times) is used in the north but 5 in the south, as well as by Columbia River Chinooks and upriver Plateau tribes. Salishans of the inland, upriver, and southern Sound also held Plateau ideals of a kin-based society, while those of the Coast emphasized class. Southern Puget Sound culture emphasizes spirit quests, with less concern for inherited privileges than the Northerners.

Socially, the South Sound also stood apart because it had a smaller population, tribes without namesake rivers, less elaborated society, specialized large-mammal harpooners, earlier European contact overland, then at HBC Fort Nisqually, more subsequent urbanization, and the innovative Indian Shaker Church founded by John and Mary Slocum.

Most Lushootseed "tribes" occupied a single river drainage, whose flow provided cohesion and identity to otherwise diverse communities, camps, and resorts. Rank and class conscious natives maintained prestigious academies for their children, social and ceremonial clubs with elaborate initiations and feasts, and intermarriage networks extolling their pedigrees and privileges. While all men hunted, career hunters were men with talents and powers to harpoon sea mammals or undertake the arduous task of hunting mountain goats. In the southern Sound, at least, these specialized hunters wore clothing and used equipment, such as quivers, made of cougar skin. Male careers were canoe maker, hunter, storyteller, gambler, harpooner, carpenter, warrior, ritualist, while women excelled as midwives, weavers, basketmakers.

Historically, Lushootseeds and Whulshootseeds raided each other for slaves. At least one prominent northern family maintained a fortified home in the South Sound at Quartermaster Harbor to take advantage of nearby Fort Nisqually, intermarry with Puyallup women, and raid Duwamish communities to take slaves. No southern colonies are known in the North Sound, though there was intermarriage among noble families in the past couple centuries. That Whulsootseed kept NL slaves is illustrated by the life of Dr Simon, born a Snohomish, owned at Minter, and redeemed by William Tolmie at Ft Nisqually.

Euro-American settlers established early hubs in the South Sound, preempting Fort Nisqually and Cowlitz Prairie founded by the Hudson Bay Company ~ HBC in 1833. Americans developed Olympia, which became the state capitol, Steilacoom, and Tacoma, which long delayed the eventually dominance of Seattle. Natives became dependent on manufactured trade goods, purchased by their trapped furs and wage labor. Logging became a source of funds for many native men, as cooking, housekeeping, and laundry did for native women. Some families soon became favorites of enterprising patrons, such as Ezra Meeker, who employed straw bosses to obtain and retain native workers for his lucrative hop fields.

Native adzed-plank houses, bastions of communal life, were early targets of American authority. In 1871, Reverend Myron Eells, missionary and agent at Skokomish, had Klallam houses on the Port Townsend beach burned in a vain attempt to force native resident to move to his reservation. Adding to his clout was his brother Edwin, Indien Agent for the region, and membership in the Masonics. About 1874, loggers desiring lands already improved, burned down the plank homes at Minter Creek on the Key Peninsula across from Tacoma, claimed it as homestead and built their own cabins. Hostilities were averted because these landgrabbers deliberately kept away from the aboriginal Glen Cove fishery where this community rebuilt, until forced on to reservations by later homesteaders and federal agents.

Across Puget Sound and Georgia Straits, the recent publication of Diamond Jenness's 1935 Saanich manuscript, tales, and fieldnotes makes it widely available, but Richling's light editing rearranged its overall organization, which is retained in its original order herein. Our table of contents compares these differences {with revised order between curved brackets} of "reducing the number of original chapters from sixteen to nine and … moving all except tabular material from appendices (and footnotes) into corresponding portions of the main body" and acknowledging the dozen sources, from their sixties through eighties, for these materials, including Saanich: Johnny Caxton of Tsawout ~ East Reserve, Edward Jim of Tseycum ~ Patricia Bay, David & Mrs Latasse of Tsartlip ~ Brentwood Bay, Louis Pelkey of Tsawout, Tom Paul of Tsartlip; along with Annie & Kaypemulthw Bob of Halalt ~ Westholme, Jimmy Fraser of Esquimalt, Johnson of Quamichan, George Kwakaston of Koksilah, Albert Westly of Nanaimo (Richling 2016: vi, vii, ix). Sages of the lower Fraser River were Peter Pierre of Katzie and William Sepass of Sardis. Saanich at Pauquachen, a fourth reserve, were skipped during his October-November 1935 fieldwork based out of Sidney, BC.

Crossborder links also involved resettlements since Tseycum ~ Patricia Bay people looted Mill Bay then "moved to Everett {Tulalip?}, in the US [and] Patricia Bay was re-occupied, by the Sidney Indians" (Richling 2016: 173).

My intent is to give a treasury trove of Salish cultures of central Salish Sea, especially the Skagit Drainage and BC Straits, for future use by interested scholars and active participants. My light editing has dealt with over punctuation, especially commas, {Miller's insertions within curved brackets}, capital letters added to identify appendices, but retaining Jenness's New Zealander spellings of camass, cohoe, though his figures, photos, and map are {AWOL}.

We begin in the US with overviews of Puget Sound, apt examples of shifting lands, and ethnographic basics, review place name maps along the Skagit system, highlight aspects of the shoreline, focus on the epitome Redeeming rite, analyze systems, with key repetitions, of temporal chronology and of prestigious namings, and then move across the Straits into Canadian BC territories of the 1935 Saanich, rivals and ritualists on Vancouver Island. At the end are a biography of Diamond Jenness, charts of language details, especially phonology, and dual bibliographies, the first devoted to toponomy and the second to cited references.

To set the stage, here are the compared Saanich tables of contents, for reference with Puget Salish materials immediately following.

Saanich

The Saanich Indiens of Vancouver Island
Diamond Jenness

1 Introduction   {1: 1}
3 Economic Cycle   {2: 6}
5 Hunting   {3: Dwellings 23}
        deer & elk 6
        deer net 6
        goats 8
        waterfowl 8
        other birds 9
        seals & porpoises 9
        sealions 9
        whaling 9

10 Fishing   {4: Clothing & Personal Adornment 35}
        Cod 10
        Halibut 11
        Dogfish 11
        Sturgeon 11
        Herring & Oolakan 11
        Salmon 12
        Purse net, count 13
        Clams 14
        Miscellaneous sea foods 14

15 Dwellings
        furniture 20
        cooking 21 camas, fernroots,

22 Clothing
24 Adornment

24 Social Organization   {5: Social Organization & Potlatch 40}

29 Warfare   {6: Warfare & Feuds 52}

34 Childhood   {7: Childhood & Adolescence 58}
36 Adolescence
41 Marriage   {8: Marriage, Childbirth & Death 71}
44 Childbirth

45 Funeral   {9: Man & Nature 83}

48 Potlatches   {10: Guardian Spirits 89}

Saanich

51 Games   {11: Illness & Medicine 107}

53 Nature & Man   {12: Spirit Dancing 117}

Appendices

56 A ~ Origin of the Willow Fishnet = sgwala   {A Saanich & Cowichan Calendars 177}

57 B ~ First Salmon Ceremonies   {B Saanich & Cowichan Kin Terms 178 }

59 C ~ Puberty   {C Cat's Cradles 180}

59 D ~ Songhese Puberty   {D Place Names 181}

61 E ~ Funerals   {E Orthography 184}

63 F ~ Funeral Feast

64 G ~ Terms of Relationship

65 Bib ~ Edits ~ Bio   Notes # 1-82   {bib 185 index 189}

PANORAMIC SENSE OF PLACE

The basin around Puget Sound, with Seattle at its center, has long been the home of the Lushootseed Coast Salish.[3] Cascading from its rim of mountain ranges, each river was graced with winter towns, villages, hamlets, and seasonal camps (resorts) of a distinct tribal community, interacting with all the others near and far to give order and meaning to Lushootseed culture.[4]

The Sound, 40 miles wide and 170 miles long, encompassing a thousand miles of shoreline, includes such ecologically diverse habitats as islands, deltas, tide flats, marshes, estuaries, shallow bays, and beaches. Away from the shore, terrain is hilly, interspersed with lakes, and dense with undergrowth beneath a mixed forest of Douglas fir, red alder, grand fir, big leaf maple, and cottonwood. Scattered parklands, kept grassy by annual burnings set by natives, included oak and Douglas fir. Edible plants ranged from a host of berries to clover, cow parsnip, fern, *wapato* (wild potato), and camas. Plentiful game, living in diverse microenvironments, comprised shellfish, ocean fish, porpoise, seal, sea lion, waterfowl, deer, elk, bear, otter, raccoon, beaver, mountain goat, and the seasonal runs of salmon, smelt, and herring (Nelson 1990: 481).

Salishans of the coast emphasized class, while those of the inland, upriver, and southern Sound held Plateau ideals of a kin-based society. "Southern Puget Sound culture emphasized spirit quests and had a lesser emphasis on inherited privileges than the Northerners" (Roberts 1975: 32, 35, 77). Each "tribe" occupied an overall river drainage, whose flow provided cohesion and identity to an otherwise diverse collection of communities and camps, except on the east and west sides of Puget Sound.

The drainage of the Duwamish once had a complex H-like trellis pattern, with an important hub on the interconnecting Black River, since obliterated to build downtown Renton in the aftermath of redirecting the outflow of Lake Washington through the Ballard locks.

The Sahewamish, now based at Squaxon Island, derived their name for a portage ('əhiw̓) between the southern Sound and Hood Canal. After epidemics devastated their community, particularly when confined to the island during the 1855 Treaty War, the toe of the canal was resettled by Skokomish Twana (see below).

The Suquamish ancestral territory was the Kitsap Peninsula between the Sound and upper Hood Canal. Their homeland, significantly, lacked any major rivers, so their subsistence adaptation required extensive travel to collect resources needed for winter, in addition to the harvesting of local foods from sheltered bays, creeks, and streams.[5]

---

[3] Lushootseed derives from the word stem <u>ləsh</u> meaning specifically the sheltered saltwater of Puget Sound, with <u>-ucid</u> for 'river, mouth, language'.

[4] Though the seasonal distinction between towns and camps is ingrained in the literature, elders speak of traditional summer camps as more like resorts. Of course, this may be more a reflection of their young age, with hard work done by adults, but the image is telling. Similarly, native settlements themselves require more varied and suitable English terms such as hamlet, haven, or town.

[5] By an irony of history, a writer at Fort Langley on the Fraser River noted the arrival of Suquamish with salmon in their canoe, which allowed US Federal Judge George Boldt (Finding of Fact #5, Order of 18 April 1975) to decree to their descendants such fishing rights in Canadian waters,

For Lushootseed peoples, closely related yet linguistically distinct Coast Salishan neighbors were, to the north, the Nooksak, to the west, the Twana (particularly the five interrelated Skokomish towns at the elbow of Hood Canal), to the south, the Chehalis, and, to the northwest, the Straits (of Juan de Fuca) Salishans of Samish, Lummi, and Klallam.

Although seldom reported, all traditional territories were carefully tended by their occupants.[6] As Richard White (1980: 20), eminent ecological historian, noted "The Salish used fire not only to maintain their nettle grounds, but also as an instrument for shaping the ecology...." While among Chehalis, Harrington (1942: Reel 017, frame 0024) was told by a local minister that tribes in Puget Sound trimmed the lower branches off trees to make some of the forest beautiful, shaded, and park-like.

After epidemics spread by diseased Europeans devastated native populations, survivors scattered to safe locations as insulated upland or island communities expanded into depopulated areas.

Stockaders

Throughout Native America, land usage was a sacred trust, derived from on-going relations with resident immortals, as well illustrated by the movement of Lummi to their present location a few centuries ago (Curtis 1913: 26-30).

Living on Orcas island, Lummis had routinely taken clams and elk from the mainland whose aboriginal residents on Bellingham and Lummi Bays, probable Nooksak speakers (Amoss 1978: 4), were known as Stockaders, benefiting from huge salmon runs through the delta of the Nooksak River. With other Straits speakers, Lummi ancestors had coveted this abundance, but specialized in the used of reef nets suspended from canoes at fixed location (Stewart 1977: 93-94).[7] Therefore, they did not know how to build river weirs, knowledge that more properly involved prayers and rituals than mere technology.

Their eventual claim is expressed in a story about a Lummi husband who insulted his Stockader wife (noting her fat legs from eating steelhead), and was beheaded by her brothers. Later his own brother quested for great power and received a club that killed whole villages.

After such depopulation from raids (and more devastating epidemics), Lummi colonists hired Stockader survivors to continue to build weirs. At the end of each season, Lummi pulled up the frameworks and hid the pieces on the north end of Lummi Island, but, knowing this location, Stockaders retrieved the posts to resell them to the Lummi every spring. Eventually, a

---

though unenforceable. Acknowledging this one instance because it was written ignores all the others known to have occurred without visible documentation.

[6] Since a standard argument for taking native homelands was that settlers were better able to "improve the land by conquering nature," it is significant that scholars have only recently, first in native California and the Great Plains, listened to elders explaining how fire was used to maintain open grasslands, hunting grounds, and berry patches. As Walter Crockett, an early settler on Whidbey Island, wrote in 1853, the primary goal of pioneer farming was "to get the land subdued and the wilde nature out of it" (White 1980: 35).

[7] Barnett (1955: 13) attributed the invention of reef netting techniques to Straits appreciation of available ocean shoals in compensation for poor local salmon streams.

few Lummi married, adopted, or befriended Stockaders to learn for themselves how to make weirs. Subsequently, this knowledge was passed down through families with Lummi descendants (Riley 1955).[8]

What accounts fail to grasp, however, is that while Lummis could easily build such a fence trap, they believed it would be ineffective because they did not have necessary *dicta* to assure success with Stockader local immortals, who spiritually provide the fish.

Duhlelip

As these Straits speakers settled at river mouths on the decimated mainland, so some Twana moved to the tip of Hood Canal, using a famous portage along a trail from Gorst on Sinclair Inlet to Belfair. Elmendorf (1960: 271) was told that a Twana looking for a lost canoe between 1800-10 "discovered" this good village site, rich in waterfowl, so he led a colony from the Skokomish to settle the village of Duhlelap on Big Mission Creek, where, in respect, these Twana retained its Lushootseed name.[9] Suquamish maintained links with this area by using Mission Lake and nearby mountains for vision quests. As recently as the early 1900s, Suquamish were camping and fishing at the mouth of the Tahuya River, southwest of Belfair.

Other trails between the Sound and Canal crossed the Kitsap Peninsula from Dye Inlet, from the villages at Chico-Erland Point to Seabeck, from Poulsbo (called Mapleville in Lushootseed), from the village at Suquamish to Port Gamble, and from Silverdale, a route so useful it has been paved as the Anderson Hill Road.

Because water travel predominated, portages were crucial throughout the area, highlighted by the self-designation of the Sahewamish. The Skagits had extensive contacts with their neighbors because those upriver had to portage over to the lower Samish or Stillaguamish Rivers to reach salt water (Collins 1974: 39), bypassing a log jam, two miles long, that blocked the river above Mount Vernon until it was dynamited away in 1878.

Across the Cascades were the Interior Salishans and Sahaptians of the Plateau culture area. Though such mountain walls have often been regarded as a barrier, sloping river valleys and upland trails enabled selective exchanges. In ancient times, moreover, this range seems to have been common territory where a resident population remained intermediate between coastal and inland traditions. Certainly, the historic closeness of the Skagit and Chelan suggest a long period of such interactions.

Indeed, given a large prehistoric population and seasonal mobility, including summer sojourns in the peaks, the Cascades were probably a distinct subcultural region. Both Onat (1990: 12) and Bruseth (1950: 13) propose ancient residents along some peaks, but little research has been devoted to their range and extent. Further south, the California Sierras did indeed form such a separate and distinct subprovince.

---

[8] A Lummi perspective on these events, now largely self-suppressed to forge unity within the modern reservation community, is provided in "How the Lummi People Came to their Present Location and How they got their Name" by Al Charles (Charles, Demers, and Bowman 1978).

[9] Variant English spellings of the same word, both Duhlelap and Tulalip mean "the end far away".

In terms of the overall Puget Basin, Marian Smith,[10] relying on her fieldwork with Puyallup and Nisqually, devised a spatial model, based on increasing levels of integration, for describing how native peoples related to their watersheds. She explicitly recognized that the greatest allegiance and loyalty coincided with the entire drainage system.

Within each watershed, group affiliations became more expansive in terms of (a) hearth mates eating together, (b) households of all residents, (c) birthright locals - those born there in contrast to inlaws, visitors, and foreigners, (d) settlements and resorts, (e) community networks, (f) tributary drainages, and (g) the entire drainage.

Culturally, these units, increasing in size, included notions of person (combining body, mind, and soul with spirit allies), of house (including hearthers, locals, and distant kin), of canoe (transport across time and space, distinguished as forest, prairie, river, or sea), and of world (the drainage linked both to resident immortals and to more remote peoples and places through marriage, ritual, and trade).

Membership within each unit derived from the subtle, discerning, and valued appreciation of customs such that insiders, in contrast to outsiders, understood the complexities of "the feud, the snub, the verbal innuendo" and accordingly "were appropriate guests for a ceremonial feast" (Roberts 1975: 79).

Major nodes in this overall system were cedar plank houses located along the shore near spots rich in local resources, such as a salmon stream, berry patch, and hunting territory. Even spirit beings lived in such houses, though rarely reported (see Jacob's quest) with the detail characteristic of the more northern Tsimshian, Haida, and Tlingit. Beyond this house node were at least three concentric rings occupied by allies, by competitors for regional status, and, third, by strangers (Roberts 1975: 82).

The mountains were thickly coated with evergreen trees, including the Western red cedar, whose straight grain made it ideal for woodworking. Native technology relied on this tree, providing planks for houses, tools for tasks, boxes for cooking and storing, and canoes – the primary transport around impenetrable undergrowth.

Lushootseed natives had an extremely complicated social life, comparable to the complex towns of farmers elsewhere, yet they largely lived by harvesting what nature provided. They did not tend fields, nor remain in one place. When natives encouraged the growth of certain wild plants, they unobtrusively left seeds and roots in well watered locales. After traders from the Hudson's Bay Company introduced natives to potatoes, these prior talents at tending wild foods allowed them to quickly raise such tubers as a cash crop (Suttles 1987: 137-151). Traditionally, people moved with the seasons to camps near available natural foods. The climate was mild, due to the offshore Japanese and California Currents, and rainy (very), so the region abounded with plants and animals.

Chief among these foods were five species of salmon which (more properly, who) spawned and died in the rivers each year, although some years the runs were more abundant than

---

[10] Smith (1941) revised this model to include pasture meadows so important for Nisqually horses, but this need does not reflect aboriginal conditions. As Gibbs (1877: 169) sagely noted, Nisqually horses are "an exception to the otherwise universal aquatic life of the coast region".

others.[11] By working hard for a few weeks, a household could catch and dry enough fish to last the winter. Yet people did not live by fish alone. After the summer fish runs, families went into the uplands to collect dozens of kinds of berries, which were also stored for winter use. Men hunted a variety of mammals, both sea and land, during the fall and winter. In the spring, fresh greens and early fish runs enriched the diet.

The dense vegetation and the rugged terrain left few level spaces where people could live, so each house in every town had about fifty occupants, with placement in the house reflecting rank in local and regional society. Thus, the owner of the house and his family had the best spot in a front corner, away from the drafts at the doorway, and constituted a nobility, providing the varied leaders for community tasks. Previously known as task leaders, this overly-economic terminology is herein replaced by "sigers," derived from sig (special interest group) and the -er suffix (Miller 1997).

Along the sides and back were common folks, who contributed food and upkeep to the household in return for the prestige of living with wealthy relatives. The least desirable and most exposed places in the house were available to slaves, who were either captured in raids, purchased, or born to their lot. Each family had its own hearth fire along a side of the house, since eating together as a commensal unit was what defined close relations.[12] Nobles usually had more than one wife, but each seems to have had a separate fireplace to feed her own and any other children.

On important occasions, particularly during winter, the head of the house hosted public events on behalf of all the residents. Accordingly, most families moved out to other accommodations, either nearby homes or tents, to make room for guests, and two or three large fires were lit along the middle axis of the house. Huge amounts of food, gathered by slaves and housemates to be prepared by women under the direction of the senior wife of the host, were served throughout the festivities. Changes in status – such as naming, puberty, marriage, or death – provided the occasions for inviting in guests. The more prominent a family, the more

---

[11] These five salmon species can be confusing because of a great variety of local names. All belong to the genus called *Oncorhynchus*, further designated by versions of Kamchatka native names for these species.
   A. *O. tshawytscha* (chinook, king, spring, quinnat), up to 80 pounds, spawns in large streams or rivers, sometimes with spring and fall subspecies.
   B. *O. kisutch* (silver), usually 6-12 pounds, up to 30 pounds, runs in early fall but may not spawn until late fall, in smaller streams far from the sea.
   C. *O. gorbuscha* (pink), 3-10 pounds, spawns early fall, smaller streams near the sea.
   D. *O. keta* (chum, dog), 8-18 pounds, spawns late fall, smaller streams near the sea, flesh is lean and smokes well.
   E. *O. nerka* (sockeye), usually a few pounds, fattest species, spawns upriver in lakes; when landlocked, known as kokanee.
In addition, steelhead (*Salmo gairdneri*) is a sea-run rainbow trout, up to 36 pounds, that, like Atlantic salmon, spawns and returns to the sea. Pacific salmon spawn and die, nourishing local carnivores and enriching poor soil (Suttles 1990: 24-25).

[12] Not eating with someone indicates hostility, suspicion, or sorcery. Native children, in particular, are told never to eat with strangers, who might poison them.

people would be invited from furthest away. Important families had far flung networks of friends and kin, forged by marriage, adoption, trade, and social obligations. By prudently using resources locally "anchored," a household could add to their regional "radiance."

The crux of the entire system and the basic reason for gathering people together was the display of bonds with particular immortal spirit powers. No one could be successful without such help. For centuries, leading families had bonded with the most powerful spirits in their locales. Lesser family members, some commoners, and even a few slaves could also have spirit partners, but these were less powerful than those of the leaders.

Spirit Bonds

Among Salish, as well as other native cultures, the hallmark of life was the existence of immortals, intermeshed within a web (rather than a hierarchical chain of being) whose positions depended on differential access to a diffuse concept of vitality, which, while deriving from a unitary source in the high god (*xa'xa*), can variously be called force, energy, potency, and power. Members of the elite, especially shamans, understood it best.[13]

Furthermore, in Lushootseed, the word for land also means nature, world, and the whole globe of earth, so "to learn from the land" was to learn from the earth and generalized nature, above all, via its spiritual aspects. Even things like rocks and tools, considered inanimate by most Americans, were recognized as having spirits and the potentiality for self-motivation.

A basic premise of this cosmos, therefore, is that everything is alive, has access to power, and is within the sphere of responsibility for a local spirit. At crux, the basis of power in this universe derived from an ultimate entity, being, or creator, known in Lushootseed as *xa'xa*, more commonly now as *shaq si'ab* (Above Chief, Above Lord), equated with the Christian God and intermeshed with individual spirits, collectively called *sqǝlalitut*, each associated with an allocation of power derived from the font of memory possessed by the Creator (Miller 1980).

In derivation, this word for spirit(s) comes from the *s-* nominalizer applied to the word meaning 'dream,' which breaks down into *qǝl* 'stop', *-al-* 'during', *-'itut* 'sleep' (Bates, Hess, and Hilbert 1994: 18, 174) and means "an interlude during sleep." The *s-* indicates that this is "someone/thing that comes during a dreamlike state," referring both to all immortals in general and to those conferring careers in specific. The other subset of such powers, much the stronger, are those for curing possessed by specialists called shamans or Indian doctors. Both the powers and these practitioners are called by the same name.[14]

According to Lushootseed mythology, all of these immortals are "persons" who shares qualities that make them akin to humans. All of them are specifically said to have human or humanoid characteristics, disguised when outside their abodes by the covering of their species ~ natural form. Sometimes, it is said that their form was not strictly human, only that they shared characteristics of gender, intelligence, and sensitivity with humanity.

---

[13] While Suttles (1987: 187) concluded "Lord Above" was historically introduced, amplifying a prior belief in a sky or daylight deity, but belief in a high god was long a guarded privilege of the elite, as with Calusa of Florida and Yurok of northern California (Miller 1980).

[14] Bates, Hess, and Hilbert (1994: 77) suggest derivations of *dx^{w}da'ǝb* from either *da'(a)* = 'call, name' ~ *da'* = 'support'.

12

The most important attitude towards all beings and life in general, therefore, was respect, fully aware that any life form was capable of both good and harm (Hilbert 1985, Collins 1952). By showing such respect a human indicated self-worth, sometimes tinged with fear of unexpected consequences. Of all, the most serious of crimes against nature was waste because this showed disrespect both for a specific spirit and for all life.

All success involved a spirit and human bond, dramatically expressed in song and dance. Through it, a human could fulfill any task, career, or undertaking to benefit both human and spiritual community.

Thus, all of life was involved in constant negotiations within a cosmos of flux and flow. Indeed, movement was a characteristic of all life, either obviously as with animals, subtly as with plants, or unobtrusively as with thoughts. In addition, cross-generational bonds set up channels along recurrent, if not enclosed, circuitry.

For instance, while immortals were always in some contact with their human partners, they themselves traveled in such a way that they were farthest away from Lushootseed communities in the summer and closest to them in the winter, expressing a fundamental duality. Summer was devoted to economic activities, collecting food for storage and winter use, moving all over a territory among set resorts. In the winter, humans stayed in or close to their towns as immortals drew near to signal the start of the winter season, devoted to the communal rituals of their ancestral religion.

Prominent families indicated their profitable bonds by sponsoring such religious events as initiations and displays for the singing of power songs, and by providing shelter and food for visitors at these gatherings, spreading their elite reputation for sharing far and wide. Sometimes, such families went deliberately outside their home territory to gather or purchase delicacies from other areas, fostering intertribal networks based of visiting, trading, and ritual which often led to intermarriage, adoption, and even closer cooperation.

Differential strengths and advantages a family derived from various partnerships became elaborated into a triple system with two freeborn social classes (upper and lower) and an underclass of slaves. These triple classes were recognized by all North Pacific Coast tribes. Wealthy families, with strong, ancient bonds, composed the nobility, known as _si'ab_ to mean an "endowment with family – with knowledgeable and resourceful relatives, rather than with wealth alone" (in Bierwort 1996: 103). Ordinary people, without a venerable pedigree or specialty career, made up the commoners, mostly honest yet volatile and lackluster.

Nobles had to be active and constantly diligent, every moment of their time used efficiently and wisely. By contrast, commoners worked intermittently, laboriously during fish runs and leisurely between them. Nobles were the managers of resources and community, constantly alert to needs and abuses that impacted on the wellbeing of all life. Their primary means for relaxing seems to have been the traveling that took them into other regions.

These twin freeborn classes were very distinct from slaves, which were acquired by birthright, purchase, or capture. Occasional reports indicate that even slaves sometimes entered into a partnership with an immortal, but elders were quick to stress that these were the least powerful sources of power. In his fieldnotes, Hermann Haeberlin (1917: notebook 39: 33) recorded the interesting fact that war captives taken into slavery went to the afterworld of their original tribe after death, but those born into slavery went to the afterworld of their masters where they remained slaves forever.

This fate suggests the strength of the bond between a human, a community, and a locale among the Salish. Clearly, the strongest bond was that created by birth at a specific place, the abode of a particular immortal. Freeborn people had full access to whatever a place could bestow, while most slaves could only benefit via their masters. This contrast suggests that the modern distinction between culture and survival (below) may somehow relate to an ancient one between master and slave, with obvious overtones about Euro-American oppressors. More than an invidious comparison between their past freedom and present role as "wage slaves," this astute observation expresses a native sense that the ultimate benefits from their fishing, logging, and carving now belong to people other than themselves.

Traditionally, all classes seem to have been further modified by terrain and location along the drainage. While everyone living along the same river shared a common identity, those who lived downriver were distinguished from those who lived inland. Generally, downriver communities, especially those at river mouths, were more populous, diversified, and prosperous than upriver ones, particularly those in the mountains, whose more arduous life, however, gave them a certain prestige derived from admiration of their forebearing diligence.

In Lushootseed languages, the greater cohesion of the downriver towns was indicated by the *-bsh* ending, while the looser organization of the upriver communities was reflected in the *-bix^w* suffix to imply a "bunch" (Hess 1976: 38.3), as indicated by one name for the little wild Evergreen blackberry. Hence, specialized nobles were more numerous and visible downriver.[15]

Moreover, each drainage constituted a "tribal" community in the sense that its inhabitants frequently and easily interacted with each other. Their relations involved economic, social, kinship, political, dialect, and, above all, religious considerations. Rather than constituting a tribe in the usual lingua-socio-political sense, the people living along a drainage represented a congregation with the same localized spirits, but reflecting differences between downriver and upriver communities such that fierce ("black paint") warrior partnerships were uniquely saltwater, while gentle ("red paint") power relations were symbolically associated with the mountains and deep lakes.

As an important aspect of drainage solidarity, foodstuffs moved up and down the drainage to balance out local specialties and periodic abundances. Thus, shells and marine foods went upriver as meat, hides, berries, and roots came down. Generally, these exchanges took place in a ritual or kinship context that set them apart from ordinary trading instances, which were regarded as overtly commercial and, therefore, somewhat crass. Thus, for the duration of a marriage, inlaws exchanged gifts with each other in a constant series to indicate on-going kindness and goodwill. On a wider scale, members of a congregation always shared what they had, only trading or selling their resources to those characterized as outsiders and foreigners. The implication, therefore, was that everything "born" (indigenous) along a drainage was shared willingly and generously among all members, whether human, biotic, or immortal.

In part, this may reflect a belief that the drainage itself (more correctly, herself) was alive, demanding respect from all residents. Over the years, my persistent questioning of valued

---

[15] Of all the discussions in this volume, Vi Hilbert had most to say about this section, insisting that I repeatedly rethink and rewrite it. While published literature makes much of this down/up river distinction, treating it like an urban/rural one and disparaging those inland as hicks, Hilbert always denied any such contrast, insisting that the riverway was itself a single unit.

Lushootseed elders confirms that rivers are associated with women: After severe flooding by the Skagit River, an elder specifically said it acted just like an angry woman.

Further amplification of such a statement is provided by other peoples of the Northwest who more explicitly equate rivers and women. In a Fraser River epic (below), a sister was placed at the head of this river and her brother at its mouth. Further north, on Haida Gwaii (Queen Charlotte Islands), natives believe that a Creek Woman lives at the head of every stream, with her head at its source and her feet at its outlet.

Today, Lushootseed and other elders still insist that the entire earth is alive and, sometimes, equate its vegetation to hair and its stones to bones. Moreover, throughout the landscape particular places are special to specific immortals. One shaman noted that local immortals and places gave each distinct language as a gift. While often overlooked, such a linkage was not unique to Salishans. In the biblical Old Testament, a parallel equation was made with Hebrew, Jews, God, and Holy Land. For traditional Lushootseeds, Puget Sound and its environs was every bit as much of holy land, most properly addressed in their own dialects.

For this reason, each winter community includes certain individuals with a special ability (conferred by a spirit partner) to project thoughts at a distance and to sense the presence of strangers in their territory. Often, they watch the area around a camp or community, paying attention to the movement of every creature so as to forecast future conditions ~ dangers.

In particular, all communal activity sites, particularly those associated with fishing – such as weirs, traps, and platforms – are closely watched, not to keep out intruders but to be aware of whether respect is or is not being shown to nature and its bounty, especially the salmon, who demand its constant expression if they are to return and stay year after year.

As with any endeavor, success is the outcome of a partnership between immortal and human. Among events that could damage or cut this tie is the refusal of any human to share his ~ her bounty with other people, particularly the needy. Selfishness violated this pact because it stopped the circulation of goods, actions, and power in the world – representing a kind of waste due to the neglect ~ abuse of a resource.

During periods when salmon runs peaked, drainages sent out messengers to invite in distant kin and neighbors, both to prevent its waste and to encourage visiting, hospitality, sharing, and local pride. Today, such invitations continue, now issued over the phone to tribal fisheries managers who then broadcast it. Such a mesh of new technology with old values has long been characteristic of Lushootseeds.

Sharing Strategies

A central tenet of all Native American cultures was the need to share with others, to give to both the needy and the great. What moved up as homage, came down as hospitality and generosity. It was perfectly in keeping with this ethic, therefore, that the predominant institution of Northwest societies was the Potlatch ~ Give-Away feast, drawing together diverse members of a community (cf Elmendorf 1971: 360, 363).

Social position and prestige derive not from membership within a local community, but from links – forged by visiting, visibility, hospitality, and generosity – among a network of such communities. People who did not share were low class, and perhaps only marginally human.

Generosity has the effect of creating a knot in the social fabric that contributes to increasing attention and regard over time.

Sharing was all pervasive, both in and out of the community. According to Dr Warren Snyder (Indian Claims Commission 1952: 157),

> for the most part there was an ideal of individual ownership, but this has to be qualified by the fact that there was a great deal of sharing, and it was sharing which was forced upon a person in order for him to remain a member in good standing in the community. It was absolutely necessary that he share with other people, say, in the village, what he had.

While all normal social relations are based on sharing, the greatest benefits came to an individual who shared with others who were both far away and unrelated.[16] Such a host was considered "real high class, a real person".

It was therefore not in the best interests of a village or its leaders to exclude anyone. The dictionaries of Salishan languages assembled by Gibbs (1877), Snyder (1968), and particularly, those of Hess (1976), of Bates, Hess, and Hilbert (1994), and of Thompson and Poggi (ms) do not contain any words meaning "to exclude, exclusive, or exclusion." Nor have I found any native speakers who can supply such terms.

The nearest equivalents were constructions based on a term meaning "to hide," with a semantic range that included being alone and selfish, both undesirable qualities for Lushootseeds. During hard times, sharing became especially important, and anything, however meager, was shared by everyone – with one exception.

While food, artifacts, and hospitality were shared with all, knowledge was private property that only passed down through direct family lines. The contrast was between survival, to which everyone was entitled, and culture, which was the privilege of the better families. Thus, while these tribes lacked terms for exclusion or territoriality, they did express the need to "seclude" valuable information, particularly details of epics, legends, rituals, and songs needed to maintain rapport with powerful immortals. Yet some of this knowledge also had a darker side, called victimizing magic by Elmendorf (1970: 152), and it too was private and secret.

While the importance of seclusion as a Lushootseed cultural characteristic has not been generally acknowledged, federal court cases involving fishing rights have relied on notions of approval – expressed through invitation, permission, or kinship – to forge a coherent system of native rights and privileges within the confines of American law. These variables, however, have not been carefully regarded.

Among Lushootseeds, the word usually given for potlatch literally means 'inviting' (_sgʷigʷi_). But, this does not mean that everyone attending had or needed a personal invitation. Rather, high class people only invited other, specificly high class people to events they were hosting so as to be sure of their attendance. These invitees could then tell kin, retainers, and others the date of the event, expecting them to come along if they were able. Given the sharing ethic, a guest who arrived with a large retinue was particularly welcome. In other words, special

---

[16] In a fascinating study of such sharing among Tsimshians, greatest prestige in potlatching comes from gifting totally unrelated guests (Dunn 1984).

16

invitations were a mark of social status, given to others of a host's own status or higher, who then confirmed his or her judgment by arriving with an entourage.

In lieu of an invitation, permission worked in much the same way, but depended much more on place than on time. People unsure of the appropriateness of fishing or conducting any other activity asked permission of a resident noble, elder, or shaman who could be expected to know in what way the rules relating to reverence for the earth and its bounty applied to such a special request.

In Salish, asking to use resources might involve a statement such as "Do you think it is a good idea for me to take X resource in order to stay alive." Clearly, when phrased this way, it was impossible for an elder to say no without very good reasons, such as depletion, stated taboos, offense to an immortal, or damage to continuing bounty. As one elder said, resources were available to anyone who needed them, as long as you "didn't run somebody else short."

Since the federal court (Boldt) decision on treaty fishing rights, kinship has been treated as the key that unlocked other resource areas for use. Usually, this was a marriage bond which naturally led to a descent line with membership and "ownership" in both places. Actually, Lushootseeds more accurately regard kinship and marriage as the simplest expression of a complex system of regional intertribal bonds based on the recognition of famed names held by identifiable persons, known and valued by a community.

Visitors were always welcome, but their arrival included dangers. Most came to visit, but a few came to scout out the community for a later raid to take booty and slaves. Resource use, therefore, involved complex and subtle evaluation of guests as they arrived and while they were visiting. Access to local resources was based primarily on proper attitudes of respect for people, resources, and spirits. The number of guests was always considered since a large group could quickly overwhelm the hosts, sell them off as slaves, and misuse the territory.

Feast, Flee, Fight, or Fidget

In all, according to local elders, any such encounter could have four outcomes: the hosts could feast, flee, fight, or fidget. The first was preferred, while the second occurred when the visiting group was large and hostile. The third required people among the hosts with "mean" spirit partners conferring the toughness of warriors. The fourth was a temporary pose to prolong the waiting until something happened to decide among the other options.

Treating kinship as the sole criterion of access thereby over-simplified the system by allowing only the option of feasting. As kin, these visitors arrived as known quantities, already part of the on-going system, though under suspicion if numerous, heavily armed, or surly.

Generally, community response was triggered by the manner of approach. As long as visitors approached in full view, they were welcomed politely before learning, in due time, their reasons for travel. Proper visitors came by canoe or walked along a recognized trail through tribal territory. Mrs. Paul Petit at Chehalis told John P Harrington (1942: reel 018, frame 819) "My grandmother told me that in the old times if we saw a sole canoe coming, it would be a messenger and all awaited news."

A host's obligations included feeding the visitor(s), with subsequent meals escalating into feasting. During peak salmon runs, many visitors were invited to share the bounty of an area and feasting became quite lavish during lulls in their hard labor.

Occasions when people would flee, fight, or fidget depended upon the size of the group of visitors and the degree of uncertainty about their intention ~ reputation. In general, the closer a large force was to a village, the more likely the inhabitants were to flee or fight. As Mary Carolyn Howard noted in her testimony (Indian Claims Commission 1952: 15),

> [People] might come in as a friend but they were always on the look out for trouble and so when any large party of people would come, they would very definitely investigate them.

Saltwater villages were the only communities to include members with warrior powers and to receive frequent unknown visitors. A few men from these downriver areas might marry into upriver settlements, but they were seldom called upon to defend them.

Fidgeting as a response occurred most often in areas along borders or away from habitations, where behavior was less governed by the conventions of social life. As JP Harrington (1942: Reel 018, frame 661) remarked for the region, if not for all of North America,

> Joint food-gathering grounds often separate American Indian linguistic divisions. Yet there were also intimate ties between a region and a tribe, based on the sharing of traditions in which primordial bonds are formed between ancestors and immortals before being perpetuated into the present.

Support for this highly diversified system of sharing – conferring status, position, and prestige across towns – spans more than the past century (cf Elmendorf 1960: 268), beginning with the statement of George Gibbs (1877: 186-87).

> The tribes are, however, somewhat tenacious of territorial right, and well understand their respective limits; but this seems to be merely as regards their title, and they never, it is believed, exclude from them other friendly tribes. It would appear also that these lands are considered to survive to the last remnant of a tribe, after its existence as such has in fact ceased... As regards the fisheries, they are held in common, and no tribe pretends to claim from another, or from individuals, seigniorage {revenue} for the right of taking. In fact, such a claim would be inconvenient to all parties, as the Indians move about, on the Sound particularly, from one to another locality, according to the season. Nor do they have disputes as to their hunting grounds. Land and sea appear to be open {commons} to all with whom they are not at war.

Arthur Ballard, who learned to speak Lushootseed from his Muckleshoot nanny and devoted much time to ethnography, also held that

> Non-village areas were open to all who cared to use them. This was a cultural characteristic of the Indians of the Sound area that they would share the area as being common territory (in Horr 1974: 116-7).

While the Northwest Coast has been characterized as a potlatch society, given to elaborate generosity, the importance given to sharing resources over its wide area was not unique. For Plateau tribes along the Columbia River, sharing (sometimes called cross-utilization) was the rule for game, fish, roots, berries, furs, skins, stone, and "other materials not distributed evenly throughout the area" (Walker 1967: 8).

To the south, Arnold Pilling (1950) extends its range to the Monterey coast of California.

The Yokuts trips to the Monterey coast {for mussels and abalones} as here described are noticeably historic, being made by a mounted, armed group. However, similar long distance travel for Yokuts described by Latta, who tells how the Northern Hill Yokuts travelled over 75 miles by balsa to Buena Vista Lake annually, is strictly in the aboriginal pattern.

Interesting, while the Yokuts sometimes fought with the local Costanoans (later known as Mission Indians), their caches of stone mortars and pestles at the coast, hundreds of miles from home, remained undisturbed until white settlement.

Culture and Survival

When trying to explain their present condition to outsiders, contemporary Lushootseed elders often distinguish between *culture* and *survival* to express the changes impacting their recent lifetimes.

At base, survival is what people have to do to keep themselves and their families in food, clothing, and other necessities, such as cars, boats, gas, gear, and utilities. Since the 1850s, it has involved work for wages from lumbering, commercial fishing, carpentry, or unskilled labor.[17] To do this, people moved out of their native community and so lost full participation in family life and public events, except for sending back money and goods.

Survival means that children are not encouraged to use native languages and traditions in the (not entirely mistaken) belief that this will interfere with their education in American schools. Today, well-meaning elders hope that by withholding native fluency, their children will profit from the perceived advantages of white Americans. Usually, this does not happen unless elders also provide a strong sense of direction and self-confidence for finding a way through the social and emotional strains of an alien, dehumanizing modern world.

In consequence, elders have had to point out that *culture*, the quality of a lifeway based in the land, is not the same as *survival*, earning a living by exploiting that same terrain. Sometimes, the two were and are incompatible, as when a new initiate into the Winter Dance has to quit his ~ her job to have the time and energy to learn this aspect of culture. Over long winter months, elders made speeches intended to instill values, attitudes, customs, and practices that were once commonplace. While in seclusion, the initiate had to rely on family, friends, and trainers for food, money, and other necessities.

When the late Martin Sampson, a Swinomish leader, was asked by Vi Hilbert, a Skagit relative, to define native culture, he said that it was "learning from the land".

---

[17] In remote areas, several native men ran dugout canoes as river ferries.

Insightfully, Sampson captured the essential difference between culture and survival. Culture involved keen attention, receptivity, and reciprocity within the resident community of sentient, sensitive, and sensory life. Survival merely consisted of a disinterested utilization of some obvious, but less important, features of this unity. Culture was a dynamic, interactive, and receptive process of insightful learning, while survival was drudgery, mechanical and uninformative. The one recognized the primacy of spirit and spiritual; the other ignored them for mundane reasons of practicality until imbalances required ritual to restore proper conditions.

Shamans

In addition to career powers, ranging from woodworking and canoe making to berry picking and midwifery, curing powers assured the wellbeing of the whole community because they were constantly available.

Leaders had spirits, themselves leaders, that empowered them to give wise council and acquire wealth, as well as to hunt the most dangerous of animals. Most chiefs had inherited power from Thunder and passed it along to their heirs for generations, giving each a booming voice and eye-catching flare. Leaders also had "riches" powers to enable them to be generous.

Most spirits, however, only visited their human partner in the winter months. During these long rainy winters, people gathered to welcome back their spirits by singing and dancing a mime of how they had first met in some remote spot on the land or in the sea. The rest of the year, the spirits lived in villages of their own "on the other side" of the human dimension, before spiralling all winter though the Salish country from the east to the north, west, and south. Towns knew their location along the route from centuries of such visits and began to prepare to host their own power displays once they had been invited to the celebrations of the towns that preceded them on the circuit.

For most people in most places, these public displays set the seasonal pattern for trafficking with powers. In every community, however, there were and are specialists who maintained personal and permanent relations with another kind of spirit power. The Lushootseed generic word for spirits referred either to career or to curing powers, with this latter named subset constituting the doctors of the universe.

Though usually known as shamans, this term for both spirits and their human allies derived from Lushootseed for "name" ~ "call" because in the native system of medicine, to correctly designate ("name") the cause of an illness was to diagnose a cure. Shamans and curing spirits were always at the ready, unlike career powers whose closeness varied with the seasons.

The head of a household and the leader of a town, who was also the head of the most distinguished house, to be effective, either acquired such a doctoring spirit or had a trusted associate who was a shaman. Just as European noble families sent various sons into the church, into business, in banking, or into the military to widen their power base, so too did Lushootseed nobles try to have members in all positions of authority, since leadership was multiplex, depending on the task at hand. Leadership relied on specialization, so each activity had its own "siger" to take charge, but only for the duration of the activity.

Moreover, modern Salish families extend this strategy to include contemporary options, particularly religious ones.[18] Thus, as families attend winter ceremonials to welcome the return of spirit partners, on Sunday they devotedly attend Protestant, Catholic, Bahai, or other services.

Shakers

In addition, for the past century, natives of Puget Sound and beyond have belonged to a religion, legally incorporated in Washington State in 1910, uniquely their own. Known as the Indian Shaker Church, it was founded by a local man, John Slocum, and his wife Mary (Amoss 1981, 1982; Ruby and Brown 1996). In October of 1882, John died and went to heaven, but God, the Christian God, sent him back to preach a new religion, founded when his wife began to shake over his body just before he revived.[19] While many of the overt actions are like details of Catholic worship – such as altars, albs, candles, and making the Sign of the Cross by placing fingers to forehead, shoulders, and chest – the use of hand bells to accompany hymns, often in Chinuk, during circular processions were creative innovations.

When natives join the Shaker Church, furthermore, their spirit powers convert with them, thus continuing the ancestral religious tradition.[20] The primary role of Shakers in the modern native community is curing, especially of addictions, but unlike the ancient shamanic tradition that also continues, Shaker curing is more democratic, done by all believers and free of charge.

Today, shamanism continues to be the career of aloof individuals who mostly work alone. Traditionally, shamans were feared for this mood, often described as mean and selfish, but they were nevertheless respected for the good that they did or could do. Whenever a shaman enters a room or a native gathering, quiet quickly falls. Since powerful spirits travel with him ~ her and cannot be seen, everyone has to be especially careful not to give offense to them.

Among the Salish, sexual equality was and remains well developed. With proper supernatural sanction, any man or woman could perform any task. Gender roles, therefore,

---

[18] Salishans are not alone in believing "the more religions you have the better for you."

[19] John Slocum and Mary Thompson came from prominent families. John's brothers were Jack and Tom, his father was Old Slocum, and his grandfather Old Chouse, a chief who died in the 1860s at great age. "The Shake" came first to Mary, who was also an Odyssey doctor (below).

[20] Shaker conversion is all inclusive because when a person becomes a Shaker, all of his or her property and possessions also convert, including spirit helpers. However, ever in command, any spirits who did not want to join the Shaker Church simply abandoned their human ally.

Nonetheless, another active belief insists on the antagonism between ancient spirits and those of Shakers. Ed Davis said that when he became a Shaker, he turned his back on all the old ways, and a Twana Shaker minister refused to tell Elmendorf traditions he knew well. A woman in the south Sound shriveled up and wasted away because, as a Shaker (Smith 1940: 64), she refused a ghost power that made her "sick to sing," yet it is unclear if her death was the result of the spirit's own intent, her refusal as a faithful Shaker, or her vocal inability because "she could not talk" to ask for help from other Shakers.

Older Shakers indeed divided their own spirit help from those of the smokehouse church, but this no longer seems to be the case, a wise tolerance helping to protect all native beliefs from attack by white officials.

existed only in a statistical sense that men tended to do some things and women to do others. Since the immortal spirits also had gender, a woman performing usual male roles was presumed to have a male spirit. Anyone undertaking a quest could expect to receive a spirit of either gender since there was no obligation for male spirits to appear only to men or for female immortals to gift only women. Dr Bill, a famous Snoqualmi shaman at Tolt (now Carnation, Wa), went to the land of the dead with the aid of a female Little Earth (Miller 1988: 18).

When someone fell ill, the character and duration of the disease determined which curer would be called to provide treatment. If it was a European-derived case of measles or a problem that required surgery, then a university-trained physician was consulted or the patient went to a hospital. But natives were and are subject to many more diseases than modern allopathic medicine can treat. Bad relations ("breaches") with the cosmos, the community, the family, and the self were manifest in particular diseases. Though psychologically derived (according to Western categories), these problems were nonetheless painfully real and could be fatal.

To improve community sentiment and general wellbeing, Shakers are now generally called in because they cure communally and never accept money for their treatments, although they are given donations to pay for gas and lodging.

For present-day instances of cosmic disharmony and spiritual disaffection, a shaman is called, loudly and repeatedly so that his or her spirits will also know that they are needed. He ~ she is expensive, although fees are returned to family if a cure was unsuccessful or patient died.

If a shaman lost too many cases, however, he or she was killed by their own relatives because of a belief that their powers had turned malevolent and would henceforth only kill and not cure, beginning with their youngest, closest, most vulnerable relatives. Such a shaman became a liability to the community, but the execution had to be performed by a family member so as to prevent a blood feud. A bereaved family, which did not wait for justice and instead killed the shaman themselves, precipitated hostilities until they paid goods to the shaman's kin.

Attacks

Illnesses cured by shamans could have either external or internal causes. Sometimes, another shaman became jealous or envious of someone or was hired by an enemy to make that someone sick. Often, the onset of this illness was caused by magically "shooting" a sharp object or barbed probe into the patient's body.

A victim could be attacked at three junctures: mind, spirit, or breath. A shaman relied on his spirit helpers to tell him or her what was wrong with a patient and how to cure it. Lushootseed shamans had a characteristic gesture, placing the upper face near the crook of an arm, for making such a diagnosis. By placing the back of the wrist against the forehead, normal sight was blocked to gain access to a curing spirit with X-ray sight that was believed to live in the lower arm. Also, entering into a trance was helped by the rhythmic pulses of the veins at the forehead and wrist.

For the Salish, as for other Native Americans, the mind was located in the heart at the center of the body.[21] The brain storaged memories, thoughts, and emotions. Therefore, sorcery applied to the heart would confuse and weaken a person, leaving him or her susceptible to worse

---

[21] Larger implications of heart = hearth = fire = sun equation are explored in Miller (1980, 1981).

illness. The shaman had to suck out whatever probing object was magically shot into the body. Often, his slack fists were stacked atop each other to form a sucking tube. Modesty required that a shaman avoid touching the patient's body as much as possible. Once the problem was gathered inside the fists, it was either sent away, if not too dangerous, or, on rare occasions, it was drowned in a basket filled with water.[22]

The second instance, spirit illness, was a common phenomenon of winter. Spirit powers were acquired in youth, before puberty in the old days and by initiation today, but they did not begin visiting their human partners annually until middle age, when a successful career and healthy family were taken as proof of a spirit ally.

Every winter, when the spirit returned to its human, that mortal became ill ("sick to sing"). The first time this happened, a special shaman was called to "draw out" the song that had lodged in the throat of that man or woman. The shaman then sang the song of the initiate so everyone in the house could hear and remember it because, thereafter, whenever that human became ill, people had to gather with drums to sing while the invalid danced to become attuned and strengthened by his or her bond.

Today, at large weekend gatherings all winter long, everyone sings and dances an evocation of their (or an ancestor's) first encounter with a spirit. Type of song and gestures help to suggest the general category of that spirit, but exact details are guarded.

Sometimes, in this second kind of illness, a shaman found one of these spirit allies attractive and stole it from its human, who then became gravely ill. If a more powerful shaman could not retrieve the spirit, then the human partner died, unless he or she could quickly acquire another strong power, which was virtually impossible.

In the third illness, a spirit, shaman, or deceased loved-one might steal the breath of someone. Since the very word for life derived from the word for breath, such a theft led to death, either quickly if that was what the perpetrator wanted, or after prolonged lingering with great suffering for maximum revenge. Breath was linked with the soul, so the delay in death was a consequence of the time allowed for the soul to wander to the land of the dead, where it became a ghost.

When someone died, everything they owned was given away because any memento might make a relative fixate on the deceased and thus become a prime candidate for being lured away by a forlorn ancestor. Natives say the dead can not help it that they kill their descendants because they are believed to be lonely and to have very little else to do.

Indeed, the dead remain more significant in the lives of Lushootseed people than anything else except the spirits. Living in close and caring communities, the bonds of the flesh, like those of the spirit, continued far beyond the grave. In the same way that only specialists like shamans and "mediums" could remain in contact with their powers, so too could they make contact with the dead. To do so, they engaged in one of the most impressive and meaningful ceremonies of Native North America and the world. Though mistitled Spirit Canoe Ceremony, its correct intent was the recovery of stolen vitality, in various intensities as mind, soul, or spirit.

---

[22] Miller once saw a water-filled plastic bowl used to drown a "bad" spirit who had been sent to harm a young boy. The precaution had as much to do with the tender age of the victim as with the strength of the intruder.

Last held in the winter of 1908, the shamanic odyssey is only vaguely known to present Lushootseed elders. Yet, at various times over the past century, missionaries, scholars, and visitors have provided glimpses of the rite assembled and analyzed so they could be compared with beliefs and practices throughout Native North America (Miller 1988).

In human societies without a tradition of scientific inquiry, the cosmos was an organic whole in which the shape of the house mirrored that of the universe, as did the body, both of biological species with essentially human underforms and of canoes as an animated means of facilitating transport and interconnections. The house frame was imagined to be a body on its hands and knees, with the face at the front. Therefore, the outer skin, canoe shell, house walls, and rim of the world were equated, as were the inner heart, hearth, and helios. In regions with gabled roofs, moreover, the ridge pole was equated with a spine, river, and the Milky Way, as were the four support posts with human limbs and sky pillars. The bow of a canoe was a head, as paddles were arms. In consequence, curing, bailing, and cleaning were all reflexes of a renewal of the world.

PLACES ALONG THE SKAGIT DRAINAGE SYSTEM[23]

Native place names (toponyms) highlight features of the land, air, and water that are both inherent there and culturally important. Instead of naming them for people or recent events, most native names refer to distinguishing features of topography, often using anatomical references such as nose, neck, foot, brow, limb, breast, and so forth. A few set aside special abodes of spirits, life-energy sources, and actors involved in mythic epics. Some refer to what is characteristically found there, whether prime foods, predominant plants or animals, raw materials, wind patterns, weather conditions, or viewpoints. Some indicate safe and sure passages across or through the landscape, including key portages. Above all, each place name provides a persistent "mental picture" of what, who, when, where, and how is reliably there for benefit or caution (Hilbert, Miller, and Zahir 2001; Waterman 1922). Yet construction, channel shifts, and massive flooding, most recently 21 October 2003, have changed some of these locations.

Two main sources provide some, but by no means, all of the place names along the Skagit drainage. The first is a compendium by Robert and Barbara Lane (1977) that assembled and mapped lists collected by Sally Snyder and Wayne Suttles, as well as input from elders Edith Bedal, George Enick, Lawrence Boome, and Ray Paul. In 1858, prolific George Gibbs drew a map of the Skagit and listed villages, with typical confusion of the sounds B~M and D~N. Another listing occurs at the end of the Star Child epic told by Susie Sampson Peter (lines 920-), who mentions the places passed by the Sun and Moon along the river: Leon Metcalf made these tapes of Susie Sampson Peter (marked as SSP) speaking northern Lushootseed in the 1950s and they were translated by Vi Hilbert, a close kinswoman. Only the transcriptions of Hilbert and Suttles are linguistically reliable. Accompanying maps appear at the end of this study.

Key for locations, activities, and sources

Delta
Sedro Woolley
Hamilton
Concrete
Rockport
Newhalem
Nookachamps, Illabot, Cascade
Stillaguamish

The Lanes use the following abbreviations for locations, activities, and sources:

SK = Skagit mainstream
N = Nookachamps Creek
Sa = Sauk River
Su = Suiattle River

---

[23] by Jay Miller & Vi taqʷšəblu Hilbert.

Skagit

I Illabot Creek
C = Cascade River

F = fishing
Fs = fishing site
Fa = fishing anywhere
W = wintering site
Sh = smokehouse, summer houses
C = campsite
L = living site

C = June Collins
G = George Gibbs, followed by number on his list
LW = Lucy Williams
MS = Martin Sampson
SS = Sally Snyder
SSP = Susie Sampson Peter, mother of MS
WS = Wayne Suttles

Skagit, Sauk, and Stillaguamish Drainage Maps
River mouths at the top

Vicinity of the Skagit River Mouths

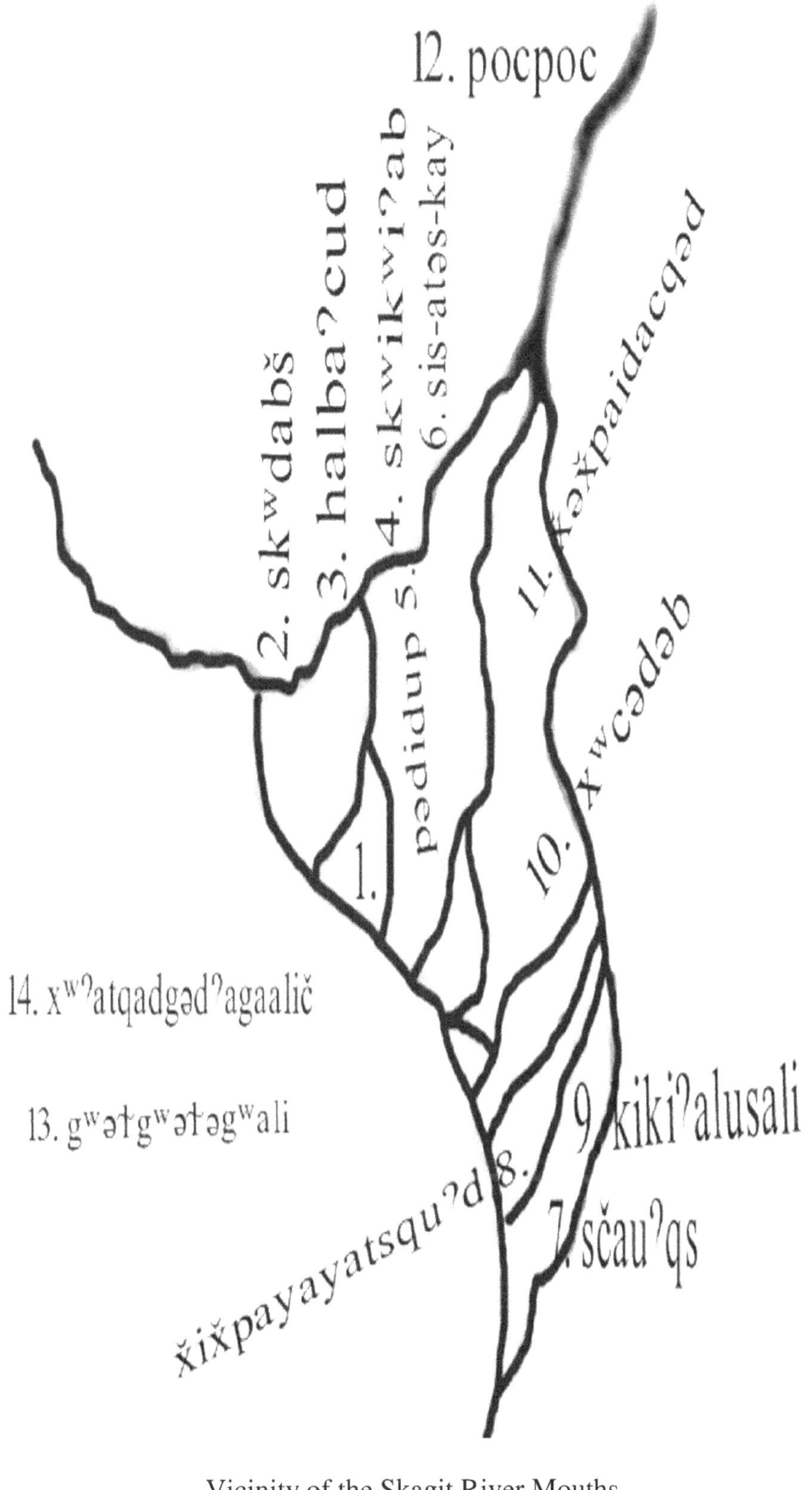

Vicinity of the Skagit River Mouths

with the bulge of Whidbey Island across Skagit Bay

Skagit Delta to Burlington #1-24 (moving upriver)

☐ Mouth of Hall? or Brown Slough FL   SK 1-33-3 (MS)

skʷdabš Fishtown N bank N fork of Skagit mouth, salmon weirs, traps FC   SK 2-33-3-7 (MS SS WS)

halbaʔcud Dodge Valley N bank W edge south end of valley, FC SK 3-33-3-8 (WS)

skʷikʷkʷab N bank of N fork, near bridge, F CW (recent) (name may refer to area rather than site) SK 4-33-3-9 ()

pədidup S bank of N fork, near bridge SK 5-33-3-9,10? (WS)

sis-ates-kay ?? N fork near bridge W SK 6-33-3-10 (WS)

sčauʔqs Milltown E bank of Tom Moore slough L SK 7-33-4-31 (WS, SS)

xixpayayatsqu'd "cedar head" Fir, near Deepwater Slough L SK 8-33-4-3 (WS)

xəxpaidacqəd Conway, W bank   C SK 11-33-4-13 (WS G1)

kikiʔəlosali Conway, E bank L SK 9-33-4-19 (WS)

kikiʔalusali = kikiyalus + -ali = 'place' also, place that looks like kiki - ?, Dewey Mitchell's sister was called skiki. SSP home of the Kikialus [Mann's Landing below the South Fork Bridge]

xʷcədab Conway, E bank W SK 10-33-4-18 (WS)

pocpoc S fork, E bank of creek, N of Conway F SK 12-33-4-18 (WS)

gʷəɫgʷələgʷali S fork, E bank below forks L SK 13-33-4?-6 (WS)

xʷʔatqadgədʔagʷalič Skagit City in the forks L SK 14-34-3-6 (WS)

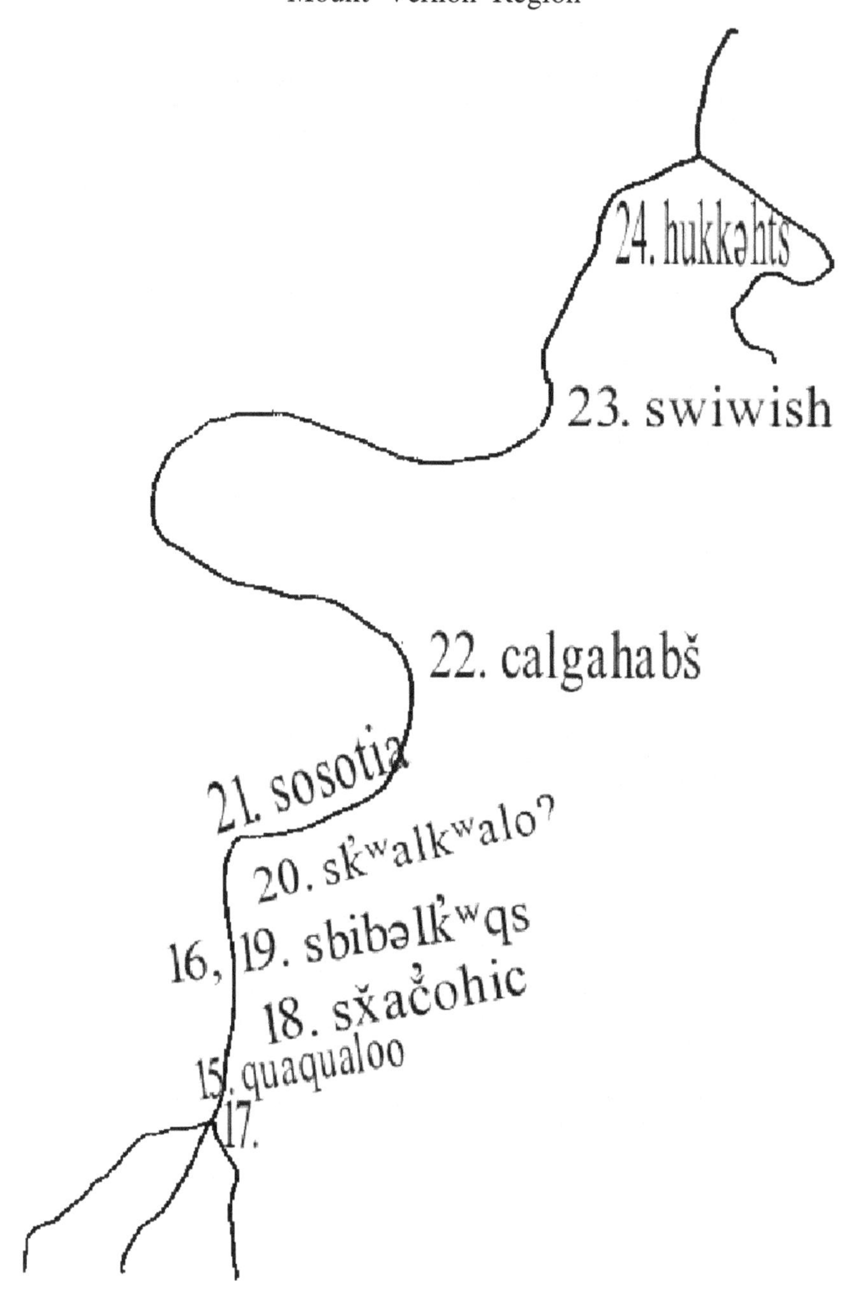

qua-qua-loo N fork, N bank FL SK 15-34-3-35 (WS)

sbíbəlk'wqs "go around a point" N bank at Forks W SK 16-34-3-6 (WS, SS, G2)

sbibulk'wqs [sbibulk'wqs] E bank, next SK 19-34-3 (WS)

□ E bank at Forks L SK 17-34-3-36 (G2, SS)

30

sxačohič E bank above? Forks L SK 18-34-3 (WS)

sk̓ʷalk̓ʷaloʔ [sk'walk̓ʷáloʔ] E bank, next L SK 20-34-3,4? (WS)

sosotia "sucks in" Mt Vernon under log jam, a 'break' in upper log jam FC SK 21-34-3-19 (WS) Salmon (chinook) fishing through logs in late spring, summer [CA AC]

susutiʔəʔəxʷ = "inhale" name for Mt Vernon because its many saloons sucked people in SSP

[xe'dobəl bluff above railroad bridge at Mt Vernon, CA's M & F had a house there, clam at Utsalady, SSP M = sʷato.]

xʷq̓ʷq̓ʷus = "White Face" old name for Mt Vernon because of its white cliffs or bluffs SSP [k̓ʷas = a smokehouse, 3-4 miles upriver]

calgahabš N of Mt Vernon, W of cemetery W SK 22-34-18 (C)

swiwíš S bank, N Mt Vernon, E Great Northern bridge W SK 23-34-4-18 (C)

hukkehts E bank, S of Burlington L SK 24-24-4-9 (G3)

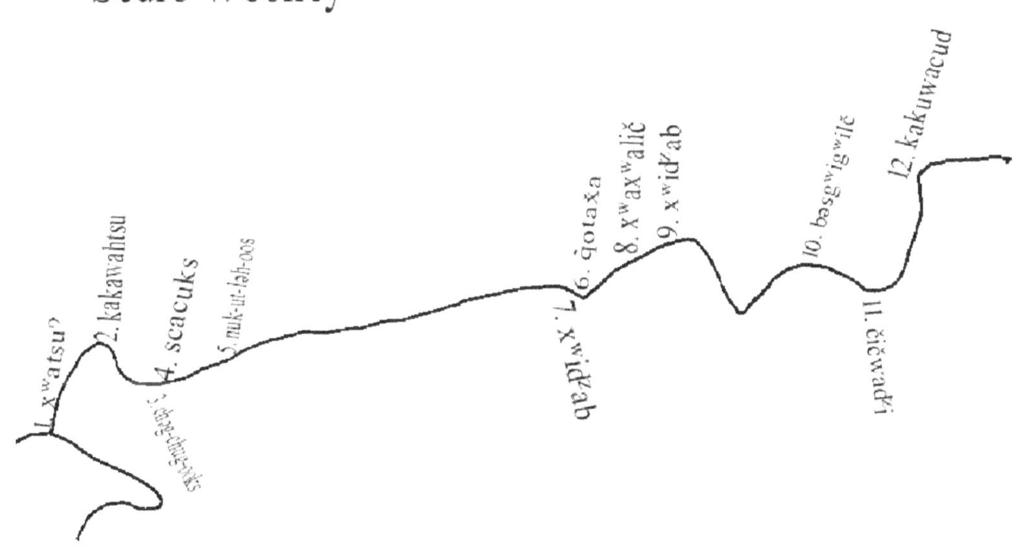

Sedro Woolley #1-12

xwahtsoo ?? N bank, below Burlington, across from mouth of Nookachamps Creek, FW winter fishing with trawl nets SK 1-34-4-4 (?)

čačxʷəχaʔ } conveys an image of arms struck off, cf čačxʷəd = strike, hit, cut it off SSP

kakawahtsu Near bow between Burlington & Sterling, same as 1? W SK 2-35-4-33 (?)

ʔabadəč = -ab extend, cf abadəb = gift, come out of the water, dried out, exposed, above Sterling; cf dxʷšigʷucid = exposed, uncovered SSP [South Fork]

cheg-chug-ooks N bank, inside deep bow, slightly upriver from mouth of Nookachamps L SK 3-34-4 (G4) river bed changed, possibly on slough W of Clear Lake

scácuks S bank, just E of mouth of Nookachamps SK 4-34-4-34 (C) may be 3-34-4

Nuk-ut-leh-oos NE bank of Skagit, SW Sedro Woolley, L SK 5-35-4-26 (G5) possibly across from Hart Island

dxʷbaqʷas = dxʷ - to, toward, concerning + baqʷas = ? SSP

q̇otaxa N bank, original Sedro store SK 6-34-4-25 (SS)

q̇ʷəbtaxa(d) = q̇ʷəb = 'get off' + tax = 'spread out', probably a place to dry nets SSP [Sedro store at Sedro Woolley, palqʷe'ca lived in a big house there, 1 child, a doctor who knew when death would come. Also downriver from Concrete AlC]

xʷaxʷalič [yalla-kwun (xwaxwalitch)] W bank, E Sedro Woolley, below Skiyou Slough FW SK 8-35-5-29 (G6, LB) fishing sloughs, creeks; basket trap for steelehead, Hansen Creek

xʷixʷhalič } sense of swampy place, cf xʷixʷ = where you throw, distribute things. [Above SedroWoolley, home of F of Fats Sampson, steelhead in creek, xʷəxʷalic] SSP

whid-zaub Island Pt N of Dead Man's (Skiyou) slough SK 9-35-5 (MS)

xʷizab Rock, S side X from Sedro Woolley dip nets for Chinook, Coho, chum, steelhead SK 7-35-5 (SS)

bsigʷigʷils [bsigwigwilsc] 'Boulders' Island (Ross?) N bank, 3-4 miles below Lyman SK 10-35-5 (SS) "big boulders," "where salmon coming in" fall chum & coho by dip net from nearby rocks

čičwazi 'little island' (Ross?) S side SK 11-35-5 () good fishing in stream from S (Sorenson Creek)

čičəwucid = a bit toward the mouth on the water side > čaʔkʷ = waterside (diminutivized) + -ucid = mouth, door SSP [čičəwu'zi home of stk̇bibtəd]

kawuwácud between E end Minkler Lake & Ross Is SK 12-35-5 (WS, SS)

kəkəwaʔcuʔ = do kəkəwaʔ to yourself SSP

Lyman - Hamilton

Hamilton Area #1-14

hwiooshoolaxah near Lyman L SK 1-35-6 (SS)

xʷixʷəcilaxad = has one side arm removed, taken off > xʷəc SSP [3 places in a row, big rocks
  below Lyman, this one above, kəkəwaʔcuʔ below]

yubəčultkw [yubəčŭltkw] Chinook salmon house S bank, SW end of Lyman FL SK 2-35-6
  (WS, SS)

yubəčaltxʷ = spawned out king salmon house, fish spawning home, fish house from < yubəč =
  king salmon + -altxʷ = house, home SSP [below Hamilton, S bank, a branch of Slox
  LW]

xʷči ʸʔágali [xʷči ʸʔágale] Lyman tripod weir FW SK 3-35-6-17 (SS) in front of Lyman, but
  weir not known to be used there

čobᵊʔabš N bank, near mouth of slough W SK 4-35-6 (SS) basket traps for coho in French,
  Etach, Day creek   for all Lyman sites?

Skagit

čubəʔabš = where you have to climb up, climbing + 'people' = abš, now Lyman SSP [1 mile above Lyman on N bank CA links with Dora Solomon]

wətacic N bank, between Lyman & Etach creeks L SK 5-35-6-17 (C)

ts'hul-1o-sulh N bank, between Lyman & Etach creeks FW SK 6-35-6-16 (G7)

skʷəb [skwəb] Mouth of Day Creek FW SK 7-35-6-20 (C)

słəkuʔub Day Creek [where SSP fasted and bathed as a girl, gravel freezing to her feet]

Soh-h' yoke kakqawacid   N bank in bend SW Hamilton FL SK 8-35-6-22 (G8, C) just beyond where "bars become stony", there was supposed to be a second kakqawacid at bend of river with big rocks below Hamilton

səloxʷ "Across" from Cumberland Creek Collins locates it on S bank W of Hamilton FL SK 9-35-6 (SS, C) coho chum steelhead with dipnets, spears, gaff hooks

sloҳ = Rancheree, north side, across from the mouth of Day Creek SSP F's home, CA GF

ṫək̓əb Arm of Etach Creek F SK 10-35-6 (SS) coho

s'qik'xʷalus [s'qik'xwalos] "upper end of bar" Mannser Creek F SK 11-35-6 (SS) Coho

čaluʔłr Mouth of Careys Creek, W of Hamilton FL SK 12-35-6-14 (SS, MS) on sand bar near mouth   basket trap in sloughs and creeks for coho

□ Alder Creek F SK 13-35-7-18 (?) salmon with spears, dipnets, gaff hooks

Birdsview – Concrete #1-11

Concrete

ƛ̓il'ɪqədab "to the head" Mouth of Grandy Creek   FW SK 1-35-7-15 (SS, C)

□ N bank X from Pressentin Creek   L SK 2-35-7-13 (MS)

Concrete

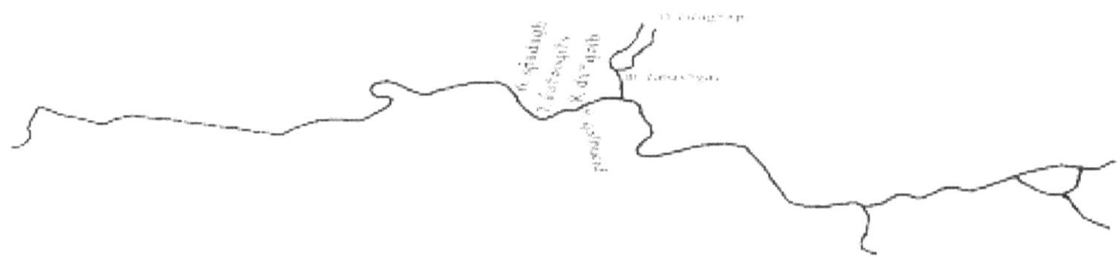

dxʷqəlb Mouth of Finney Creek   W SK 3-35-7-13 (C)

beh-ose SW tip of Cape Horn   W SK 4-35-7-12 (G, SS, C)

diʔus = look the other way, Snee-oosh SSP

liłq̓ixʷəxʷ = by way of {lił-} going upriver {-q̓ixʷ} SSP

gʷdədołdqł Whirlpool below rapids at foot of high bluff at NW side of river F SK 5-35-7-12
        (SS) dipnets, drying on NW bank

s•p̓adaqh N bank, downstream Dalles Bridge at Concrete FW SK 6-35-8-16 (C, SS) dipnets

sp̓aʔdaq = where you try in a tight space, recalling that trout there are eager for bait, Channel
        Gorge at Concrete SSP

k̓ałeoqiłs "otter bank trail" Head of Dalles FL SK 7-35-8 (SS) Living site on N, dipnets
        from rocks on S. Duck nets on poles where bridge now is [sq̓aƛ̓ = otter, šəgʷł = path ??]

dxʷqəlb Smalehu W of mouth of Baker River FW SK 8-35-8-11 (C, G10)

ʔilucid ʔə dxʷqəlb = mouth of Baker River; dxʷqəlb = rain water colored, toward the rain like, in
        contrast to the milky color of rivers with glacial runoff SSP

qəlbúcid E side Baker River FW SK 9-35-8-11 (C, SS) [beargrass kagʷal traded from Mt
        Baker for golc nets PW]

čəbəxʷgəs "where meat hooked under gills" Baker River Falls FC SK 10-35-8 (SS) sockeye

čičagʷəp Peninsula in Baker Lake FC SK 11-35-9 (SS) dry fish

sčačigʷəqs = narrowing down SSP

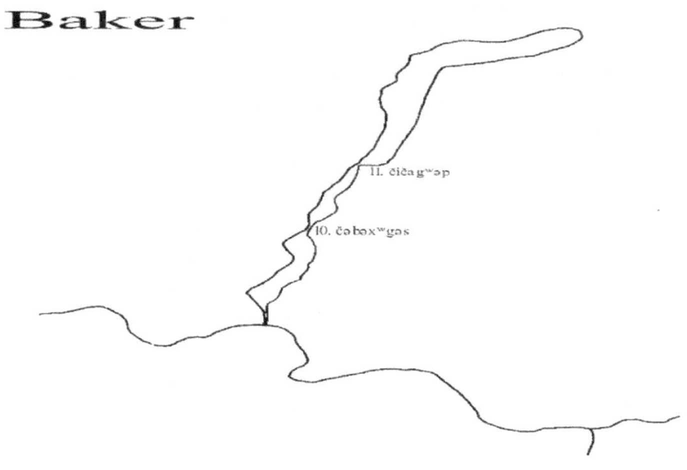

Rockport #1-13

dxʷqəlb S bank, near mouth of Baker R W SK 1-35-8 (C)

hahilwáykid mouth of Jackman Creek FL SK 2-35-8-13 (C)

dxʷququs [duxqoqos] "white face" S side F SK 3-35-8-24 (SS) S of Van Horn dipnets from
    canoes in big eddy

ko-whatch sʔílayucid Point inside bow S of Van Horn L SK 4-35-8-24 (G11, C, SS)

□ S bank X from 4 L SK 5-35-8-24 (?) village

dxʷəq̓ʷq̓ʷəq̓ʷ [dʷəq̓wʼqwəqʼʷ] "white" Foot of slide E of Van Horn FW SK 6-35 (C) same as
    3?

jijəqšəd "foot of mountains stuck in river" NW of Rockport L SK 7-35-9-21 (C) A town of
    Sauk [Cascade R Moses home]

xok̓ʷadis [xok̓wadis] "cooking spit" Sauk Station FW SK 8-35-9-33 (SS) trawl nets for
    salmon, whitefish in sloughs

xʷuk̓ʷadis = like a fastener, pin, now a safety pin SSP

sx̣ad̓x̣ad̓ədis = very crowded for space, cf d̓adis = teeth SSP

sq'ixʷucid "whitefish" N side, bend W of Rockport L SK 9-35-9 (C)

Sakumehu S bank, W side of mouth of Sauk R L SK 10-35-9 (G11) Sauk mouth has shifted,
    probably farther upstream at earlier time

saʔkʷ = Sauk, cf bəsʔaʔq a fern root used to make bread by Nooksacks and others   SSP

(bis)ilocid Mouth of Sauk R FW SK 11-35-9 (SS) same as 9?

ʔaytalúshay E & W of Rockport W SK 12-35-9-26.25 (C)

dukʷdukʷala [dukwdukwala] "posts" S bank few miles above Rockport L SK 13-35-10 (SS)

duqʷduqʷala(d) = many house poles, supports often carved with emblems of the home owners
    SSP

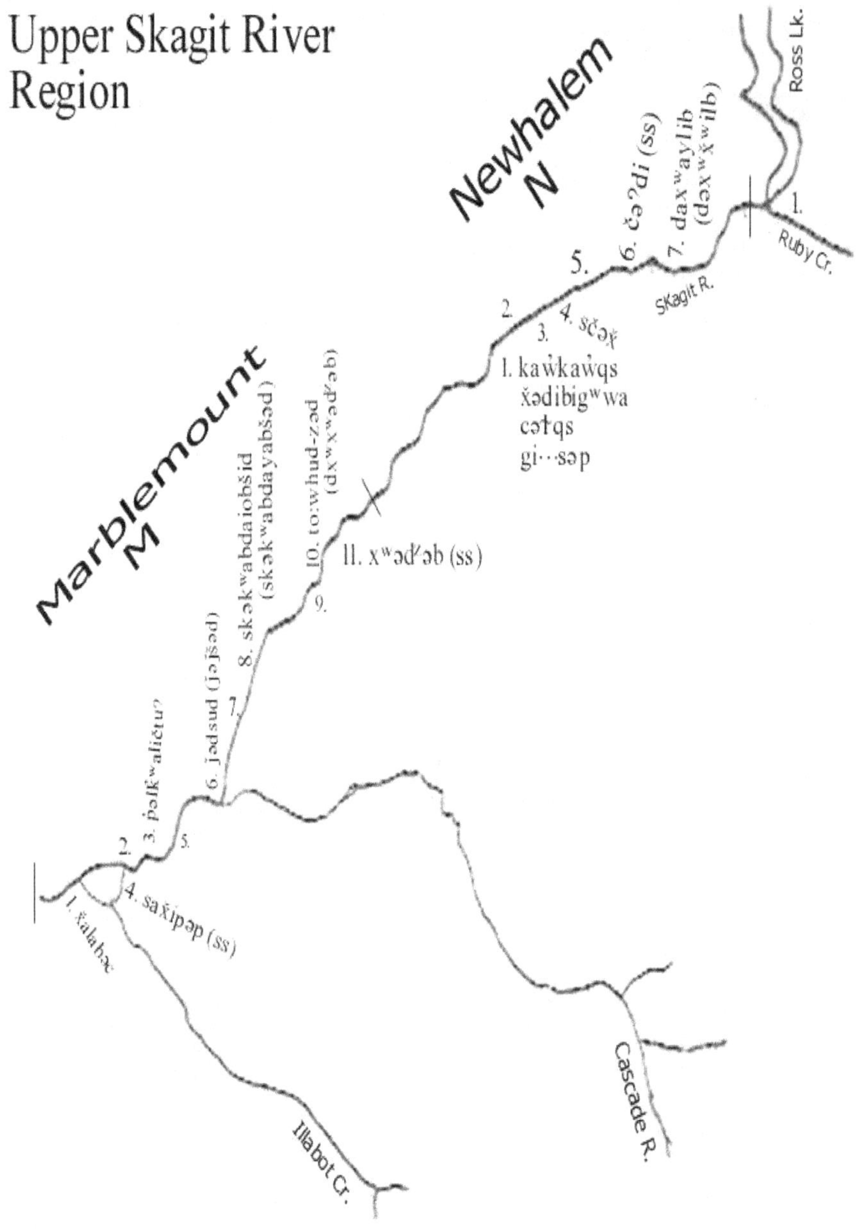

Marblemount #1-11

x̣alabəc [xalab-c] "hollow cedar stump" mouth of Illabot Creek FW SK 1-35-10 (SS)

□ N bank, bow 3 miles below Marblemount L SK 2-35-10 (G12)

pukʷalicu "lots of whirlpools" N bank, near Rocky Creek FW SK 3-35-10-22 (C, SS) traps in sloughs, tripod weir in one of the channels downstream. Rocks and rapids good for fishing

ṗəlkʷaličtuʔ = ṗəl = chase, shoo out, k̓ʷal = look at, aličtuʔ = juice of it SSP [lots of whirlpools, mouth of Sauk. ṗəlq̓ʷałičduʔ fishtrap in front of Cuthbert place, above Rockport]

saxípəp S bank, X mouth of Rocky Creek FW SK 4-35-10 (C, SS) same as 2, 3, 1 confusing sloughs at mouth of Illabot

□ S side, SE of Marblemount, by cliff F SK 5-35-10 (?) spearing pink and other salmon

jídšud N bank X from mouth of Cascade R FW SK 6-35-11 (G13, C) Big house for festivities hosted by Moses family [see Sauk section]

□ W bank, mile below Diobsud Creek W SK 7-35-11-6 (C)

skəkʷabdaiobšid Diobsud Creek F SK 8-36-11 (SS) salmon fishing

□ S side, X from mouth of Bacon Creek W SK 9-36-11-29 (C)

To:whud-zub S bank of mouth of Bacon Creek L SK 10-36-11-20 (?)

xʷəzəb Bacon Creek [house & fishery, dip net, at rock upriver X from Sedro Woolley; first hostilities with Thompsons when iron pot hook missing, kill 3 Thompson brothers, 150 years ago according to Harry Moses M, who died at 70 in 1902 LW] [furthest Skagit camp upriver is Portage, for steelhead]

Newhalem #1-7

Portage canyon F SK 1-36-15,10,11 (?) between Alma and Damnation Creeks Canoes taken above rapids in canyon to be portages. 4 fishing sites there for salmon, steelhead

    A qáuqáuqəs raven at bottom of canyon
    B xedíbigwa big rock in eddy – limit of salmon migration?
    C cəł(s)kəs "on top of a nose" rapids near head of canyon
    D gi•səp at head of canyon

□ N bank at Portage, W of Damnation Creek W SK 2-36-11 (?)

□ head of "Great Rapids," E bank of Skagit FC SK 3-36-11-4 (G13)

s•čhəx "spread open rock" SE bank 4½ miles below Newhalem, near Thornton Creek FC SK 4-36-11-1 (SS) house for smoking fish

□ N bank, E of Thornton Creek W SK 5-37-11 (?)

čəʔdí Goodell Creek   FC SK 6-37-12 (SS) camp was W of mouth of creek, fishing site was above first little falls big trout

daxʷáylib "thread" N bank at Newhalem F SK 7-37-12 (?) called thread because shed wool of mt goats was collected where they came down to river. Spear steelhead in three rapids

Ross Lake #1

□ Ruby Creek F SK 1-37-14 (SS) trout [Thompson camp here in Upper Skagit land LW]

SKAGIT RIVER TRIBUTARIES

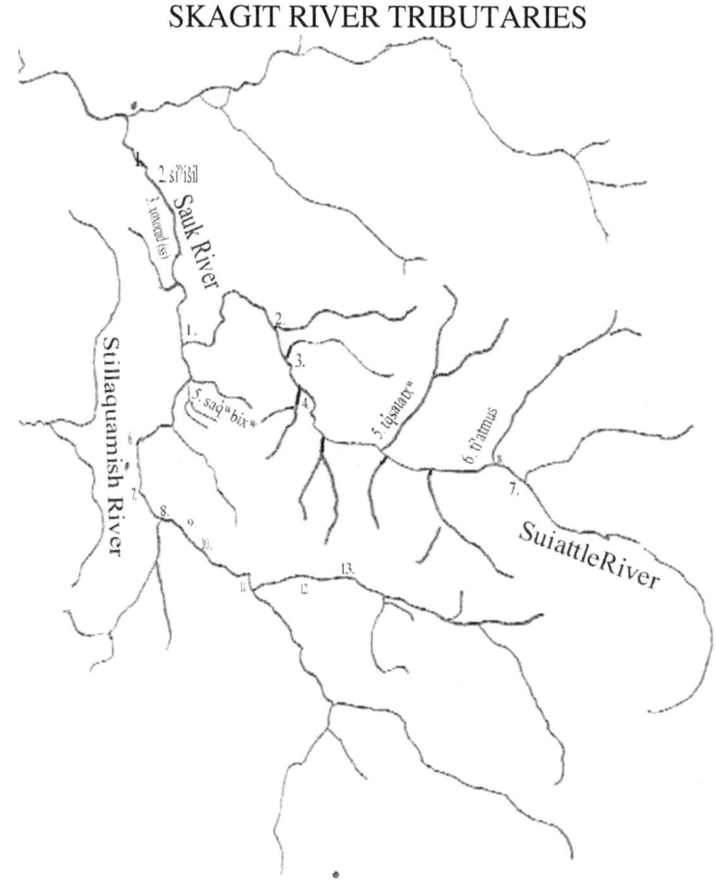

NOOKACHAMPS CREEK 1-12

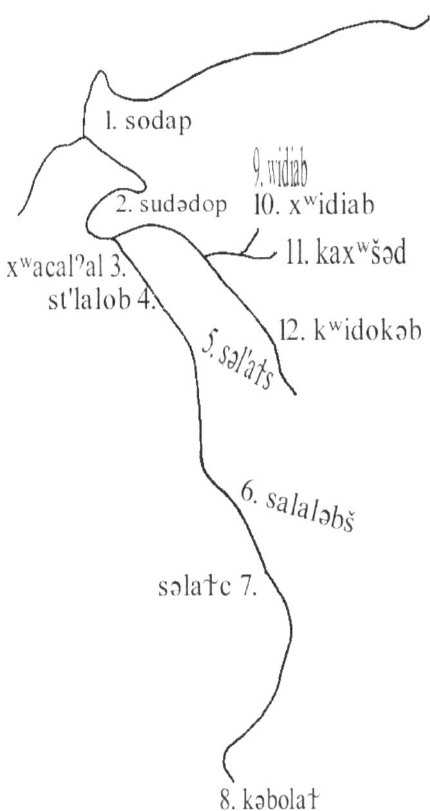

sodáp Barney Lake, little below W N 1-34-4-10 (SS)

su•bədop E fork, mile E of 1 W N 2-34-4-11?,14? (SS)

hʷacálʔal "high ground" W Nookachamps Creek , on rise W N 3-34-4-15 (MS, C, SS) S of
    & overlooking Barney Lake

st'lalob Small rapids NW of Big Rock F N 4-34-4-14 (SS) creek above & below also fishing
    grounds using rock dams, impounds, picket weirs, gratings, basket traps, dipnets, spears.
    Coho driven in shallows toward spear fishery. Trout taken with spears. Coho, chum,
    trout, chubs, two species of sockeyes. Productive throughout the year

stl'aɬs Big Lake F N 5-33-5 (LB) chum coho steelhead other fish

stlaɬc SW end of lake, W bank of stream from Lake McMurray FC N 7-33-5-7 (?) probably
    name for Big Lake

salaɬabš Montborne, E side Big Lake L N 6-33-5-6 (SS)

kabólał Lake McMurray F N 8-33-5 (SS) trout duck (nets) beaver

widiab Clear Lake Creek   F N 9-34-4-11,2,1 (SS) between Nookachamps & Clear Lake coho

xʷidiʔab [xwidiab] Mouth of creek entering Clear Lake FL N 10-34-4-1 (SS)

káxʷsəd Clear Lake F N 11-34-4,5 (SS) trout, coho basket traps duck nets in nearby marshes

kʷidókəb [kwidokeb] Beaver Lake F N 12-34-5-7 (SS) beaver trapped, duck nets in marshes

ILLABOT REGION

xʷalabəc Illabot Creek [Andrew William's F, GF lived there LW]

x̣ʷadᶻabac = prickly dried fir bark slivers SSP

sək̓ʷabadᶻalgʷił = trees peeled off by the side of the river SSP

dadəč̓ulqi(d) = 1 standing tree SSP

xʷqəlbucid = xʷəlb + ucid = mouth SSP

šabš = where things get dry; Samish SSP

dxʷ(h)adᶻəb = long place SSP

stkʷab = falls SSP [farthest extent of canoe travel LW]

CASCADE RIVER 1-4

jídsud N bank at mouth FW C 1-35-11 (SS, C) Big house for festivities hosted by Moses family.

šəkšid Small rapids F C 2-35-11 (?) 2½ miles upstream

jəkaləp "leg of a person in the water" (a rock formation) rapids F Sh C 3-35-11-14 (?) 5½ miles upstream just above Day Creek , rapids with eddy and whirlpool "There was a ritual associated with this site. A fisherman could 'shout' at the rock formation and, with the proper words, cause large salmon to appear."

sk̓éčai Rapids F, Sh C 4-35-11-12 (SS) rapids 7½ miles upstream, just above Irene Creek. "There was a rock "grand man" here. If anyone appealed to and thanked it [him] in the proper way, salmon would appear from behind this rock."

STILLAGUAMISH #1-19

In his booklet, Bruseth (1950, 34-35) listed place names along the Stillaguamish in rough English spellings. These have been checked with Vi Hilbert, a native Lushootseed speaker, and are respelled at the beginning of each entry, followed by more literal translation within single quotes. If there is no other translation, that of Bruseth still serves. Though he abbreviated Stillaguamish as Still, here it is replaced by Sl. The last version of this file is dated 4 July 2004.

1 qʷač 'mustard color'	Qaudsak	Lower Sl	
2 dxʷl(ə)hi'idačab 'wealth'	Toli Da chub	Lower Pilchuck	Plenty game - meat
3 siqabalqʷu?	Skabalko	Forks Sl, Arlington	Forks
4 baqʷab 'prairie'	Ba Quab	Kents Prairie	Open dry land
5 ƛacqʷu? 'cinched water'	Klatsko	Jim Creek	Closed in or folded up
6 ?ačalič	Achalitch	So Fork, to Granite Falls	Swifter falling water
7 ?ačaličabš	Achalitch ubsh		People on this river

8 šəqəlusəd 'high side'	Hak chlosid	Trafton Indian Camp	High bank
9 ʔilqsadiʔ 'rock point side'	Aogsadi	Near Trafton	Rock point
10 ƛəχalqʷuʔ 'huge water'	Hlohalko	Down river from Trafton	Whirlpool
11 lililqs 'point way out there'	Lae lilks	Gorge in N Fork of Sl	Referring to echoes
12 sqasalič	Ska Kalitch	Past hill above Trafton	Referring to wind, noisy
13 shudilč 'burnt edge'	So Dilts	Ebey Hill, N side	Burned off
14 šikʷigʷilč 'rocks in water'	Se queguilch	Creek below Trafton	Rocks in stream
15 tatac(u)losid 'animal talk'	Tata chlosid	Next creek below	
16 tuləkʷəb 'rivery'	Kloe ekub/Tulekub	Oso, near Deer Ck	Muddy or colored water
17 qələbqʷuʔ 'bad/left water'	Kalub	Boulder Creek	Referring to roily water
18 sgʷistalb 'sandy'	Queest Alb	Three Fingers Mountain	Sand and rock
19 ti stiqayuʔb 'the wolf-like'	Te Stekiub	Hill, N side Sl above Trafton	Wolves

These images were produced on the computer and scanning equipment of Zalmai (ʔəswəli) Zahir, whose tutoring and many kindnesses are here acknowledged with thanks. He also began the process of the most reliable analysis and translation of these terms currently possible. We both honor the memory of Vi Hilbert who was long integral to this project, supplying biographical details to this ethno-geography.

ANCESTRAL TRIBES

After epidemics devasted Puget Sound, people shifted to better locales along the saltwater shores.   Along the Skagit River lived Lower Skagit, Kikialus, and Swdabsh (Swinomish proper) along Fidalgo Island.   Along the Samish River were the Samish and Nuwaha (dxᵂʔaha), both now known as Samish. While the Straits speaking Samish, Lummi, and Klallam were moving to the mainland during this traumatic aftermath, the Nuwaha (dxᵂʔaha) were Lushootseed speakers long residing along what became known as the Samish River.

To the south were the skᵂədəbš (Skwidabsh, Skwinamish), a blending of Lower Skagit and Swdabsh, with villages at Oak Harbor on Whidbey Island and on the north side of the Skagit's North Fork. The major treaty signer Goliah came from this group, though via his traditional role as a spokesman rather than as hereditary chief.

The Lower Skagit trace themselves from k̓ək̓ədəb, the first man of the Skagit, who was sent down to Sneatlum Point by the Creator and founded three ancestral families. Later young warriors trained by running from Sneatlum Point to Coupeville and on to Fort Casey, a strategic lookout (Snyder Box 108, Folders 2: 10).

For the Swadabsh, major villages along Swinomish Slough included those at the present reservation town, called   txᵂiu'udᶻ ~ txᵂiwuts, led by ləxalbid, and at the Wilbur homestead, called   waxtadači ~ xᵂtadači, (from sweathouse = wuxta ?), led by bəloʔl and his brother yitq̓ᵂəb. bəloʔl was a famous gambler and the inside walls of his house were decorated with guns, piles of blankets, and other winnings. The last longhouse there was built by Peter Charles's grandfather, sdaxui ~ yitq̓ᵂəb, who was a cousin of ləxalbid. His grandmother had a scar on her arm where she fell onto a stake in the trench at the fort on Sullivan Flats. An old village (čayəlq̓ᵂo) was at the spring below the Lyons place.

In the spring, Swadabsh people left their longhouses to camp in mat houses at various places, such as Dewey, Similk Bay, and Snee-oosh (sdiʔus), where   ləxalbid had another longhouse. Some women dug and oven steamed camas on islets off Deception Pass and along Fidalgo Bay in May, then clams at Similk and Snee-oosh in June, while men trolled for springs and silvers, hunted deer, and used line for rock fish and gillnet trout. In late summer and early fall, many people moved back to the slough to weir net at private locations.

In the early 1800s, the village at Swdabsh still had a woman who served as "youth leader," keeping the children occupied each night before bedtime. The last woman who was raised this way was ai'ol'tsa, who was probably ədəltsa (Jennie Thomas) (Snyder Box 108, Folder 6).

Span Joe said Blower Bluff was a good place to catch herring, and Susie Sampson Peter added Greenbank and a beach near Camano City for both herring and smelt. Sturgeon could be taken at Utsaladdy. Harpoons and gaffhooks were effective at the edge of the great Skagit logjam near Mount Vernon, though the best fishery was claimed by kᵂəskadəb as one of his house sites (below, in Renowned Names).

Seals were harpooned while asleep at night, or fighting each other during the day. A net with a ten inch mesh was used for seals, while a drive into a land net was used for deer. Nets placed underwater, in the air, or hand held in canoes were used for ducks, along with snares on the flats.

A fort, on the flats beside Sullivan Slough (tiq̓ʷil 'murky, smoky', bəkʷigʷə?), was a longhouse surrounded by a 7-8 foot trench with pointed stakes embedded along the bottom. The top of the trench was covered over with branches and grass, except for hidden planks that gave safe entry. Further up this slough, a house (sgʷadəqs) stood on the eastern slope at the north end of Pleasant Ridge, providing another refuge. At least once, all the Swdabsh wintered over there. Other settlements were reported at Whitmarsh at the north end of Swinomish Slough, at Whitney between Telegraph and Indian Sloughs, and at qeliqet near the north bridge.

Today, the Swinomish Indian Tribal Community (SITC) and its Senate is the legal and political successor of four tribal authorities from the lower Skagit and Samish Rivers and adjacent islands, and includes both Lushootseed and Straits speakers.

SITC were involved in the most complex rituals and sects of the region, including the Growlers, feast for the dead, shamanic redeeming odyssey, and inherited sacred shield-like objects (sacra) such as the sgʷədiləč.

Growlers

Spread from the central coast of British Columbia, north to Alaska and south to the Columbia River were specialized groupings initiating only children from elite families, more to indicate status within regional ranks than complex doctrines.

Modern "tribes" who once participated in the Growler sect (x̌ədx̌ədəb) were the Songish, Lummi, Klallam, Samish, Swdabsh, Twana, Puyallup, Nisqually, and Suquamish. It was inspired by Wakashans to the north, both from dancing societies of the Kwakiutlans and the Wolf Dances (ɬuqʷali) of the Nootkans, who passed it on to speakers of Straits languages such as Songish, Lummi, S'Klallam, and Samish. These, in turn, initiated Twana and Lushootseed members (Amoss 1978: 72), particularly at the large Samish longhouse on Guemes Island (Elmendorf 1993: 68) in the late 1800s. Among its important emblems were ducks, who arrived in the spring at the same time as the namesake patron spirit of this guild. Indeed, he was believed to travel with ducks and other waterfowl.

Ghost Feedings

Both Swdabsh and Lummi once held periodic feasts for the dead under the direction of shamans, such as famous SITC member John Fornsby. Until the early 1900s, families placed cooked foods intended for the dead near the hearth in the center of house, and then hid under mats along the side bunks of the house before the officials summoned the dead to eat these foods. "The food was placed there to show respect to the ghosts, to reduce their feelings of jealousy toward the living, and in general to placate them for the remainder of the year" (Collins 1974: 236).

Redeeming Odyssey

On 22 October 1976, Martin Sampson told how he went around the region helping Jerry Kanim set up a model of the spirit canoe to tell how shamans used to go to the land of the dead (Miller 1988: 45-46; 1999). The actual trip was done in spirit while the doctors acted it out in a house filled with a large audience. As narrator, Martin told of the need to make the trip to the first land of the dead to cure someone with lingering lethargy. In the process, the shamans walked most of the way, using a canoe only to cross two rivers and then a bay in front of the longhouses of the dead, a beautiful settlement visited during its summer bounty, since the times of mortals and ghosts were reversed.

To lure the dead outside and locate the stolen spirit, the doctors made an elk decoy swim in the bay until it was noticed and the village alerted. Everyone rushed outside, including a ghost holding the hand of the lost spirit, who had been taken for any one of several reasons, often because the person was grieving at a funeral. The shamans thereby saw it, recaptured it, and brought it back to the patient, who got well immediately.

On 21 March 1977, Alfonso Sampson gave a fascinating account of one of the last Odyssey ceremonies, held during his childhood on the beach under where the present Rainbow bridge was later built over the Swinomish Slough between La Conner and the reservation. The location is significant because it was below the cemetery and at the end of main high road.

His family had come to visit his grandmother Annie McLeod and encountered the shamans preparing to leave for the land of the dead. Four shamans, including at least one close relative, announced that they were going by water over to the "other side" to retrieve the spirit of their patient. After some discussion about the perils of crossing a big river, they decided they needed five in the canoe, apparently for stability. His kinsman selected Al to go along, although he was a child, and positioned him in the middle of the canoe, the safest spot among the crew.

They sang the whole way, until they arrived in the land of the dead and became very quiet. It was beautiful there, full of flowers. A doctor found the spirit and stole it back, placing it just below the left side of his neck [in the depression near the collar bone?]. Then, they hurried back to restore the patient to health. Because it was weak from being with the dead, they added breath to his spirit, helping it strengthen the patient.

Joyce Wike (1941: 75) says that SITC members denied knowledge of an elaborate ceremony. She was told, however, that shamans, including a woman "if she has a strong mind," would gather and sing their songs in turn to recover a soul from the land of the dead. "This treatment embodies the concept of group curing but on a relatively unformalized level. The most recent case of this kind was reported at Swinomish two years ago." This seems to have been the same one that included Al Sampson. Wike (1941: 71) also includes a map to the land of the dead as described by a famous shaman. The next chapter is fuller description of this rite.

sgʷədiləč

The enormously complex beliefs associated with sgʷədiləč involve an epic in which at least four brothers go up the Skagit River, placing men and women at various locations to create future generations there (Collins 1974: 158-59, Snyder Tale 73, Amoss 1978: 66-70, Miller 1999: 60-62). These brothers, oldest to youngest, were sgʷədiləč, Knife, Fire, and Baby, each giving powers and abilities appropriate to their names.

Knife taught the proper ways to butcher and prepare game, Fire how to cook it. Baby instructed these couples on how to fix family talents, skills, and abilities on their children. The others went away upriver, and Knife may have stopped at the Hozomeen Quarry, adding great cultural dimensions to its archaeological significance. šgʷədiləč became a rock in the upper

Skagit near Portage where he might be heard singing about 3AM by those who had fasted and prepared to learn his song to be able to hunt and fish successfully.

Because all water sources are interconnected, it was also possible to dredge up, net, or hook specific forms of these guarding powers from the bottoms of lakes, rivers, and bays. Similarly, a special mask was brought up from Lake Samish by ancestors of the Edwards family (Sampson 1938: 13).

As Thom Hess (Amoss 1978: 70) noted, this term has an etymology only in Lushootseed, indicating its origins there, meaning "the thing that bends down over to protect." At least five varieties or outward forms of sgʷədiləč were used in the past, made from cedar (planks, boughs), rock, goat wool, and vine maple (*Acer circinatum*). Indeed, the great cultural significance of vine maple throughout this region is indicated by various dialect names.

For example, the latest *Lushootseed Dictionary* by Bates, Hess, and Hilbert (1994) provides kyuʔkiwəc on page 119 as the Snohomish term, təq̓qac on page 238 for Skagit, and sč̓uč̓uɫəc on page 74 for Suquamish. Vine maple splints were used for openwork baskets, fishtraps, salmon tongs, roasting sticks, spoons, snowshoe frames, and, most recently, knitting needles (Turner 1979: 154-55). More important than these helpful tools, the upriver was the home and heartland for the distinctive form of the vine maple sgʷədiləč, now inherited through family lines throughout the region to give spiritual and religious help to natives.

Indeed, vine maple sgʷədiləč are very closely associated with the upper Skagit River, and mountain goat wool may also be, but this was never confirmed. Vine maple groves, clusters, or stands serving as traditional cultural properties used for sgʷədiləč reveal themselves in active and obvious ways. "Look for a clump of young vine maple that twist and sway when there is no one around" (Bruseth 1950: 29-30; Box 1, folder 6). "Sometimes they found that vine-maple which was bunched-up and all and would shake" particularly "above Marblemount at Naiumsi [Diobsud] Creek" (Sally Snyder Box 109 folder 4: page 24 LW). In other words, without wind or ground shift, these stems churn up the ground to leave telltale marks of their vitality.

Dora Williams Solomon, married into Lummi, implied that the founding person in the upper Skagit River appeared at the same time as the Cedar Tree and first sgʷədiləč.

> My mother seen that place where this skwedilech and where this tree and where this one human were. Her uncle brought her there when she was very young, first got married with my dad, and they went up there to – that's way up there – you know where Ross Dam is? Well the mountain from Ross Dam. They walked up that way – hiking you know. And her uncle brought her to this place where the skwedilech was created and where the cedar tree was created. She says that place is just as level as could be. That's why the Indians used the cedar tree for everything (Solomon 1982: 17).

Legendary Beginnings

Because all important knowledge was private information, Lushootseed have both popular as well as privileged accounts of their origins. As Martin Sampson (1938: 7) wrote "Family tradition was never taught in public, but was whispered to the children in the family's own council." Most of the popular accounts deal with the immortal called dukʷibəɬ, the transformer or changer, who, by purpose, blunder, and accident, prepared the traditional world for humans.

Public

As per map, in the vicinity of Portage, at Bacon Creek below Newhalem, according to Charlie Anderson, were four places, whose spiritual associations derive from their transformation by dukʷibəɬ before the dawn of human history (Snyder Box 108 File 5 CA), given here in her transcription followed by its updated spelling within square brackets.

1)	raven qauqauqes [qaẃqawks]
2)	big rock xʷədibigʷa [xʷədibigʷa = xʷəd push, -əb- , igʷa inside] shaman transformed into
		a twelve foot rock with his hanging heart protruding from the ceiling of an open
		chest cavern
3)	atop nose cət(š)kəs [čə̓tqs = near the nose]
4)	s.čəx̣ [sčəx̣ = split in half] = four miles below Goodell Creek, a
	smokehouse & open rock

Privileged

A private epic of creation is hinted at by John Fornsby, a famous Skagit River shaman, in his wide-ranging autobiography (Collins 1949: 296). He mentioned that God devoted considerable thought to how the first people were going to make a living. He created fish and animals for them and taught them how to make and use a variety of traps. He decreed that Europeans would have tame animals to feed them, but that natives would rely on wild creatures, who required prayers and rituals before allowing themselves to be killed. In consequence, return (first) foods rituals were instituted to give thanks, along with prayers and taboos applied to hunting, fishing, and berrying.

Violation of these taboos caused disasters so the world was remade and destroyed several times. At least once there was a Flood, but six canoes of people and animals survived to repopulate the earth, while a seventh drifted to settle China (Peter 1995: 145-157). One of these landed on the massive Warrior Rock behind the SITC tribal offices and its crew came down to found txʷiwuts village through the efforts of Robe Boy and his sons (Snyder 108-6 AJ, SSP)

Its most informed and privileged version was told by Dora Solomon (Hilbert 1980a: 1-4), who said "people were forbidden to tell it unless they were from that family of the woman named tsiʔ əgʷas." A man who knew the flood was coming tied four seagoing canoes to the top of haẏqiʔd, the rock behind the tribal offices, with four long ropes that stretched out as the waters rose higher. As the flood receded, the high top of the mountain broke off and the other canoes drifted away, but the man, his wife, son, and daughter came to rest there at the village of modern Swinomish. They soon built cattail mat houses for dwelling and storage.

Slowly, life returned. Little fish came into the slough and the girl went to play with them, until, one day, a great fish took her away. Saddened, her brother wandered away, began to shoot small animals, prepare their pelts, and eventually sewed them into a blanket. When he finally came home, his parents were gone and the mat houses burned because they thought both their children were dead.

In great despair, he wept until a voice told him to gather up and match all the animal bones he could find, lay them out, and wave his robe over them four times. Immediately, all these bones became people, but they were chilled. The voice said to gather charcoal from the burned houses, wave the robe over them, and thus fire was recreated. Next he waded into the slough, where herring swarmed as soon as the hem of his robe touched the water. These fed the people. A mountain goat appeared to give everyone wool blankets as clothing to keep warm, and may have provided the first goat wool sgʷədiləč.

In another version, which better matches his image on the Swinomish pole, his only companion was his dog, who eventually was changed into either his wife or the mother of new people (Upchurch 1936: 289).

Robe Boy (x̣uyałič̓a)

After this Flood, according to another account, a boy was abandoned by his family at txiwuts because he refused to fast and quest for spiritual help. Starving, he was forced to purify and, thereby, made contact with God, who instructed the boy to make a special blanket from the skins of many small animals (Sampson 1938: 14-16, Matson 1968: 29-38). Then he gathered up all the refuse from the Flood and waved the blanket over it, creating an abundance of foods. People too were revived, but they had no sense, so the boy made brains for them from the very soil of that place, according to Andrew Span Joe (Snyder ms: Tale 68). These people spoke many different languages, drifted apart, and thereby scattered all over the earth.

In another version, human kin rejoined Robe Boy and those he had created were sent off to live by themselves. Perhaps they went to Dugualla (dugʷalał) Bay on Whidbey Island, since people there were obligated to provide firewood to Swdabsh during the coldest times of winter, supposedly in return for having been saved from famine. Though their pedigree was suspect, their women were valued wives because they made such fine mats (Snyder 108-6 AJ).

Robe Boy (x̣uyalič̓a ~ 'made from a robe') and his two sons, tuxʷiqədəb ('first daylight') and ləx̣albid ('daybreak') founded villages of

(a) dəxʷiuʔudᶻ on the west side of the slough from the Flood rock near Rainbow bridge to American Hall, using the land to March Point. Recent chiefs were bəloʔl and stodəbqəd, older and younger brothers

(b) xʷkaykayohəli, probably 'bluejay place' from kay̓kay̓ = Stellar's jay, the name of the nephew who succeeded Goliah as leader (Snyder Box 108, File 10), although skayu = 'ghost' is possible, at Martha's Bay and Pull and Be Damned, for the south end of this peninsula and offshore islands; their chief was k̓əlk̓alč̓əcu whose last descendant was Henry Cladoosby

(c) shore from Snee-oosh Point to Similk Bay and on to Deception Pass, including Hope Island. Their chief was ləx̣albid, through Joshua Obidiah at Lone Tree Point, Swinomish George (Tommy (č̓ubəhad) George's father, Bertha Dan's grandfather), and the Willups family, who presently hold the name

As a boy, the first ləx̣albid of this name slept late every morning and was thought lazy, but he had secretly been up all night looking for great power. One morning he was out in the bay in a canoe, singing "Goodbye, my people, Goodbye," warning of a coming epidemic from the north. His father moved his people to Snee-oosh (or Coupeville), but lax̣albid stayed behind at the present village and saved everyone by having them pray for a long time.

In another version, after the epidemic he recreated people from sweepings to populate the earth, but his father returned with human survivors and these lesser creations went to live at someplace like Dugualla Bay on Whidbey Island (Sampson 1938: 13).

Starchild

The most elaborate epic of this entire region, told in many versions, explains the institution of chiefly family lines from the children of two boys, less than twins though more than brothers, mystically descended from stars. The version below builds on Miller and Hilbert (1996: 141-155) blending accounts from Susie Sampson Peter in 1950, Dora Solomon in 1975, and Martin Sampson (1972).

Two sisters of high rank were camping on a prairie, digging fern roots. The world was new and there were few males so, one night, each fantasized marrying a white or a red star. The next morning they awoke in the sky next to these husbands. The older sister was married to an old man with white matter in his eyes, the younger sister was married to a handsome young man. They continued to dig fern roots in their new home, but the husbands warned them not to dig any root that went straight down.

The older sister was soon pregnant by her wiser, older, kinder husband, but, dejected, she wanted to escape. Digging deeply, she broke through the sky and looked at her home below. She convinced her sister, who remained in the sky, to dig twice as many roots so she could make a cedar bough rope to lower herself down. Later this rope broke and fell to earth to become Big Rock, a holy place (above, in Legendary Beginnings).

On earth, she was advised by a voice to change a log into an old woman to babysit her newborn boy, Starchild, and to build a house using four living trees as corner posts and a fish weir to sustain them. Easily confused, the grandmother sang lullabies appropriate for a boy instead of a girl, as the mother had demanded. Overhearing, two women fleeing from the Chehalis River stole the baby as they went up the Skagit River toward the Sauk.

Devastated, his mother took a soiled diaper left behind and washed it in the river. Blinded by tears, she was startled to hear a baby cry and discovered Diaper Boy in her hands, cross-eyed, bald, and twisted in her agony.

Raven took the defenseless mother and babe to be his slaves, treating them badly. Diaper Boy was warned never to go east, as his wives warned Starchild never to go west, so, ever defiant, the brothers eventually met, the younger was healed, and they planned revenge on Raven. Starchild came to the town with an elk in his canoe, announcing that the girl who lifted it out would become his wife. Dainty Green Frog won and everyone feasted. Raven gorged on their elk-fat-rich feces, becoming the scavenger of today.

At the wedding, the brothers decided to finish the modern world. They threw everything that they could find – tools, clothes, baskets, bowls, and house planks – into a huge fire that burned for many days. Later the cooled ashes were placed in a pouch and scattered over the earth so that humans would ever after be able to find most of what they needed wherever they settled. Thus, the brothers made the world ready for humans, towns, and tribes. Trees and stones were now available at most locations to allow humans to make a variety of necessary tools, clothes, buildings, and traps.

In addition, during this scattering, the brothers confirmed the sacred qualities of the world and acknowledged the supreme importance of immortal beings for achieving success. As they re-created the world, they named all of its aspects with special words (instituting magical phrasings known as "dicta"), which were only learned by the most important chiefly families.

These words controlled the world because they linked together minds by the sheer force of disciplined will power to accomplish a variety of personal ends. Known as χačadəd, *this mind control concentrated all intelligence. Its strongest form was called* siyu'id, *derived from the high god, and was very privileged. By its means, animals were summoned and killed, people's moods shifted, and catastrophes averted.*

When the brothers finished, an old woman asked about light and they decided that the earth needed a soul so they prepared for sun and moon. Star Child attempted to be the sun, but as he rose into the sky, the earth became very hot and people jumped into the water to stay alive. When he returned, Star Child was told that he would not do. Instead, Diaper Boy became the sun and Star Child became the moon, going into the sky with his wife, who became the Frog on the back of the moon concerned with women's health.

Things continued for some time until Mink, introducing deceit, claimed to be a son of Moon and went along through the sky. Daily, Moon took along a cane to vault over the river in the sky, which was the Milky Way. A few days later, Mink decided to go alone as the Moon, but he forgot the cane. When he came to the river, he tried to jump, but missed, fell in, and drowned, causing the first eclipse.

The brothers met and decided that they needed to move away from the earth so they would have no more unwelcome visits from people like Mink. Besides, the world was now ready for humans. They named every bay, nook, cranny, bend, confluence, and prominence. They named every lake, hill, mountain, and spring, allowing some duplicates. They named the tribes who would live in each place, taking the name from the characteristics and spirit of that location.

Though these men now live in the sky, their children became chiefly families all over Puget Sound after humans arrived to occupy this prepared land. They grew and prospered, filling the region and learning from ancient traditions, while adding some of their own. Their most famous members passed on outstanding names.

Renowned Names

Mostly native people lived common, uneventful lives, but Collins (1953, 1966, 1979) has distinguished as "renowned names" a set of famous chiefly names that acted more like regional

52

titles. It was the holders of such names who owned several big houses in various endowed locales. Indeed, in Lushootseed, such a person or family is called <u>hik^w</u> <u>siʔab</u>, in the sense of a grandee, "big, high, most, very" in terms of authority, respect, ability, and, above all, presence.

In a few instances, such an owner might have several large houses, each placed near an important seasonal and localized resource. Each house was a few days travel away from the others to justify all this labor. That he (or they) could coordinate the building of more than one large home further spoke to his (their) leadership abilities. As brief examples of some of these renowned names for those living on the SITC reservation, a few well known from a variety of publications and historical documents, including treaties, are discussed.

ləχalbid

As discussed, for the modern community on Swinomish Slough, the name of ləχalbid remains a strong link with their ancestral past, a child of Robe Boy who landed after the Flood.

k^wəskadəb

John Fornsby (Collins 1949: 296, 326) said that his own Lower Skagit grandfather k^wəskadəb ("scorched head") had a potlatch house above Skagit City where the house posts at each end were painted to represent his powers. His fame extended along the entire Skagit River since his ancestry closely bound him to Whidbey Island, while his name itself is that of the rock (a petrified person) in the eddy just below the furthest limit of salmon going up the length of the Skagit River (Snyder 108, file 5: 58 AC).

His children also became famous. One daughter married among the Chehalis, and a son was Sneatlam, a Lower Skagit who was renowned throughout the Northwest, a Catholic prayer leader, and an important broker in the fur trade based at Fort Nisqually. After his death on 16 December 1852, a carved wooden effigy of Sneatlam stood on a high bank on the eastern side of Whidbey Island, "dressed in his usual costume, and wearing the articles of which he was fond" (Gibbs 1877: 203). His family has remained important in intertribal and international trading and brokering.

His granddaughter named ma'na'yl (ba'da'yl in Lushootseed) was captured by Klallams from Dungeness, who quickly realized her high rank and so married her. A year later, the Klallams returned to formalize this wedding by giving over twenty slaves, a canoe, and many goods to the grandfather, who, in turn, gave them ten slaves, a seagoing canoe, and many blankets. As they landed at Swadabsh, the groom wore an enormous rawhide mask. Everyone exchanged clothing and feasted on local shellfish and game. This international marriage among these leading families opened a channel for sharing, cooperation, and ritual participation between the Straits and Puget Sound, abating prior hostilities. Elmendorf (1993: 108-100) dates these events to 1780-1810.

When the grandfather k^wəskadəb died, he was placed in the back of his own potlatch house until later buried at the SITC cemetery. After this building washed away in a flood, one of the houseposts was found downriver at La Conner. John Fornsby held a potlatch to set it up on his own behalf.

pətiyus

Prominent among the treaty-signers for SITC was Patius [pətiyus], leader of the Nuwaha (Upper Samish) village called "cedars" between Bayview Park and cemetery (Snyder 108-7 JJ), where he was buried, until SITC led by tsiʔ əgʷas [named for the woman ancestor from the Flood, above] decided to move the old graves to the reservation. Martin Sampson said on a private tape,

> They brought in, took in all those cemeteries, brought in the people from there. Out of these graves they discovered Patius's body. Patius had a broken leg, lower part of the leg. It healed crooked. They identified him by that. He was taken there to Swinomish. Patius the signer of the treaty is at Swinomish now. Now Tom Patius was a distant relative. He was a nephew of that same one, but I don't know how it is. Maybe third or fourth cousin. The name Patius was a family name, they were entitled to that name. Tom Patius took it. The descendant of Tom Patius, of course, is Casey, married into Lummi. And Thomas Scott married into Snohomish. That family came from Patius. And of course afterwards, Tom Patius married Sally, who we know as Fat Sally, then on to Frank Tom. That is the story of Patius family. Tom Patius died in maybe 1898. He got drowned in the Skagit River. So his body has never been found. People took first names as last names like Casey Tom. Patius was Bayview Tom, the father of Casey and Thomas Scott.

Other important leaders had their remains moved to Swinomish. "Indeed, in 1938, when Whites were buying up waterfront property on Whidbey Island, and displacing the gravesites of Tslalakum, Goliah, and others of the first Lushootseed converts to Catholicism of the 1840s ... the parish priest responsible for Swinomish ... officiated at the reinternment services" (Vecsey 1997: 330).

sλ̕əbibtəkəd

The most specialized, and perhaps recent, role throughout this region was that of the prophet, a position whose importance increased with white settlement, forced change, and intermarriage with families like those of Patius. Today, in the best known case, while the name discussed below has recently been passed on to descendants of the first wife, the direct male line has long lived and been enrolled at SITC Swinomish.

The most famous example was sλ̕əbibtəkəd, the prophet known as Captain Campbell (or Camel), who centralized religion and politics along the upper Skagit River. His father had moved from Nespelem, now headquarters for the Colville Reservation, and married a woman from the native town at the mouth of the Snohomish River. As he grew up and returned to visit relatives along the mid-Columbia, he was introduced to native versions of Catholic rituals, to aspects of the Plateau prophet cult, and, eventually, to Catholic missionaries like Father Eugene Chirouse, an early and important Oblate missionary, then active at the Catholic mission among the Yakama. After the 1855 Treaty War, Chirouse came to the Tulalip Reservation in 1863, then ended his career among the Canadian Okanagan (Sullivan 1932).

The prophet and priest worked closely, particularly in translating liturgy into Lushootseed. Apparently, they communicated with each other using the Okanogan dialect of Interior Salish. The prophet established his home longhouse, one of several, across from Rocky Creek, where he led Catholic services in the summer and native spirit dances in the winter. His links with Chirouse expanded his authority into Euro-American and Catholic contexts.

By introducing his own form of prophet cult, and later serving as the translator for Father Chirouse, sx̌əbibtəkəd also gained recognition from outside authority which aided his centralizing of Upper Skagit polity and religion. In other words, he used prestige in both systems to augment native society with increased organization.

For years, near Day Creek, when the first Spring salmon was caught in a šəbəd trawl net at slox̣ and dispatched with a deer ulna spike, it was taken to the prophet who used it to consecrate those annual fish runs. By assuming a leading role in this first salmon ceremony, the prophet reaffirmed his own authority.

Like any rich man, he had several homes, but his base was a huge plank house on an island across from Rocky Creek near Marblemount, where his wife managed the domestic affairs. In keeping with their rank, however, most of the work was done by slaves and retainers. At Rocky Creek, he was also close to the Cascade River Pass into the Interior at Lake Chelan. Downriver families would leave home on Thursdays so they could be at his home for Sunday services (Snyder Box 108, Folder 5 AC).

He is also sometimes associated with the huge house at the mouth of the Sauk River, but this hall was within Sauk tribal territory. He went to this longhouse to consult with Sauk and other leaders, each speaking as distinct Nuwaha, Skagit, or Sauk tribal authorities. Similarly, he often presided at the largest Skagit town, located five miles above Marblemount, where a large cemetery was eventually located (earning it the place name of skaiyu'ali 'ghost place'). Gatherings there were so large that only canoes were large enough containers to cook food in, and only men did the cooking (Snyder Box 108, File 5: page 51 LW).

ẏagʷało

Captain Campbell married two women from powerful families who further encouraged him. First, he married a woman from Big Lake along the Skagit. After she died, he married the daughter of Patius. Her name, ẏagʷaɫiẇ, was that of a male Samish ancestor, assumed later in life (Snyder 1964, 383: note 9). In this marriage, she outranked him, as indicated by her escort of body guards and attendants. Sometimes she is misidentified as her own daughter by the prophet, who also held the same name.

ẏagʷało "used to talk to the Indians when they had meetings and told the men what to do. She told her grandchildren and the people that it was their land and that they didn't want to give it away, and tell the younger children how they had to be. She was always kind of busy and was always tied up drying fish and getting the people to work because she was a chief's wife. The Indians used to gather at the upper side of the Skagit River (around sosotia ~ Mount Vernon) with the upriver people who piled their fish in one place while the down-river people piled theirs in another. And then they would all cook it and exchange it. yagʷało used to organize these gatherings. When the people gathered she had certain people cook and others who called out for the food. She had a man who had a loud voice like a bell, so he called the people to come and eat and he always called the people when they were going to pray (SS Box 109 folder 4: page 102 AC).

His dynasty continues among the SITC and Upper Skagit (Collins 1953). After the captain died, the office passed to his son John, then to his daughter, who was remarkably forceful, like her mother, but had no children so John's son Joseph inherited the position and passed it to his sons John, then Peter, who died a few years ago. Most recently three males in the same Upper Skagit family have assumed the name.

Present Ross Lake includes the contact zone between the Upper Skagits of the Coast Salish branch and the Lower Thompsons {Ntlakapmuk ~ nɬəʔkəpmxʷ}, locally known as Steetathls [stitaɬ], of the Interior Salish branch. While their historic relations were not always calm, their degree of interdependence could be intense, as reflected in a report by Martin Sampson in a private tape that his uncle, a SITC native doctor, had a Thompson Indian ghost who served as his spirit guide after he encountered it ("Came on me, stays with me") along the Thompson River in British Columbia, north of the border in Canada. Thus, while economic resources were localized and carefully guarded among the living, in religious matters, including possible intertribal associations with the ghosts of "enemies," wide latitude existed.

An important distinction applied to the seasonal use of the Skagit. Winter was a time when people stayed close to their plank longhouse communities eating stored foods, while summer found them traveling extensively up and down river to traditional camps and resources, as well as visiting far afield along the coast, into the mountains, and through the interior to harvest and prepare fresh game, fish, berries, and plants for such storage.

During winter,

The last village upriver on the Skagit itself and deep in the Cascade Mountains was ḱʷabatsabš, consisting of ṫskʷab, a large winter house at Portage, west of Damnation Creek on the north side of the Skagit; one small winter house with three families to the east of Thornton Creek on the north side of the Skagit; and one large winter house, dawaylib (meaning "thread" or "rope") at Newhalem on the north bank of the Skagit (Collins 1974: 19).

As noted and mapped previously, four places in the vicinity of Portage, at Bacon Creek below Newhalem, had spiritual associations deriving from their transformation by dukʷibəɬ (Snyder Box 108 Folder 5 CA). While the presence of these landforms was public knowledge, their specific locations were guarded by families who knew their formal names and attributes.

Of great import for the history of native and European farming in the Northwest, both in terms of ancient tending of garden plots owned by native mothers and daughters on burned over prairies and later commercial farming of potatoes introduced by the early European fur traders, is

garden spot səqpəda'ləkʷ above Rockport for growing camas and fern (saʔq) root, then potatoes, after these were brought over the Cascades from the Wenatchi by the grandfather of Harry Moses, they were tried at Sauk Prairie, then here on the Skagit (Snyder Box 108 Folder 5 AC, HM, LW)

Also, Collins (1974) included other comparable named places that represent momentous beings and events influencing the life and history of the study area. The following, in particular, inspired chiefly families by providing them with wealth and resources to sustain and enhance their leadership.

tiyułəbaxʷəd   a man-like wealth spirit who lives under the water at The Dalles in the Skagit River near Concrete (1974: 146, 151)

čagʷalq̓ʷ "brought something down," referring to a man who split a rock (see above) to make a seat for himself opposite Rockport. He started off with his elder brother to listen to marmots (whistlers) in the high mountains, but his brother turned back and shortly after died. The younger brother persisted and got power from Timber Wolf for wealth and stamina that can now also be received by fasting and praying near this rock (1974: 147, 151)

kalalitabiqʷ a giant wearing moss on his head, knocking over trees with his walking stick, and seeming to appear as fire swarming up a tree (1974: 157)

kayəʔ "grandmother," an old woman turned by dəkʷibəł into a stone near Portage who is believed to control the fish runs upriver from where the Cascade River joins the Skagit at Marblemount (1974: 212)

bubuxʷəd a huge cedar near Rockport hung with long moss that it used to capture the souls of people who came too close and then tossed them back and forth across the river with another cedar tree until that person died (1974: 214).

Nels Bruseth (1950: 14-15; Box 1, Folder 6), long a forest ranger at Darrington, published an account of a battle between the Skagits and the Steetathls [Thompsons], but only in a generalized account. In some versions, this feud is given an historic context because an iron pot hook disappears and the battles are the result of conflicting accusations. Bruseth's original notes, however, specifically locate such a battle at the site of the present Diablo Dam powerhouse at the mouth of Stetattle Creek, as does Jenkins (1984: 124), another local.

The Duhkwautsub War

On the upper Skagit, just where the City of Seattle [Diablo] power house now stands, was the summer camp of a family of Upper Skagit Indians. The surrounding country was their fishing, hunting, and berry territory. Other families were welcome to enjoy it.
Here lived a father, mother, and four sons. The oldest son had a wife. The youngest was an adopted son. A daughter of the family had married a Thompson River man, from the country north of the Skagit.

One day, this daughter with her man and his two brothers came down river to visit. One of the men in this party, a boastful, quarrelsome character, got into an argument and a fight with one of the Skagits and was killed. This created a very bad feeling between the families. The visitors left and on their way north traveled up Steetathl creek to cross the mountain.

A year later, when the Skagits were again at their summer camp, the wife of the married son said, "We had better move down the river again. If we stay here we will all be killed."

This woman was known for her ability to see into the future.

The old man said, "No, we won't move away. We have the right to stay here. If trouble comes, we will take care of it."

Finally came a day when the woman said, "Something has to be done. There are enemies near us."

The old man then sent the adopted son up the river to see if this was true. The boy looked for signs and the first day did not find any. But the next day, when he stopped at one of his fish traps, he found it molested. A fish had been cut up into small pieces and bird feathers had been strewn over and among the pieces. This was clearly a declaration of war. He returned home, bringing bad news, saying "We are sure to be attacked. Perhaps we should leave for down river. We are not many enough here to be safe."

That day the woman said, "I am going to leave." She also persuaded the husband to move down to the mouth of Bacon creek where another family lived. Before leaving, the man said, "If anything happens, send the boy down to tell us and I will come back up to help you."

The boy began planning for a quick get-away. He untied one of the small canoes, and left it so it could be easily pushed into the water.

Just at dusk that day the dogs sensed intruders, and began barking. Suddenly out of the woods dashed several men and began an attack on the family who rushed into the house.

The house was built of poles and long cedar slabs, the corners tied together with ropes of cedar root and bark. The attackers sneaked up and cut the ropes on the two front corners and, with a jerk, pulled the front out, exposing the people inside. Arrows flew thick. The two sons fell first. The father and mother lasted a long time, finally falling, so full of arrows that they hardly touched the ground. Then the house was set on fire and everything burned.

Meanwhile, the adopted son had sneaked out and, among the barking and milling dogs, crawled down to the canoe, shoved it off, and steered down river. When he reached his brother's camp and told what was happening, the woman said, "We can't be of any help now. They are all dead. But we can go up tomorrow." They did and found the burned camp and charred bodies.

Now was the time to plan revenge. The two remaining brothers talked it over and decided that this [moment] was not the time. The attackers had probably gone clear back to their own country. The best way was to return down river, tell the other families of the tribe, and get them to pledge their help in the campaign to rid the country of the enemy next summer.

So it was that one day, a year later, several braves of the Skagits traveled up river bent on revenge. When they reached Sedieh (sdi), now called Goodell creek, the foremost scout smelled smoke and, watching carefully, saw it coming out of the ground on the creek bank a short distance up stream. This was reported to the others. The older brother then stole quietly up along the bank opposite the camp to a point above it. Then, putting a tuft of moss over his head, he got into the water and drifted down stream. When near the point where smoke was *coming out of the ground, he crawled out of the water and up the bank, and saw that it came from an underground dwelling with entrances both at front and rear.*

After getting back to the helpers, further plans were made. The two brothers were to get near the rear entrance and the other were to make a bold rush at the front.

The plan worked. The inmates dashed out of the rear entrance and were beaten to death by the brothers. The helpers got the spoils of war, much smoked meat and fish.

The brothers were still not satisfied. They dismissed their helpers and went further up into the mountain meadows. There they found four others of the same tribe as their enemies.

The brothers were outnumbered but pledged each other to do or die to complete the revenge. They caught their victims off guard and killed all four.

All this happened many generations ago, but out of it has come many a story about the Steetathls, becoming more and more legendary. These people from the north, who used to come down along Steetathl creek into the Skagit, have become mystic creatures given to petty thievery. To this day is often heard the expression: "The Steetathl must have been around." They are never seen, but sometimes heard signaling to each other with birdlike whistling.

For the lower river, including ancestors of modern Swinomish, other ancient feuds involved communities at Barney Lake and the islands, as assembled from several sources (Sampson 1972: 56-59; Peter 1995: 187-202; Collins 1974: 161).

Clues that these war stories form an interwoven series come from Martin Sampson's (1972: 57) title referring to "Battles of Whats-al-ul and Ut-sa-laddy" involving a youngest son whose name he spells as Pa-och (paq̓ʷ). Moreover, he (1972: 58, 59) noted that "The era of the Squa-de-lich was after the Battle of Whats-al-ul," located "just above Barney Lake on the Nookachamps River." In other words, the gift of these guarding powers was somehow in compensation for the deaths, pain, and hardships of these fights.

paq̓ʷ

High House was the winter abode for the duqʷəčabš tribe, comprising at least five longhouses for those from Big Lake (čəɫaɫ) led by <u>spik-cum</u>, from Clear Lake (?) in the house of <u>Be-bash-cad</u>, and those of <u>Za-ta-sub-ki</u>, <u>Ch-lah-ben,</u> and <u>Scha-ha-lab-ki</u>.

Long ago, spring snow melt filled the Nookachamps River to flood Barney Lake in front of High House (x̌ʷatsʔalʔal), trapping the people inside during a sudden dawn attack and massacre. As was the custom, when the house was surrounded, the enemy leader announced they were Skagits in order to give any of their inmarried or captive relatives a chance to come forward for rescue. Only a pregnant girl and her brother-in-law escaped in the final moments. After hiding in the woods for some time, they returned to the plundered houses and took enough to survive "by a stream in the foothills of the mountains to the east" (Sampson 1972, 57). A few months later, she gave birth to a boy. Later these inlaws married and had three more sons.

As the brothers grew into elk hunters, they were warned never to go over the ridge to the west, but, after much discussion among themselves, they went there and discovered the old village, returning with discarded weapons. Their father wept when he saw these, eventually telling them about their massacred ancestors. The children insisted they move back.

The youngest boy was paqʷ *and he had a magic hat of weasel fur decorated with red feathers [red-shafted flicker?], that made the oldest brother, born the nephew of their father, uneasy because he was very literal minded. This hat was in some way compensation for the many lives lost in the massacre and the sincere diligence of the tiny boy.*

Later, attempting to destroy this hat, the oldest boy scorched it, driving the youngest in despair to quest and gain great power from inside Big Lake. His mother wove him a four-strand belt of cedar bark. Then he went to xalabač *["marked all over" near Illabot Creek flowing into the Skagit near the Sauk River] to make a special cane and clothing, caching it there.*

Finally, when the hunters could not approach any game, paqʷ *waved his hat in the air and chanted "Herded by Wolf" and the elk dropped dead. Sometimes, they netted already baked salmon and meat from the river. Jealous, threatened, and confused, the oldest son plotted revenge. The day they found an entire side of elk, roasted and ready to eat, he resolved to end these "tricks" against him and, when the chance came, threw the hat into the fire. Immediately* paqʷ *began to wither away, becoming increasingly feeble. After many consultations and treatments, a doctor decreed that the hat be replaced.*

A gathering was called so that paqʷ *could sing of his Wolf Power. Many refugees from Skagit attacks heard about this healing and came together. After many attempts, an old man heard the correct tune and insisted that the oldest brother kneel beside the boy to learn it and, stretching out his neck like a heron, sing it for everyone. Thereby,* paqʷ *began to gain strength. Then he was able to eat. He asked each community to make ten distinctive bands of woven cattails so as to identify their share of elk that Wolf would drive into Barney Lake.*

He sent his brother upriver to Illabot to fetch his gear and return, placing that bundle on a special mountain goat wool blanket spread on the floor. Then paqʷ *took it into the woods and dressed in a weasel fur hat decorated with red feathers, raccoon skin apron, buckskin shirt, leggings, and moccasins. Every family head floated their ten marked cattail loops on the lake so an elk could stick its nose though each as it died to provide an even distribution of this meat. Then everyone went inside to crouch under cattail mats while* paqʷ *went outside to forcefully sing and dance before waving his cane and shouting to collapse the entire elk herd.*

Fully restored, the oldest brother pleaded with paqʷ *to undertake a revenge raid on the Skagit, but* paqʷ *said his hat was only to feed and nourish people, not to kill them. Yet those gathered strongly insisted that, as a display of power, only the father and four sons attack Utsaladdy at midday after landing at Miller's Point [sx̌ʷəlgʷas]. Dressed in full war gear,* paqʷ *alone stepped out on a fallen tree that projected over the bluff above this village to attract everyone's attention. Then he waved his hat and chanted as they all fell dead, oozing blood. Those who were only stunned were killed with war clubs by his family. Any Lower Skagit survivors fled to Whidbey Island so Kikialus took over this place on Camano.*

Long after these hostilities were settled, another boy quested by diving deep into Big Lake and was rewarded by awesome immortals there with the gift of power boards constructed of cedar shields. Later when this gift was transferred upriver, it took the form of loops of vine maple. Such sgʷədiləč *cleansing and nourishing power can have five forms in rock, vine maple, goat wool, or cedar.*

Most recently, High House was devastated by the first smallpox epidemic on the Skagit, though the surviving family of four moved upriver to be able to assure continuity.

REDEEMING

The epitome of Lushootseed culture, especially in the north, was the Redeeming Rite {*spəłtədaq, spədaq*}[24] relying on the remarkable cooperation of shamans with the special power to venture to and from the land of the dead. Specific accounts of the rite exist from the Skagit, Swinomish, Snohomish, Snoqualmi, Duwamish, Suquamish, Puyallup, and Nisqually, along with version from the neighboring Lummi, Klallam, Twana, and Chehalis.[25] Miller (1988) considered these in some detail, prior to this overall synthesis of long reflection.

This retrieval rite, for all its importance for comparative religion, also brought together every aspect of Lushootseed culture. For the duration of the ceremony, realms of spirits and ghosts, efforts by shamans, and complexities of a person's life (and death) were drawn together inside a house, which was decorated with specialized artifacts.

A plank house was used for the rite, either owned by the patient or borrowed for the occasion. Its floor space was cleared so that paired planks could be stood up and carved effigies of each shaman's Little Earth placed in a row down the middle.

What was unique about this rite is that, instead of a doctor working alone as usual, shamans worked together in unison to mime a trek to the land of the dead,[26] a fight to regain some spiritual aspect, and a hasty return to put that lost vitality back into the patient.

Along the way, central concerns of Lushootseed culture were epitomized and validated in a public community setting during the coldest, wettest months of the year. To balance the depicted vehicle, an even number of shamans, usually four or six, co-officiated during the rite, although one of them took the lead. Along with their power from Little Earths, their other spirit allies were called upon periodically to help so that the shamans could safely go to the afterworld and return. As noted above, the Little Earths were synonymous "owners" of the earth itself and so could draw the shamans back home. Almost all of the shamans were men. Women were not prohibited from joining the rite, but very few female shamans had the necessary spirit helpers.[27]

---

[24] spəłtədaq derives from s- = nominalizer + bəł = 'curing by shamans' + təd = 'in a line ~ queue ~ row' + -aq = bounded ~ tight; all together meaning "aligned shamanic healing". In Straits Salish, it is called *smətnaq* by regular B > M & D > N shifts.

[25] While now living in southwestern Washington, the Chehalis name for themselves indicates they moved from Mud Bay on the Sound, accounting for this parallel with Lushootseed.

[26] As Marian Smith (1940: 81) explained, Lushootseed shamans sometimes cooperated for a single cure, but when they did so, they alternated so that one sang while the other worked on the patient. For the odyssey, shamans worked in unison. Only the Midewiwin (Shamans Academy) of the Great Lakes tribes involved a comparable cooperation among shamans. While clearly ancient, its modern procedures trace to a religious revival about A.D. 1700 at the Ojibwa capitol near Ashland, Wisconsin.

[27] Chehalis mentioned Queen Susan as a woman shaman with the power to go to the land of the dead and return (Miller 1988: 24). Twana named five men with retrieval power, along with one woman with a Wolf familiar, who could also make two bundles of cedarbark dance in the air. Most dramatically, when the odyssey vehicle seemed to get to the top of a mountain, her hair blew straight up; then, when coming down, her hair blew back toward the mountain top. At the bottom, she howled like a wolf (Elmendorf 1993: 74, 227, 230).

The shamans went at midwinter because everything in the afterworld was the reverse of their own. When snow covered the ground here, there it was summer with warm, flower-lined trails. Similarly, our day was their night, our high tide was their low one, and objects broken here were whole there.

Everyone in the community was involved in the preparations. Women cooked food and cleaned the house, while men hunted and helped out as needed. Children gathered nearby, ready to run errands and carry messages. A sense of place was so profound that every odyssey enactment was customized specifically to the locale and people involved. In other words, specific features of that place and population were explicit in that version of the rite, with the local graveyard doubling as the land of the dead.

Meanwhile, the shamans, or that shaman associated with the house, went into the woods and selected a large cedar tree, which was hauled or floated to a convenient location near the community. There it was split into planks,[28] each shaped into a particular form, either with an arched top, snout, or disk. Every drainage had its own style of plank. For example, the Snohomish cutout the snout because they traced descent from a legendary marine mammal.[29]

Each plank was coated with a chalky white layer of paint to provide a background before thick black outlines were drawn along the edges. The day before the ceremony, each shaman was assigned a plank where he painted an image of his primary power in the very center, colored in combinations of red, white, and black. Sometimes, dots in red or black surrounded the figure to represent the song that linked shaman and spirit. Since humans were alien in the afterworld, shamans felt as though they were traveling through an engulfing viscosity. Whenever they sang or talked, their breath escaped as bubbles, represented as painted dots, moving through thickness.

Poles were also made for or by the shamans to serve multiple purposes during the rite – as bows, punts, probes, spears, paddles, or place markers.

Every shaman kept a carved humanoid figure about a yard high representing his Little Earth. Before an odyssey, this figure was repainted and dressed, as appropriate, to look its best. When the Little Earths, primordial male and female spirits who lived in forest marshes, heard the shamans singing as they departed for the afterworld, they rushed into the house to help out by lodging in their carved effigies.[30] According to common belief, these earthlings actually made the voyage which their shamans merely depicted.

During the arrival and setting up of the objects for the ritual, spectators had to keep very still and silent since these actions were fraught with danger. The membrane between worlds was being thinned or breached and much could go wrong that could lead to fatal consequences.

---

[28] The best evidence that a single log was used to make all the planks is the graduated widths within any single set and identical knotholes in all the boards at the American Museum of Natural History in New York (Miller 1988: 80).

[29] Marian Smith (1946: 310, figure 3) shows five styles of plank tops drawn by a Suquamish, but these have no other documentation.

[30] Details of the manufacture of ritual objects are not well known. The only comparable descriptions were provided by John Fornsby (Collins 1949: 297-298) in terms of the making of power boards. Fornsby himself used three power boards, a spirit he inherited from his grandmother's father. Apparently, while a pair "ran" through the house, Fornsby sang behind the third one. These triple boards are pictured in Haeberlin and Gunther (1930: Plate 1B).

Ghosts might be attracted to vulnerable spectators or shamans might decide to steal souls and hide them in the other world. Other supernatural beings might be unleashed because of a miscue or a wrong move at a crucial moment.

When all was prepared, spectators sat quietly near the walls of the house. Meanwhile, the shamans and their human helpers lined up outside, ready to march in and set up the paraphernalia so they could start their odyssey.

Surrounded by drumming and singing, the procession entered the house. The shamans were wearing special cedar bark headbands and painted faces. Sometimes, long strips of woven cedarbark were draped around the neck. Each curer carried his Little Earth, with an assistant carrying the painted plank. Sometimes, the planks were held so that they appeared to peek inside the door, making their power seem more life-like. Each shaman placed his figurine in a line down the center of the house and sat down on the sidelines. Helpers arranged the planks in pairs so that each shaman faced the image on his centrally painted spirit power. The boards at the ends were painted on only one side, while those in the middle were painted on both. In this manner, the images looked at each other and provided protection for the shaman both front and back. When the schematic vehicle had been constructed in the middle of the floor, the shamans returned to stand in the cubical spaces between each board. Then they acted as if departing.

They had to hurry because, in Lushootseed belief, any illness was a prelude to death (Collins 1974: 206), not a temporary disability. Their patient was wasting away without any obvious cause because the dead were sapping his or her vitality. During the entire ritual, the victim rested unobtrusively on a cedar mat at the rear of the house.

Along the way, the voyagers made routine stops to gather power, influence the future, and collect information with great caution and circumspection. For example, a shaman used his cedarbark scarf to wipe off sweat and other body secretions so they could not be used against him by ghosts and other doctors. Lost souls and images of other objects from the land of the dead were also brought back in its tangles.

At the first stop, shamans visited a land filled with the spirits of artifacts, each of which sang its song. Moving among them, the healers learned and repeated these songs since knowing them would help people to use tools more efficiently. Artifacts themselves represented the full cooperation of natural products, human resourcefulness, and spiritual inspiration. The manufacture of useful items required supernatural assistance because career powers enhanced any personal abilities. Melville Jacobs (1958: 85) noted that principal foods and major tools were regarded throughout the region as akin to "spirit-powers, kindred, or co-villagers. Foods and tools themselves wanted relationships with people just as spirit-powers and kin yearned for their relatives. All must help and lean upon one another."

Since this was the initial encounter with the "other side," everyone was reminded that it was the spiritual aspects of existence which were the most important, a logical beginning place for any such journey, and for life in general. Tools and other artifacts often served as appropriate "houses" for spirits, contacted through song.

After some time, the trip continued until they got to a berry thicket, which was also spiritual because the berries were the size of birds, hopping about in the shape of human babies. Since everything was believed to have an essential human form under the cloak of its species or appearance, this visit was a reminder of the common humanity of all life. Shamans tried to pluck a berry or two with their poles, and their clumsy antics created much humor for the audience. If they managed to get just one, there would be a plentiful berry harvest the next fall.

The Nuxalk had a similar belief that berries in their true forms looked like goggle eyed little boys (MacIlwraith 1948: 691). Among the Katzie, berries and mollusks were primordial foods, available from creation and later augmented by foods provided by beings transformed into modern species.

Continuing on, the shamans next came to a lake where their vehicle was reconfigured into a flat-water canoe. Since deep lakes were and are the abodes of powerful spirits, this place was a particularly important source of power. Indeed, a shaman with a lake-dwelling spirit like Otter called out its name to speed the canoe across the water. In addition, lakes and marshes provided a wide variety of foods, which were also being celebrated at this stop.

Next, they came to a wide prairie where the shamans used their poles as bows and seemed to hunt meat. If they were successful, then there would be plenty of game in the fall. Those crews who used planks carved with snouts took time to offer pieces of meat to each mouth in a symbolic feeding gesture.

Fifth, they came to Mosquito Place where they were attacked by such insects the size of birds. They fought these off with their poles, being careful not to be stung for that would be fatal. Since Mosquitos were shamans in the spirit world because their ability to suck blood was useful in curing, this encounter was a test of shamanic ability.

Moving on, the doctors came to Beaver Den, where they hunted using their poles as spears. If they killed a beaver, furs would be of high quality the next year.

Afterwards, the shamans went on to meet the Dawn after they had been traveling most of the night. The appearance of light added to the heaviness of their thick surroundings, so the curers had to pause to "lift the daylight" by passing their poles over their heads.[31] Because Dawn had different intensities, they had to lift it five times, the sacred pattern number for southern Lushootseeds, to safely move underneath and beyond this light. What was dawn for the shamans was sunset for the ghosts.

After their exertion, the shamans rested all day long, since it was night in the land of the dead, preparing to resume the next evening. Sometimes, the lead shaman, if he had great power, would take time to make a quick trip to the land of the dead to better plan the final assault.

The next day, after the trek resumed, the major challenge was a raging river with collapsing banks and on-rushing boulders. Shamans held a quick conference and decided to tip up one end of a plain cedar plank as a ramp to help each jump across the river, using their poles to vault. A shaman was most vulnerable when he was suspended in the air supported only by his spirits. If his spirit were weak or another shaman held a lingering grudge, that shaman would lose his balance. If a shaman slipped or fell, he was expected to die within that year.

By now the crew was close to the town of the dead, whose physical surroundings looked like the location of the nearest human graveyard, customizing the rite according to the characteristics of the participating shamans, the tribe and family of the patient, and the locale where the ceremony was held.

---

[31] Gulf ~ Guelph of Georgia Salish believed that Dawn had four phases or aspects, each one was prayed to while facing east (Barnett 1955: 212, note 20).

Near the ghosts's town, the vehicle was beached. While a few shamans reversed the planks and figures so they could head back home, the rest went along the trail to the town. There they sometimes encountered a ghost, played by a member of the audience, out picking berries. They knew it was a ghost because he or she walked by crossing and recrossing the feet. Pretending that they too were ghosts, they asked for news and learned the quality and name of the newest occupant and where it dwelled, "it" being soul, mind, or spirit of their patient.

Once informed, the shamans quickly killed the ghost and buried it in a shallow grave. Such murder was possible because there were at least two lands of the dead. The first, where they were, was inhabited by people who were still remembered by the living. When all memory of them was gone, they died again and passed to the second land of the dead. From there, according to some shamans, they were reborn into a descendant and began living again. The cycle, in theory, was endless, either through rebirth or increasingly more remote abodes of unremembered dead.

By learning from the ghost what they were after, the shamans planned a strategy for when they got to the town. Sometimes, they created a diversion by having one of their spirit powers appear in front of the town as an elk, deer, or beaver.[32] When everyone rushed to the river to hunt that animal, the houses were left deserted. Then, acting like a ghost, the most powerful shaman entered the house where the patient's vitality was, quietly leading it away. Outside, other shamans joined them to protect the retreat as they rushed to the vehicle. Once they had boarded and pushed off, a shaman "threw his meanness" at the ghosts, who swarmed from the town. Apparently, by successfully fighting for the lost spirit, shamans were able, in fairness, to keep it. If they merely lured it away, the ghosts could take it back.

In some towns, this final battle was enacted with long flaming splinters shot at the shamans by youngsters acting the part of the ghosts. If a shaman were hit or burned, he died within the year. Since the enactment took place at night, often inside a house, these flames were both dramatic and fraught with danger because of hazardous, old, wooden buildings.

Having made their escape, the shamans paddled hard, with their Little Earths providing protection on the way home. Sometimes, they took a short cut used by those who died suddenly, which brought them back in a few hours instead of days.

The patient was still lying quietly on a mat in the back of the house when the shamans arrived, each quivering with power.[33] Their leader came forward with the missing vitality and acted as though he was pouring it into the head of the invalid. Slowly at first, then with renewed vigor, the victim began to sing his or her power song.

Sometimes, shamans saw the souls of other people, seemingly well but soon to sicken, in the land of the dead and these too were brought back, carried in a shredded cedar scarf or warmed in the skin crease between neck and shoulder, and restored to the owner. These patients liberally compensated their healer.

Among Twana, before the doctors returned, the patient and spectators were protected by a rope barricade. "Those people inside the rope are all the souls that are coming back from the

---

[32] An account of the rite from Lucy Williams (Collins 1974: 202), in which a shaman assumed the form of his Beaver power to float in the river as a decoy to lure the ghosts out of their homes, was overlooked in Miller (1988).

[33] This quivering may survive as the curing mode of the Shakers.

ghost land. The sick man will be singing too now, shaking his head. And they keep pulling them all toward the sunrise" (Elmendorf 1993: 231).

Once the vessel returned safely, everyone in the house heard about future conditions. Any artifacts, berries, or meat brought back were given out to families who might need them. Usually, berries went to a woman since picking was her job. At least once, a baby was brought back to a childless woman, who gave birth nine months later.[34] Other predictions were also made, both to delight or to warn everyone.

Though they might rest briefly, the used paraphernalia had to be dismantled to close off the route to the afterworld. Planks were taken into a remote area of the woods to rot, returning to their elements. Only in the most dire of circumstances could boards be reused for an immediate return to the land of the dead, always accompanied by special songs. The only reason for such reuse was to enable a crew that had gone to the wrong town to immediately take the correct route to the other abode of the captured entity. Any delay gave the ghosts time to pass on word ("telephone") that the shamans were coming and allowed them to hide the spirit away so that the patient would die. Having made the journey once, the planks were contaminated and unsafe.

The poles may have also been abandoned, but some seem to have been reused in later rites. Kept for a lifetime, Little Earth figurines were carefully washed, losing much of their paint, and hidden in special places in the woods, often a hollow tree.[35] There each awaited the next ceremonial use by its shaman partner. Only after the shaman died was the Little Earth left forever in the forest.

Though not well reported, a counter attack by ghosts was described by Jerry Kanim, a Snoqualmi leader (Miller 1988: 33). They came late at night, their day, and spit down the smokehole at individuals, who became comatose, foaming at the mouth. While relatives attended them, shamans rushed down the trail to the land of the dead, not pausing to set up effigies or grab paraphernalia. By starting specific songs, they alerted Little Earths who rushed on to slow down the ghosts by engaging them in conversation. When shamans caught up, they killed a ghost, took back the souls, and immediately restored to health the stricken individuals.

Great urgency was required because if the ghosts got to a particular place on the trail, probably the sticky lake, then the souls stayed in their keeping until the shamans mounted a full odyssey and fought to get them back. Though this attack was revenge for the killing of ghosts during a final fight, the victims were not shamans but those with less spiritual protection.

In Puget Sound, intertribal contacts were long an aspect of the local social, political, and religious complexity. Important leaders fostered these interchanges at their feasts, namings, marriages, funerals, cult initiations, and winter dances. These activities in turn had repercussions throughout the larger environment and enabled spiritual connections to be made that facilitated the complex cultural elaboration that was the shamanic odyssey.

---

[34] The best known instance was Moses Seattle, a dwarf grandchild of the famous chief.

[35] As a boy, Mark R Harrington, later a prolific Americanist anthropologist, discovered such a hidden effigy in a tree in West Seattle, presumably a casualty of the 1893 burning of that Duwamish community (Tollefson 1992). It subsequently joined the collections of the NYC American Museum of Natural History.

BETWEEN A ROCK AND A LOGJAM:
Salishan Chronologies

The Salishans of the central Nortwest Coast have less-well-known yet elaborate epics featuring "begatting" founders (with inherited ancestral name-titles) who were sent to earth at specific places. Equally localized were anchoring features of technology and economy, such as net usages. Culturally radiating from these, however, were privileges of rank, dynastic marriage, literary expression, trade, potlatch, and ritual interweaving elite families along the entire Northwest Coast and beyond in space and time.

Intro

Eager to help, some boys went to pick salmonberries at a thick patch above the abandoned town of Skagit City. The grandfather, named kʷəskadəb, of one of the boys had once commissioned half a dozen Lower Skagit carpenters to build him a potlatch house there, with a painted post holding up either end of the gable. Years later, as a grown man, that boy recalled, in fine laconic style, how

"There were lots of berries. We crawled around and got to the middle back of the house. The body of my [great] grandfather kʷəskadəb was right there. We got scared. We went home. We never picked berries. I laughed [with relief] when we got back into the canoe" (Fornsby to Collins 1949: 295-96).

For most Salishanists, that startling encounter was our first introduction to Johnny Fornsby and to kʷəskadəb, a famous Skagit leader based on Whidbey Island around Coupeville. In his autobiography, Fornsby added that kʷəskadəb was father to the equally famous Sneatlam; was uncle to Goliah, the spokesman drafted as signer for the northern Lushootseed tribes at the 1855 Treaty of Point Elliot - Mukilteo; and had one daughter married among the Chehalis.

Sneatlam became renowned throughout the Northwest as a Catholic prayer leader and an important broker in the fur trade at Fort Nisqually. At least one of his wives was a Makah from Neah Bay. Yet one of his brothers flaunted the strict rules of the culture by having an affair with a slave girl who thereafter became known as dᶻaƛəb ~ 'mistake'.

After his death on 16 December 1852, a carved wooden effigy of Sneatlam stood on a high bank on the eastern side of Whidbey Island, "dressed in his usual costume, and wearing the articles of which he was fond" (Gibbs 1877: 203). To this day, his family has remained important in intertribal and international trading, now brokering as far away as China.

Sometime after the boys fled, the body of kʷəskadəb was buried behind his potlatch house, which eventually washed away in a flood. One of his house posts, 3 feet wide, 4 feet thick, and 8 feet long, landed in the back of the bay at La Conner. Johnny Fornsby hired Lummi to help him move and set up this housepost at a potlatch that was held when the dead were gathered up from a gravehouse on Deadman's island and also moved to the community cemetery, where kʷəskadəb himself was eventually reburied.

A granddaughter of kʷəskadəb by the name of ba'da'ɬ (in Lushootseed, ma'na'yɬ in Straits Salish) was captured by raiding Klallams from Dungeness, who instead quickly married her, receiving ten slaves, a seagoing canoe, and many blankets from her grandfather in exchange for twenty slaves, a canoe, and other goods from these Klallams. At the wedding, the groom appeared inside an enormous rawhide mask. Elmendorf (1993: 108-100) dates these events to 1780-1810.

Extending their range of dynastic marriages, both Sneatlam [sniƛ̕əb] and kʷəskʷadəb appear in the journal of Fort Langley for June, July, and August of 1830 (Maclachlan 1998: 150, 156-6). This time, Sneatlam's son was marrying the daughter of a Cowichan leader, a chief variously known as Shashia, Joshua, Josia, or Old Joe. By luck, portraits of him and his son Cul-chil-hum were painted by Paul Kane in 1847. A brief biography, alas, mentions only two sons, leaving uncertain the fate of this daughter married among Skagits when he died blind and heirless in 1870 (Maclachlan 1998: 228-230).

While negotiations had been decided in the spring of 1830, the formal exchange took place in late summer after the Vancouver Islanders had moved to their Fraser River fishery.

"This afternoon [June 17, Thursday] the two Scadchats Chiefs – Neetlum & Wheskienum accompanied by a half dozen of others & Sinaughten the Sinnahomes Came here – They have about 20 Skins Lar[ge] & Small…"

On June 29, Tuesday, Nanaimos and Cowichans of Vancouver Island arrived at the mouth of the Fraser, only to be attacked by Lekwiltok (southern most Kwakiutl) about July 4th, before the Nanaimo settled into their summer village on Friday the 16th. On July 10th, the Cowichan Shashia demanded 2 guns and 10 blankets in exchange for a dozen skins, but he left empty handed "for we have hardly So much property in the Fort." His concern was, of course, not routine fur trade but his upcoming wedding responsibilities.

Neetlum himself visited the fort on August 7th, Tuesday; the Cowichan Shashia on the 8th, before the 9th when "In the evening two very large & three Small Canoes full of Scadchads made their appearance at our wharf – Their Chief (Needlum) was already in the Fort – he immediately embarked with them & pushed over to Joe's [Cowichan] camp – All the great men of the river are now assembled there – Our night watch is doubled & every thing in readiness in Case of the worst."

On Friday, August 10th came the culminating exchange in "A great Ceremony – going on the other Side solemnising a marriage that took place last Spring between a Boy of Needlum's and a little Girl of Joe's – Canoes – Guns – Blankets – Slaves etc. etc. are exchanged on the occasion".

On Saturday, the Skagits came across to propose trading, "for which they would have nothing but Blkts [blankets]" but were soon rebuffed. "They returned to the Cawitchin Camp in the evening & Spoiled Children they are." On Sunday afternoon, August 12th, the Skagits left for home.

Clearly, through pedigree and alliances, kʷəskadəb and his family held and hold high rank, meeting elite criteria by having a Wealth spirit power (below) and by inviting (to a potlatch) four times at least (Sally Snyder Box 108 Folder 2 page 17 Joe Joe). Accordingly they kept affirming it with generosity, as indicated by the specially built potlatch house where he was entombed. Its location just above Skagit City served to remind everyone of a major source of his bounty, namely the dense fishery at the lower end of a logjam, two miles long, that blocked the Skagit River from above Mount Vernon to Hamilton. Spawning salmon clumped there before managing to weave their way upriver. They were so abundant that more fish-selective harpoons and gaffhooks could be used along with nets.

Until the jam was dynamited away in 1878, peoples along the Skagit had extensive contacts with their neighbors because voyagers either had to drag a canoe through the brush around the jam, or, more readily, portage over to the lower Samish or the Stillaguamish Rivers to reach salt water (Collins 1974: 39).

This fishery, potlatch house, and generous leader, therefore, account for the logjam in my title. They also, as it happens, account for the rock since, according to notes taken by Sally Snyder from Alice Campbell,

> Long ago there were people who turned into rocks [because of the Flood]. This kʷəskadəb was the name of one [of them] way up on the Skagit. It is the name of one of Andrew Joe's relatives. They came up to ask the people there for a name (certain people used to go to certain places to obtain a name). If they had known, they could have asked the *sbalix* here [around Concrete] for a name (Snyder 108 5 58 Alice C).

Ancestors

But what of the ancestors of kʷəskadəb, prior to his own relocation by the Flood? Surely they must have been equally great. Indeed, they were not only great, they were primary ancestors for this entire region, the first generation in the founding of the Skagit world. Their names were indeed mighty.

While most native people lived common, uneventful lives, those with what June Collins (1966) called "renowned names" were entitled to form a set of famous chiefly leaders who owned several big houses in various richly endowed locales. That he (or they) could coordinate the building of more than one large home further spoke to his (their) leadership abilities. Indeed, in Lushootseed, such a person or family is called hikʷ siʔab, in the sense of a grandee who is "big, high, most, very" in terms of authority, respect, ability, and, above all, presence.

According to Lower Skagit, k̓ək̓ədəb, the first (Lower) Skagit man, was send down to čuba'aɬšəd (Sneatlum Point) by the Creator to found three ancestral families who each first lived in one of the three compartments within a huge plank longhouse set inside a stockade. Nearest the beach lived the čətčətqs, in the middle were the highest ranking abd̓udadagʷabəts, and furthest back were the absəlalagʷəbš, the source for the people who settled further up along the Skagit River (Sally Snyder, Box 108 folder 10 page 33 AJ).

Once this first family was established, they found themselves lured into adopting a new member with long ranging consequences. Taking the shape of a young man, the Underwater

Wealth Spirit tiuɫəbaxad, who was usually both ugly and pitiful to humans, mentally compelled the family of k̓ək̓adəb to adopt him after he made himself look presentable as a baby. A daughter took him to raise, then became pregnant by him. Since he appeared handsome and hard working, they were quickly married, and had a son. The husband fixed it so his family could live underwater and took them back home. But his son was never happy there, and the family came back aground when he was old enough to quest for a spirit power.

The son was gone a year. Times became hard and famine loomed when the son went to Sneatlam Point and to the bottomless lake across from Greenbanks. There he got power from the sea and a pair of *sg^widelitch* (in the form of cedar shields). On his return, he told his cousin, who was "pure" from fasting, to have his own parent's home cleaned up and renewed in four days in time for his return. Everyone worked hard and all was ready when he came into the house with the twin panels and sang the middle part of his song, which filled the beach with food. From then on, aided by all these spirit powers, the Skagit grew mighty (Sally Snyder Box 109 folder 2 page 12 -13 AJ, cf Wealth married daughter of k̓ək̓adəb I Sally Snyder Box 109 folder 2 page 39-40 AJ).

Eventually, trade up and down the Skagit River was managed by k̓ək̓adəb at Coupeville for everyone on Penn Cove and by daxalx^wəd, a member of the *sbalix* community near Concrete on Lake Shannon at present Baker River, for those above (Sally Snyder, Box 109 folder 1 page 42 AD).

One of these, named xk̓ək̓adəb, later married both a Swinomish wife, giving their son his same name, and a Samish wife tsi ʔag^wɫ, having four boys and three girls.

Of these seven children, the oldest son (sakoblk̓əd) married a Lummi woman, the next was a k^wəskadəb (aka~ sk̓əltk̓ədəb), who had two daughters (šisadk^wɫ, pipsišəbol) by one wife, and a son (bəskidob) by another who became a treaty signer and father of Chief Joseph. Another son was sx^walus (a Samish name), who had a daughter cəx̓o and a son colog^wad, who signed the treaty. His second wife left no descendants (cf Sally Snyder, Box 108 folder 10 page 71 AJ, Box 109 folder 2 page 2 AJ).

The half-Swinomish namesake son xk̓ək̓adəb, in turn, had 5-6 wives, with their sons marrying 3 Swadabsh women (sisters ?) from Oak Harbor, a woman from Dugualla Bay, and 2 women (cousins, one named čəłox̓) from Sneatlum Point.

The children of the Oak Harbor women included full brothers Goliah and dukdak^wtx̌^wd of one mother, and full brothers x^wabšdəd and x^wiyaldapədəd of another. The third wife had children of the x^wiax̌asdəd family.

The Dugualla Bay woman (xaix̌ud, xiyax̌ud) had a son Detius, who had many children, and a daughter, also xaix̌ud, whose son was ski.sax̌ad, who had a daughter tsi ʔəg^wɫ (Mrs Peter John) and another daughter, whose son was Eugene Joseph. Detius was half brother to Goliah and zolog^wadk^w, and his grandchildren included a boy also named Detius ~ Little Bob, and cacaik^w Mrs Johnny Fornsby, mother of Charlie Wilbur (Sally Snyder, Box 109 folder 2 page 31 AJ; cf Detius was son of xk̓ək̓adəb III, Sally Snyder, Box 108 folder 10 page 43 AJ; Box 109, folder 2, page 3 AJ).

Overall, the name of k̓ək̓adəb seems to first occur at the very beginning, but actually goes even "deeper, really, from the Flood. That's why it was hard to tell the history, because the

Indian only had one name" [over many generations] (Sally Snyder, Box 109 folder 2 page 57 AJ).

One kʷəskadəb also had a famous warrior son taχ̇taɫ who was an endurance runner and athlete. He would test himself by spitting on a rock and running around Sneatlam Point and back before it dried. He could outrun deer, elk, cranes, and eagles, killing them with his bare hands (Sally Snyder, Box 108 folder 2 page 97 AJ). Later young warriors trained by running from Sneatlum Point to Coupeville and on to Fort Casey, a strategic lookout later fortified in cement by the US military (Snyder Box 108, Folder 2, page 10).

Other founders were sent by the creator to specific locations, either at the founding of the world or to repopulate it after the Flood. For example, χačdəd was sent to found the Oak Harbor Swadabsh (Sally Snyder Box 108 Folder 2 page 96 AJ). Yet for the Swadabsh proper on their slough, the important founder was traced to a third generation after the Flood, the son of Robe Boy known as ləχalbid.

ləχalbid

The family of the woman named tsiʔ əgʷaɫ came into their own after the Flood (Sampson 1938: 14-16, Matson 1968: 29-38), and thereby "own" the story about a man who sensed the Flood was coming. He tied four seagoing canoes to the top of a mountain with four long ropes that stretched out as the waters rose higher. As the waters receded, the high top of the mountain snapped off and the other canoes drifted away, but the man, his wife, son, and daughter came down safely. They quickly built cattail mat houses for dwellings and storage.

Slowly, life returned. Little fish came into the slough. The girl went to play with them, until, one day, a great fish took her away. Saddened, her brother and his dog wandered off. He began to shoot small animals, prepare their pelts, and eventually sewed them into a blanket. When he finally came home, his parents were gone to Coupeville and the mat houses were burned down in mourning because they thought both their children were dead.

In great despair, he wept until a voice told him to gather up and match all the animal bones he could find, lay them out, and wave his robe over them four times. Immediately, all these bones became people, but they were chilled. The voice said to gather charcoal from the burned houses, wave the robe over them, and thus fire was recreated.

Next he waded into the slough, where herring swarmed as soon as the hem of his robe touched the water. These fed the people. A mountain goat appeared to give everyone wool blankets as clothing to keep them warm. These reformed people had no sense, so the boy made brains for them from the very soil of that place (Andrew Span Joe, Snyder ms, Tale 68).

Eventually, his own human relations returned and these impromptu beings wandered away. Everafter known as Robe Boy (χuyaɬiča, made from a robe), he married a human woman and had two sons, tuxʷiqədəb (first daylight) and ləχalbid (daybreak). These boys, withstanding snide criticism like that once directed at their their father, seemed to refuse to quest and had a hard time. In time, though, they revealed they had indeed quested successfully and founded several houses and villages at resource locations and fisheries, each harvest celebrated with appropriate thanks-giving rituals.

ləx̌albid had at least four houses around Fidalgo Island, located in modern terms on the east side near the Swinomish tribal police station, further east at the ancient fort on Sullivan Slough, on the southwest near Martha's Bay and Pull and Be Damned Road, and on the northwest at Snee-oosh (sdiʔus) Point.

Among the Lushootseed, importantly, socio-cultural institutions were arranged as concentric circles, from the most restricted concerned with food economics to the most expansive of religious expressions – an "anchored radiance" – with everything situated within the drainage of a major river flowing into Puget Sound.

Drainages

In terms of the overall Puget Basin, Marian Smith, after fieldwork with Puyallup and Nisqually, outlined a comprehensive spatial model with expanding components for each watershed, the maximum extent of allegiance and loyalty for most Lushootseeds. These units were (a) hearth mates eating together, (b) within a cedar plank household, (c) among houses of all local residents, (d) of birthright locals – those born there in contrast to inlaws, visitors, and foreigners, (e) including all seasonal settlements, towns, and resorts, (f) inter-community networks, (g) tributary drainages, of (h) the entire drainage of a watershed.

Culturally, these units, decreasing in size, included notions of tribal world (the drainage linked both to resident immortals and to more remote peoples and places through visits, marriage, trade, and ritual), of canoe (transport across time and terrains on mountain, forest, prairie, river, or sea), of house (including hearth mates, locals, and distant kin), and of person (combining body, mind, and soul with spirit allies).

Membership within each unit was based on well-informed understandings, both subtle and discerning, of local customs such that insiders, in contrast to outsiders, fully appreciated the complexities of "the feud, the snub, the verbal innuendo" and accordingly "were appropriate guests for a ceremonial feast" (Roberts 1975: 79). To be involved in Lushootseed culture required formal training in and experience with the complexities of oratory, rank, and proper public expressions.

Major nodes in this overall system were cedar plank houses located along the shoreline near spots rich in local resources, such as a salmon stream, berry patch, and hunting territory. Even spirit beings lived in such houses, often on the bottom of river or sea, or at the top of a peak. Easy access, depending on features of current and terrain, allowed some houses to interact as neighborhoods along certain stretches of a river, as distinct from separate towns. Beyond these house nodes were at least three concentric rings occupied by allies, by competitors for regional status, and, third, by strangers (Roberts 1975: 82).

Every drainage had customs that set it apart, often with obviously different styles of making fire or using nets, for example, as well as in venerating certain spirit powers and abilities. The most complex example of net use occurred along the length of the Skagit River.

chronologies

Nets

Nets – placed underwater, on land, in the air, or hand held in canoes – were used for fish, fowl, and other foods. Along the length of the Skagit River, three major types of fish nets were used, according to divine sanction. Out in the saltwater, the reef net (sxʷaɫo), developed by Straits speakers, was deployed. In the lower river, the weir net (qʷəɫʔits) was developed and used by Swinomish and others. Upriver, the trawl net (šəbəd) was featured.

Each weir net was about 20 feet long and 15 feet wide, with a square pocket (x̌ʷšəbədab) about four feet wide and three feet deep. To use a V-shaped weir (təqʷapəd), a pair of two-man canoes anchored at the open apex and spread between them a willow bark twine net. Since the opening had to face against the current to be effective, there were specific flood tide and ebb tide locations claimed by families, each extending only half way across the slough to allow some fish to escape. The forward end facing the tide was held down by a pole from the bow of each canoe. At night or when water was murky, men held signal strings attached to the net front to indicate when fish brushed past. Using poles and strings, the net was worked so that these fish entered the pocket to make sure they could be secure during removal of the net.

Throughout the length of the Skagit river, the šəbəd trawl net was used, made from twine twisted from a grass (k̓ʷaagʷaɫx̌ʷ) that had to be traded from Mount Baker or eastern Washington across the Cascades. Martin Sampson (1972: 57) described the "shub-ud" as "a net used for drifting, held in the water by poles in each corner between two canoes for night fishing."

This net was deployed by five men in a pair of two-man canoes, the fifth keeping a fire burning in the middle of one craft. The haul, therefore, was placed in the middle of the other canoe. If not enough men were available, women filled out the crews, as Susie Sampson Peter did for her father. As this technique was used for all salmon, steelhead, and trout; the size and mesh gauge had to be customized for the catch. For spring salmon, it was 12 x 6 feet with a 6 inch mesh, while the mesh for trout was only a few inches. Once hauled out, the fish were dispatched by severing the spinal cord with a 8-10 inch spike of deer leg bone (čq̓ʷač, čəq̓ʷačəd) kept in a hole drilled into the stern.

Beliefs

Today, counterbalancing this specialized and restrictive use of technology, Lushootseed observe four semi-autonomous expressions of their religion (cf. Amoss 1978: 43) in terms of the high god, guardian spirit powers, *dicta* special words, and ghosts. These modern complexes were reduced from the much more complex ancient religion, relying on a wide variety of past religious specialists (mediums, priests, ritualists) that have now been subsumed by modern shamans (Indian doctors) filling these formerly distinct roles.

What we have all failed to notice, however, is that these expressions have a strong chronological aspect such that the Creator high god preceded everything, both empowering and engendering all subsequent life forms, whether immortal, mortal or intermediate. Further, these fading Lushootseed beliefs best make sense in comparison with the fuller accounts from the Fraser and Bella Coola rivers.

Katzie

Based on what the Katzie shaman Old Peter Pierre (1860s - 1946) told Diamond Jenness, the details of creation were known only to chiefs and shamans belonging to "high families" because of their special relationship if not actual kinship with the Creator high god called χaʔχa, who was closely associated with the sun.

Among the Katzie, allowing for intermittent cycles of population overcrowding, destruction, and recreation; spirits were ranked in terms of degree of power and priority in both time and space, cascading down and radiating out from the creator. For example, Katzie were instructed to pray to deities in sequence, beginning with the creator (now known as Lord Above), then the Sun, Khaals (their Changer), the Moon, and any personal spirit powers.

In the beginning, the creator decided to send specific groups of people under a named leader to particular locales along the Fraser river. Instead of one pair like Adam and Eve, there were many couples, each entrusted to start a community at Musqueam (north of the river mouth), Point Roberts (south of the mouth), Port Hammond, Sheridan Hill, and Pitt River (all upriver).

The names of these ancestors were secret, kept by the elder of a family. Indeed, Duff (1952: 85) noted that Franz Boas, Diamond Jenness, and Charles Hill-Tout were all told these traditions, but each received a different set of names for the first ancestors. These names reflect the teachings of different families from those learned by Old Pierre. Throughout his region, the wonderful thing about such private knowledge was that many variants existed side by side among families and neighbors, with each family glorifying its own at tightly monitored public events sponsored by the family who "set the table" for everyone.

Initially, at the very beginning, the world was grim and silent, with only invertebrates such as shellfish to feed these primal shape-shifting people. There were no birds, animals, or winds. The Lord Above made the sun to give warmth, which the people needed and craved; the moon to measure time; and the rainbow to indicate that the next day would be nice and sunny.

People built their houses and towns at their own distinct locales. The leader at Point Roberts married and had a son, but his wife was unfaithful. Mortified, their son used a sling to send father, mother, lover, and self to become winds of each of the four directions.

Other powerful semi-human leaders were Swaneset at Sheridan Hill, who made the sloughs on Pitt Meadow by first painting a diagram of them on his own face in red ocher. His many wives on land and in the sky provided particular foods for posterity. For example, his Sockeye wife taught the making and use of fishing gear to everyone. Only one man in each tribe, however, learned the *dicta* enchantments, rituals, and taboos demanded by Salmon to assure respect and bounty.

Despite these divine gifts and extraordinary deeds, people faltered, failing to observe proper restrictions or to show gratitude. So, by decree of the creator, Khaals came, from the west, with two younger brothers and twelve servants. Through the power of his thought, he fixed the world and changed its inhabitants into people, places, and, sometimes, modern species, after first sending their souls back above.

Throughout, Khaals was just, following the laws given by Lord Above. He sorted the good from the bad, and again made the world a better place, allowing those people who showed respect to remain human. Finally, Khaals went far away up the Fraser River.

The world continued and the population again increased, resulting in another crisis. Families settled all over until they overcrowded the world and Lord Above sent a flood. Many people died, but some saved themselves by fleeing to mountain tops enabling them to resettle the land, just like at Swinomish.

Eventually, the world became crowded again. Knowing their past, people grew fearful. That October, snow fell and covered the world. Half of all the people died of starvation.

Again, the survivors multiplied and spread. Again, the world became crowded. The smoke from their fires filled the Fraser valley like a dense fog. Too many people were living too close together. Then word came of a great sickness from the east. Smallpox killed many people before Europeans actually arrived and pushed native people off their lands.

Today, as traditionally, their High God creates each humans with a soul, vitality-thought, empowered talent, and shadow-reflection. At death, the breath and special talent perish with the body, the soul returns above, and the vitality and shadow merge to produce the ghost that roams as a barely visible form in the neighborhood of its old home, dangerous to surviving relatives.

Nuuxalk

The other well described system of Salish beliefs is the Nuxalk (a/k/a Bella Coola, McIlwraith 1948: xx, 23, 32), whose world was created by a high god known as *ałqʷuntam*, who employed four immortal carpenters.

Covering the earth was the huge dome of the sky, made clear to allow the sun to shine through. The top of the dome was another flat land where the creator lived in an enormous house called *Nusmatta*, with many rooms. His carved seat rested behind the central fire, and he was closely associated with the sun, which he used like a canoe to cross the sky. When traveling, he wore a cloak lined with salmon, which, when reversed, caused salmon runs to start in the rivers of earth.

The land itself was a round, flat island held in place by a being named *Sninia*, who lived in the icy north holding a rope that kept the world tight against his outstretched feet. Whenever he shifted this rope, an earthquake resulted. The undersea was controlled by a leader called *Qomoqwa*, who lived in a huge house with all other marine beings. This wealthy chief always wore a large hat to shield his face, which was painted black and covered with eagle down. Humans visited him in the past to receive power, and he himself sometimes visited Nusmatta.

Under the earth was at least one subterranean world where the ghosts lived and shamans often visited. Everything there, such as tides, seasons, day and night, was the reverse of the earth surface, as Lushootseeds and many others also believed. Its river flowed from west to east, and was the source for all the springs in this world. What was cottonwood fluff on earth, was snow there. Ghosts themselves had green faces, weird actions, and spoke with sounds humans heard as whistling or gurgling.

Along the inside walls of Nusmatta hung the cloaks of many species, especially ravens, eagles, whales, grizzlies, black bears, and seabirds. The creator asked those dwelling in his house to chose a cloak and put it on, immediately transforming into that animal or bird. Then he entrusted each of them with hereditary names, tools, houses, clothing, and foods in compressed form. He sent them to earth as Nuxalk founders, with groups and couples landing on particular mountain peaks. From these summits, each cloak floated back up above. These ancestors, returned to human form, hiked down to found various of the forty-five or so Nuxalk towns.

Other ancestors came to earth in only human form because they climbed down a set of temporary pillars between sky and earth. After the first constructed dome collapsed because it had no supports, this second one was braced by pillars that were eventually removed after these solely human ancestors had descended.

All these first beings founded ancestral families (*minmints*) which were the social units of Nuxalk society. Each one guarded the privileges of its ancestors, especially knowledge of the names, species cloak, landing place, and the crest (emblem. logo) conveying these claims.

Since a Nuxalk belonged to all the ancestral families of both of his parents, he or she represented these memberships with tattoos. For example, a design representing the primary family of the father, whose ancestor wore a Raven cloak, adorned the right breast, while the eagle cloak worn by the mother's ancestor was on the left side. Similar designs were painted on the prow of a canoe or the front of the house.

The more details known about these privileges, the more noble the family. When a Nuxalk died, each went back through the line of ancestors to the original mountain top and ascended to live in *Nusmatta*.

Every winter solstice, the creator entered his house but his intense heat drove out all the immortals living there, except for three who then conferred with him about the fates of humans during the coming year. Births, deaths, and initiations were set, with the creator giving final approval. Dreams sometimes forewarned humans of what their coming destinies would be.

The animals and plants made by the four carpenters' crews had human forms and minds, and lived in plank houses, but humans, because they were usually impure, rarely saw these dwellings as they really are. For example, some mountains were the homes of mountain goats, though humans did not realize they were hollow until a goat befriended a lone hunter and took him home. All species were given fire by the creator, with the color of their smoke matching that of their outer covering. Thus, the smoke from a mountain goat home was white, from a beaver's was black, from a squirrel's was reddish, and from that of wolves was grey. Species lived much as humans did, with health and illness treated by Grizzlies and Wolverines, who were the animal's shamans.

Each of these species was also said to have a Mother, much as the earth itself was regarded as Mother, nourishing the lives of all those who dwelt with her. Nothing was said of a Father, but the logical surmise would be that he was the creator himself, who ordered the world.

Humans maintained good relations with spirits and deities by fasting, praying, sacrificing, and observing "ceremonial chastity." These acts made the person pure and able to succeed at hunting, raiding, questing, gambling, building a salmon weir, or hosting a potlatch.

In the beginning, the creator gave to every Nuxalk person three spiritual aspects: a spirit in the body, along with a tally post and a water basin set up at Nusmatta. Each post was decorated with the crest (species cloak) of their first ancestor and it leaned over when its person became ill and approached death. During a cure, shamans went above to try to straighten it upright. When it fell over the person died, so shamans could estimate the duration of the patient's life from its angle of incline. A shaman diagnosed by consulting the curing power that lived in his or her own wrist.

76

The person's spirit resided at the back of the neck in a thin, palmate (maple-leaf-shaped) bone that trembled to increase wealth or remained inert with misfortune. Associated with the spirit were mentality and vitality. Mentality provided awareness and was localized in the heart, while vitality stretched as a force field between the little fingers and little toes of a person. Any damage to these circuits was often fatal.

At death, the person divided into a corpse, shadow, and ghost. The spirit became a ghost who traveled back through its generations of ancestors to the family mountain peak, donned the cloak of the ancestral species, and ascended to Nusmatta. Existence above was like that on earth, except all personal skills and abilities were enhanced.

The dead were never far from the minds and emotions of the living. Indeed, the hallmark of the Nuxalk potlatch, setting it apart from those of their neighbors, was the dramatic enactment of the return of a deceased relative in the guise of a crest. Unlike their neighbors, moreover, Nuxalk only sang but did not dance during these events.

In sum, these systematized beliefs of Katzie and Nuxalk provide both Salishan and Northwest contexts, and likely details for Lushootseeds, otherwise missing from their record.

Lushootseed Chronologies

Based on this background and comparisons, then, a Lushootseed chronology must start with the creator high god (χaʔχa) who empowers other immortal spirits (sqəlalitut) who dwell in the sky, on and in the earth, and under the water. Foremost among these spirits were four brothers who traveled up the Skagit River, placing pairs of men and women at various locations to create future generations (Collins 1974: 158-59, Snyder Tale 73, Amoss 1978: 66-70, Miller 1999: 60-62). These brothers, oldest to youngest, were sgʷədiləč, Knife, Fire, and Baby, each giving powers and abilities appropriate to their names. Knife taught the proper ways to butcher and prepare game. Fire showed how to cook it. Baby told these couples how to fix family talents, skills, and abilities on their children.

The others went away upriver, and Knife may have stopped at the ancient Hozomeen Quarry, but šgʷədiləč became a rock in the upper Skagit near Portage, where he can be heard singing about 3AM by those who had fasted and prepared to learn his song so as to be able to hunt and fish successfully.

This era ended with the time of Starchild and Diaper boy, created by Stars married to human women. After the "twins" had rescued their mother from slavery and found industrious wives, they gathered up everything useful on the earth and burned it in a great conflagration. Then they scattered these ashes everywhere so the essence of these materials, resources, and abilities could be more easily found by future generations.

Their children became the chiefly families throughout northern Puget Sound, each leader learning and guarding the special words of enchantment (instituting the *dicta* system) to benefit his family and community. These incantations were specifically given in compensation for the renewal of the world at the time when mortals and immortals were moving away from the bodily contact of marriage toward the immateriality of adoption.

The land repopulated and thrived until people failed to respect the rules, regulations, and avoidances needed for proper living, so a Flood set things right again. The few survivors included Robe Boy, his son ləẋalbid, and their many descendants at Swadabsh, as other ancestors refounded communities in other locales. Though unstated, the host of dead from the Flood must have provided the incentive for the Ghost system still important today, since the deluge obviously left behind more refuse and remains than did Fire.

The occasionally references to those few who "drifted away" during the Flood also suggest that one of these Flood casualties was one of the kʷəskadəb who ended up petrified far up the Skagit. Thus, resolving the conflicting attributes and locations of this name, the Lower Skagit who went upriver to ask for this name were actually showing respect for the people among whom this kʷəskadəb ended up lodging. That is why they did not ask more important tribes around Concrete and elsewhere for a name. Presumably, that kʷəskadəb revealed his location to a descendant in a dream that was followed up by this delegation.

Most recently, the creator high god has again asserted his priority by empowering John and Mary Slocum to establish the 1882 Indian Shaker Church, incorporated in Washington State in 1910, and still thriving (Amoss 1990, Collins 1950b). As Martin Sampson, Swinomish leader, noted, the advantage of Shakers was "worshipping God direct, they increased their healing over much greater distances." Unlike shamans, whose spirits remained localized, Shaker spirits could expand into the world as far as needed since they were affiliated with a universal God. Moreover, though a shaman's spirits left at death, the Shaker Spirit led that member "home."

Simultaneously, immortal spirits remain active among initiates of modern Siyowin, the use Religion that allows modern members to "inherit" family spirit powers in the context of this organization.

In modern Lushootseed beliefs about immortals or guardian spirits, such a power attaches itself to a person at birth, but only reveals its presence at puberty through at least two aspects, a being and a song, along with a personifying of the vision itself. Some or all of these aspects "travel" during the year and only join together during the winter when the person becomes "sick to sing" with the return of his or her spirit partner. For a woman, her spirit power was regarded as a personal friend, while for a man it was an impersonal force that infused his entire body when it returned (Amoss 1978: 51).

The song, at least, came from the east in the fall, curved slowly south and westward during the winter, and, in late April or so, headed east again. As a group, spirits came to the Nooksak on Mt Baker before they reached Vancouver Island, where they lingered until spring.

In contrast to these lay or career powers, shamanic curing powers were available at all times. According to Joyce Wike (1941), while the song traveled, the spirit itself stayed close to the human partner. Fierce black paint spirits traveled more widely than did those of calm red paint, who stayed nearby and could be used to cure or help others.

During the day, spirits also move around, hovering in the air (rather than treading on the ground), lower in the early morning then higher in the afternoon. They are constantly aware of human actions and leave if their partner becomes ritually impure or disrespectful. Then the spirit was said to "lift off" until it could be coaxed back by a shaman. Spirits liked daylight but, lacking form or substance, were truly ethereal. Marian Smith (1940: 97) reported that spirits had the most nebulous of existences, with their appetites and pleasures supplied vicariously through their links with humans, especially relatives who were kind enough to remember them and send food and treats through an open fire.

78

Finale

Usually, in discussions of the Northwest Coast as a culture area of Native North America, the north section of matrilineal nations is contrasted with the mid-section of ambilateral tribes like Lushootseed. Yet my analysis has shown that despite these differences in ancestor-focused lineality or ego-focused immediacy, the pedigree and position of high rank is treated the same in both regions. In this way, the "begats" of the Bible are given greater relevancy for all humans, where pedigree underscores position.

Particularly fascinating are the echos of the sacred histories of the matrilineal Northwest Coast, where immortals provide names that chiefs inherit over generations. Because marriages and interchanges unified the elite along the entire coast, these Salish examples clearly place their chiefly families within the overall system. The Skagit founding ancestor descended to a point of land on a strategic island in Puget Sound. Canoes, trade, marriages, and rituals drew his name and prodige into the regional cultural system.

NAMING CULTURE AMONG LUSHOOTSEEDS OF PUGET SOUND

Hereditary **names**, today as in the past, bind together Lushootseeds of Puget Sound. They crosscut considerations of culture history, gender, age, rank, descent, kinship, pedigree, residence, territory, and waterway. They are the focus of the basic institutions of **person**, **place**, **sept**, and **power** from immortal spirits. They are at the heart of the crucial factors of "blood" and of "mud" – kinship and landscape. By good fortune, examples of the renowned names who "begat" the present day world can be retrieved from fieldnotes and documents, and confirmed by living holders of these names. In sum, these data allow a fuller integration of the Coast Salish into wider patterns and traditions typical of the whole Northwest Coast.

Introduction

For the Lushootseeds of Puget Sound, **names**, above all, provide the nexus (lynchpin) intersecting their concepts of kinship, pedigree, territory, and culture history. Any full understanding of this ethnohistory of naming, however, has been obscured by a lack of available data, especially in publications. Indeed, most of the supporting information occurs only in fieldnotes provided by fluent speakers of high rank, who were themselves holders of crucial ancestral names.[36] Once these data were assembled, moreover, the relationship between these Coast Salish and other cultures of the North Pacific becomes much more clear. Salish is a language family distinctive of the Northwest, divided into Coast and Interior branches.[37]

Like the "begats" of the Judeo-Christian Bible, a sequence of names establishes family lines of descent which standout distinctly within these bilateral societies. Over time, these names are successively embodied in a person within a household which is anchored to a series of locales specifically keyed to needed resources. Today that household is conceptual, but until a century ago it was physical and multiple.

Unlike the Tsimshian with over a dozen chronological episodes in their ethno-ethnohistory (Miller 1997b), Lushootseeds recognize fewer eras.[38] Little is said about creation

---

[36] The prime trove of these fieldnotes come from the amazingly productive years in the early 1950s when Sally Snyder, a graduate student of Melville Jacobs, worked on the Swinomish reservation and among landless ("unrecognized") Skagits and Sauks living upriver. Her life or career was never easy so we are especially fortunate that copies of her notes are preserved in Special Collections at the University of Washington, though they were once closed to the public and their use requires permission from a board of trustees. My admiration of her notes has been confirmed by thirty years involvement with these communities, where I am honored to be a friend of today's Goliah, Lahalbid, and Kwaskadub.

[37] Lushootseed (Puget) belongs to the Coast Salish Branch and, for English speakers, seems daunting because of its complex phonemes, the same sound often pronounced with four variants, and a shift of the sounds of B to M, D to N that confounds the ethnohistoric record.

[38] This paper builds upon my prior work with Tshimshian eras (Miller 1997b) for the matrilineal north coast, and vastly improves my prior discussion of kinship and naming

<u>de novo</u> of the world. Instead, successive recreations mark distinct eras, each following a global destruction caused by human arrogance, overcrowding, and disrespect for the world.

Elders now dead hinted that there was a local genesis which was known only to shamans, while the recreations were largely common knowledge. Key members of chiefly families, however, had much more detailed versions of these changes that included *dicta* – special words, spells, and formulae that profoundly affected all other beings in the world, and could be used to help or harm. Invoking the Creator in these *dicta* and prayers also suggests an original creation.[39] Though now mostly known as *shaq si'ab* "above lord" under missionary influence, the persistent use of <u>xa'xa</u> "taboo, sacred, forbidden" for that being indicates great antiquity for this deification.

Because important names are eternal, all fieldworkers in the Northwest have had disconcerting moments when it is unclear if an elder is speaking of a mythological person from the dawn of time, a protohistoric figure, or one of their current relatives – all of them with the very same name.

The reformers, by convention, are known as Changers, sometimes Transformers, who set the world right and prepare the way for modern humans. In the past century, as natives have stopped speaking Lushootseed in favor of English, what seem to have been teams of siblings have now been individuated as a single named person. In Puget Sound, the major Changer has become identified with the Moon, while his less powerful brother became the Sun.

All of the standard cataclysms seem to be reported, firmly based in local geology, including destruction by flood (with canoes as escape arks), quake (viewed as the world capsizing), fire (easily correlated with volcanic eruptions like that of Mt St Helens), and plague (with survivors protected by special rituals envisioned by named prophets). Among Lushootseeds, at least one renowned name is associated with each of these destructions, as well as systems of power provided in compensation for the lost lives. In a later section, the famous name of *Lehalbid* provides an example of this close association with a crisis.

Institutions

Native Lushootseed society in Puget Sound involved concepts of territory, kinship, pedigree, and culture history. It was and is organized around practical considerations of gender, age, rank, descent, residence, and waterway. In more general terms, these are concerned with *person*, *place*, and *sept*, a kinship grouping traced through both maternal and paternal lines over

---

among Lushootseeds (Miller 1997a, 1999). More recent effort has used native names from fieldnotes to reconstitute aboriginal villages burned out so such prime "vacant land" could be homesteaded by white "pioneers" (Miller 2000).

[39] The significance of high-rank names are better known closer to the northern coast. Wilson Duff (1952: 85) noted their importance among the Sto:lō of the Fraser River, while commenting that each researcher (Franz Boas, Diamond Jenness, Charles Hill-Tout) was given a different list and pedigree of these important hereditary names -- indicating that the actual name was merely a marker for the crucial concept of rank. Creation epics are reported in some detail for the Sto:lō, from Old Peter Pierre, a shaman, and for the Nuxalk (Bella Coola), as summarized in Miller (1999).

at least four generations. Over all of these was and is the all-important fourth factor of religion, namely *power* from immortal spirits. Subsets conferring power variously focus on the high god (*xa'xa*), immortals (guardian spirits), ghosts, and *dicta* (special words). As appropriate for this rainy climate, the basic symbolic opposition underlying these factors is that of "blood" and of "mud" – kinship and landscape.

Culturally, the building blocks of this society, increasing in size, included notions of the individual person (composed of a gendered aging body, a mind, and souls with spirit allies), of the house (including hearthers, locals, and distant kin), of the canoe (transport across time and space, distinguished by habitat as forest, prairie, river, or sea), and of the world (the entire drainage, linked both to resident immortals via rituals and to further remote peoples and places through marriage, ritual, and trade).

Person ~ "blood"

Personhood was characterized by gender as male or female, by age as older or younger, and by ranking as freeborn or slave. The leaders of households and communities constituted the elite, "owning" (in the sense of holding and hosting) famous names attached to resource locations. Other members of the freeborn rank were commoners, valuable for their labor and support but otherwise undistinguished.

A few transgendered individuals are known from fieldnotes, but these did not constitute a "third gender". Instead each was identified anatomically since natives once wore few if any clothes beyond rain gear when necessary.

Lushootseeds along the coast emphasized rank and class, while those inland, upriver, and in the southern Sound held more Plateau ideals of a kin-based society. "Southern Puget Sound culture emphasized spirit quests and had a lesser emphasis on inherited privileges than the Northerners" (Roberts 1975: 32, 35, 77), and hence provided the birthplace for more democratic beliefs known as the Indian Shaker Church, recognizing a universal, omnipotent God.

Space ~ Place ~ "mud"

In terms of the overall Puget Basin, Marian Smith (1940: 7), relying on her fieldwork among the Puyallup and Nisqually, devised a spatial model, with units decreasing in size, for describing how native peoples related to their watersheds. She explicitly recognized that the greatest allegiance and loyalty coincided with the entire drainage system of Puget Sound. Taking these units in reverse or increasing size, however, better indicates the progression.

Therefore, within each riverine watershed, group cohesion, dialects, loyalties, and affiliations grew in terms of (a) hearth mates eating together at the fires within a household, (b) residents of all neighboring houses, (c) birthright locals - those born there as distinct from inlaws, visitors, and foreigners, (d) seasonal settlements, camps, and resorts, (e) wider community networks, (f) tributary waterways, and (g) the entire drainage of a river.

Each river constituted a "tribe", designated by the endings of -bš (-*bsh*) (if more cohesive) or as -bix̌ʷ (-*byuh*) 'bunch' if more dispersed. The ending -*mish* in English (Snohomish, Skykomish) is the pre-shift Lushootseed form of -*bsh*. Rivers and streams with shoreside trails linked all of these together, while trails along and across ridges gave access to separate tribes.

Membership within each drainage derived from the subtle, discerning, and valued appreciation of customs such that insiders, in contrast to outsiders, understood the complexities of "the feud, the snub, the verbal innuendo" and accordingly "were appropriate guests for a ceremonial feast" (Roberts 1975: 79).

Traditionally, the crux of the entire system and the basic reason for gathering people together was the display of bonds with particular immortal powers. No one could be successful without such help. For centuries, leading families had bonded with the most powerful spirits in their locales. Lesser family members, some commoners, and even a few slaves could also have spirit partners, but these were less powerful than those of the leaders.

Kin

In addition to considerations of space and place ("mud") within an overall drainage, Lushootseeds also traced kinship through the bloodlines of both parents. The immediate family grouping (derived from four grandparents) is technically called a <u>kindred</u>, while the huge extended family, which was and is transnational or intertribal (though eight great grandparents), is a called a *sept*.

Among ordinary kinspeople, a <u>*nodal kindred*</u> formed around its senior member(s), often the grandparents as a married couple. After the death of the last surviving spouse, the kindred regrouped around the marriage of their oldest child – if fit and able – and so on, through a generation or two. Leading families, however, formed a <u>*stem kindred*</u>, which continued across generations because the stem consisted of the line of holders of its famous, renowned name, conferring control ("management") of locations and resources that made up the "estate" of these nobles. Influence from Wakashans of Vancouver Island may have led to occasional *ramages*, descent based on birth order, especially a line composed only of eldest sons or eldest daughters.

Traced through all of the bloodlines of great grandparents, a *sept* had its own network that even now extends beyond space and time, as a "nondiscrete, nonlocalized, property-holding group" (Suttles 1987: 210). It existed wherever its members lived, and included ancestors from the past and children yet unborn. It had no fixed size nor place, except in family lore explaining the origin of its famous names. It was managed by the oldest able elder (male or female), who provided guidance and 'advice' about the proper use of resources and the transmission of names, positions, and artifacts within the kindred. If it held a famous name, stories about past holders of that name and their fea(s)ts served to specify places where the kindred indeed had a birthright through past actions, particularly on-going partnerships between the spirits of these places and family members. These most powerful spirits (conferring wealth, power, bounty) dwell in remote locations, either high up in the mountains or deep in the water, either ocean or river. Its most prized possession has been called 'advice' (x̌ʷdikʷ, also teachings, knowhow, wisdom), which included special formulae (*dicta*) to compel ~ control activities for good or ill, genealogical details, and a body of stories from the beginning of time.

House

Major nodes in this overall system were cedar plank houses, once located along the shore near spots rich in local resources, such as a salmon stream, berry patch, and hunting territory. Even spirit beings lived in such houses, though only special people could see ~ visit them. Beyond this house node were and are at least three concentric rings occupied by allies, by competitors for regional status, and, third, by strangers (Roberts 1975: 82). During the late 1800s, officials broke up these communal homes. Instead, single family dwellings were built with milled lumber, though many people shared these rooms. Today, these households are conceptual and symbolic, though periodically reconstituted inside local school gyms, tribal halls, and ceremonial smokehouses when they host family namings, potlatches, and other displays of their generosity.

These community halls, sometimes inspired by styles of ancient housing, are still used for ceremonies, feasts, and gatherings, particularly in winter. These buildings and events continue such traditions. Regional networks also continue, now discussed according to modern reservations instead of former watersheds, though there is considerable overlap between these past and present locations.

The park-like old growth forests and rugged terrain left few level spaces where people could live, so each house in every town had about fifty occupants, with placement within the house reflecting rank in local and regional society. Thus, with a door at the front or side, the owner of the house and his family had the best protected spot in a back corner, away from the drafts at the doorway. They constituted a nobility, providing leaders for varied community tasks (Miller 1997a). The hallmark of such nobility was being hard working, steady, and reliable.

Along the sides were families of ordinary common folks, who contributed food and upkeep to the household in return for the prestige of living with wealthy relatives. The least desirable and most exposed places in the front of the house harbored slaves, who had either been captured in raids, purchased, or born to their lot. Each family had its own hearth fire along a side of the house, since eating together as a 'commensal unit' was what defined close, caring, trust relations. Nobles usually had more than one wife, but each seems to have had a separate fireplace hearth to feed her own children and their playmates.

On important occasions, particularly during winter, the head of the house hosted public events on behalf of all the residents. Accordingly, most families moved out to other accommodations, either nearby homes or mat tents, to make room for honored guests. Two or three large, public fires were lit down the middle (along the long central axis) of the big house. Huge amounts of food – collected by slaves and housemates and prepared by women under the direction of the senior wife of the host – were served throughout the festivities.

Changes in social status – such as naming, puberty, marriage, or death – provided the occasions for hosting, for inviting in guests. The more prominent a family, the more people would be invited from furthest away. Important families had far flung networks of friends and kin, forged by marriage, adoption, gifts, help, trade, and social obligations. They also named their infants at the youngest possible moment, when it was clear the heir would live.

Today, all of the religions and sects of the modern world can be found among the native peoples of Puget Sound, but they co-exist with much more ancient beliefs and practices based in the landscape. Even the modern churches, morever, have distinctly native features because families and communities continue to worship together. In the northern Sound, Catholic for 150 years, cedar boughs freshly cut from the forest and flutes carved from cedar limbs are used during the Mass. Similarly, Protestant churches on reservations will feature native designs and concepts such as the "Great Spirit" in their services.

Two modern religious expressions, especially, continue ancient beliefs and traditions associated with the spirits of the land. One is sometimes called the Smokehouse Religion because it uses public buildings in the form of ancestral, communal, cedar-plank houses. It continues the tradition of personal spirit helpers and special regard to certain places, often remote and sacred, on the land and in the water. The other is the Indian Shaker Church – founded near Olympia in 1882 by the death and revival of John Slocum – incorporated under the protection of Washington state law in 1910. It blends ancient beliefs with those of Christianity into a distinctive pattern of worship now spread from California to Canada and Montana (Miller 1999).

Resources

Lushootseed natives had an extremely complicated social life which was comparable to the complexity of farmers elsewhere in the world. Here, however, they largely lived by harvesting (mostly without the effort planting) the bounty that nature provided for them. They did enhance plots and fields of plants with edible roots, such as wild carrots, onions, camas, and other bulbs; but this wise cultivation of nature was not the same as intensive farming (Miller 2005). When natives encouraged the growth of certain wild plants, they unobtrusively left seeds and roots in moist locales. After traders from the Hudson's Bay Company introduced natives to "Irish" [Andean] potatoes, these prior talents at tending wild foods allowed them to quickly raise such tubers as a cash crop (Suttles 1987: 137-151). Traditionally, people moved with the seasons to camps near available natural foods. The climate was mild, due to the offshore Japanese and California Currents, and rainy, so the region abounded with plants and animals.

Chief among these foods were five species of Pacific salmon which (more properly, who) spawned and died in the rivers each year, although some years the runs were more abundant than others. By working hard for a few weeks, a household could catch and dry enough fish to meet winter needs of the family and its guests. Yet people did not live by fish alone. After the summer fish runs, families went into the uplands and mountains to collect dozens of kinds of berries, which were also stored for winter use. Men hunted a variety of mammals, both sea and land, during the fall and winter, depending on where they lived. In the spring, fresh greens and early fish runs enriched the diet of stored supplies. By prudently and generously using resources which were locally "anchored," a household could spread their "radiance" throughout a larger region (Miller 1999).

Kʷaskadub

The best-known name from fieldwork, fieldnotes, and documents is that of Kʷaskadub [k̓ʷaskadəb] "roasted, burnt head". Chiefly names are usually distinguished by the endings –*qd* ~ –*qn* 'head' or –*qs* 'nose, point' indicating their duties as deciders ~ "lead-ers" (Bates, Hess, and Hilbert 1994: 127, 178, 179).

The lone appearance of this name in print is dramatic. In his dictated autobiography, John Fornsby, a shaman, told how, as boy picking berries near Skagit City, he entered the overgrown feasting house of his great grandfather, and found him still laid out on the rear platform. Later, the body was reburied behind this house and then moved to the Swinomish Catholic Cemetery. After this potlatch house washed away in a flood, one of its carved houseposts (3 x 4 x 8 feet) was later found and installed by Lummi workmen paid by Fornsby at a famous potlatch when graves from a nearby island were moved to the same cemetery.

That Kʷaskadub was a famous trader with several homes at strategic locations. His winter and thus primary home was on Penn Cove at Coupeville on Whidbey Island. The home at Skagit City where he lay in state was at the lower end of a two-mile-long logjam that forced migrating salmon to pool before they wove their way upriver. Local gardens grew huge nettle plants (some eight feet tall), processed into fiber for nets and other fabrics. These nets were specifically adapted and colored to microhabitats. This logjam directed canoe travel on to other rivers until it was dynamited away in 1878 (Collins 1974: 39).

Kʷaskadub has several adult children who forged dynastic marriages. More famous and much better documented is the son named Sneatlam (*sditləb* in Lushootseed), who was a fur trade middleman for Ft Nisqually, founded in the south Sound in 1833. Sneatlam was also a Catholic lay leader. At least one of his wives was Makah, from the far northwest tip of Washington State. After Sneatlam died 16 December 1852, a carved wooden effigy dressed in his own clothes was set up on what became Sneatlum Point on eastern Whidbey Island (Gibbs 1877: 203). Another Kʷaskadub son flaunted the rules of rank by taking up with a slave girl, who thereafter was named 'mistake'. One of his daughters married into Chehalis.

Kʷaskadub's nephews (cf pages 48, 65) included Goliah, a community spokesman ~ document messenger who was drafted by Governor Isaac Stevens into signing the 1855 Treaty of Pt Elliot (Mukilteo) as "chief" of northern Sound tribes. As official speaker, though not of noble family, Goliah, having the advantage of some English fluency, appealed to American authorities.

Goliah's brother, known only in fieldnotes, was sadsəhəbixʷ ~ sadʔəhəbixʷ, who maintained a fortified home at Quartermaster Harbor between Maury and Vashon Islands, an important portage in south Puget Sound. Both Penn Cove, the Lower Skagit homeland, and Quartermaster Harbor were sheltered bays deep into islands, providing portage shortcuts. Famous as a warrior and slaver, he also had crucial access to the fur trade at Fort Nisqually. Because he raided the nearby Duwamish for slaves, his fort was under constant threat so in old age "this village moved to Gig Harbor. The movement took place not long before the treaty" (Smith 1940: 11).[40] Throughout this region, competition took many forms, not all of them involving weapons and warfare.

Moreover, a clearer view of the international and intertribal complexity of the region is shown by the ability of important families to set themselves up in foreign territory and to take advantage of slaving upon locals and trade at the British fort. Of especial note, via intermarriage among local chiefly families, these famous hereditary names thereby become legitimately claimed by widely dispersed heirs.

------

[40] *The Puyallup-Nisqually* (Smith 1940: 11) is based on Marian Wesley Smith, Microfilm Roll 3 (Reel A1738), British Columbia Archives, MSS 2689: Box 6, Folder 9 (Houses 26); Royal Anthropological Archives, MSS 2794, Houses p26.

Both K^{w}askadub and Sneatlam appear in the Fort Langley journal during June, July, and August of 1830 as "the two Scadchats Chiefs – Neetlum & Weskienum" (Maclachlan 1998: 150, 156). On Friday, August 10th, Sneatlam's son married the daughter of a Cowichan leader, variously known as Joshua, Josia, Old Joe, or Shashia. In 1847, Paul Kane painted portraits of him and his son Cul-chil-hum. At least one other son is mentioned, but the father died blind and heirless in 1870. Cowichans, then as now, had winter villages on Vancouver Island. After Ft Langley was founded by the HBC in 1827, its journal noted that these island villages had permanent camps on the mainland along the Fraser River to take full advantage of salmon runs.

Between 1780-1810, Ba'da'ɫ (ma'na'ɫ in Straits Salish), a granddaughter of K^{w}askadub, was captured by Klallam raiders from Dungeness who quickly realized her rank and married her to a noble son. At the wedding, the groom wore an enormous rawhide mask. K^{w}askadub gave his family ten slaves, a seagoing canoe, and many blankets, and, in return, received twenty slaves, a canoe, and other goods (Elmendorf 1993: 108-10).

Alice Campbell, married to the Upper Skagit chief descended from the famous prophet Captain Camel (Campbell), explained the upriver source for the name K^{w}askadub.

Long ago there were people who turned into rocks [in the Flood]. This Kwaskadub was the name of one [of them] way up on the Skagit. It is the name of one of Andrew Joe's relatives. They came up to ask the people there for a name (certain people used to go to certain places to obtain a name). If they had known, they could have asked the Sbalix here [Concrete, Wa] for a name (Sally Snyder, Box 108, Folder 5, Page 58).

What is noteworthy about her report is this transport of a renowned name from an earlier era into a later one. K^{w}askadub survived the Flood by being carried upriver and then turned into stone, with his powers intact. When the renewed coastal family came looking for an ancient name, they were reminded of the upriver rock and so revived that name, neatly bracketing the all-important salmon runs between the downriver resource site at the lower logjam and the farthest point upriver where salmon came to spawn.

Elsewhere in the notes the "begets" of the name itself are listed, descended from the first being send down from Heaven to what became Sneatlum Point. As founders of the pedigree of human chiefly lines, these "renowned names" (Collins 1966) constituted the *hik^w si'ab* (highest rank), based on words for "big, high, most, very" and "wealth, rich, treasure, abundant" (Bates, Hess, and Hilbert 1994: 15, 109).

The first ancestor of the Lower Skagit, sent down by the Creator to this point, was named KeKedab [k̓əkádəb]. He sired three families, each living within a compartment of a huge cedar plank longhouse inside a stockade. Like the Iroquois Confederacy whose symbolic longhouse paralleled the Mohawk River across central New York, the Skagit occupants of each section settled along the Skagit River, with those in the back of the house furthest upriver, as compared to those who stayed in the middle, and those in the more prestigious front section who took over the river mouth, delta, and islands (Sally Snyder, Box 108, Folder 10, Page 33, AJ).

Each compartment took along or developed specialized artifacts and technologies appropriate to the ecology of their new homelands. Such distinctions are most clearly indicated by different types of nets. Those out in the saltwater used the reef net (*sx^{w}alo* = 'willow') named for the twisted willow bark that formed its tough cordage. In the lower river, the weir net (*ql'its*) also of willow bark was used, and upriver the trawl net (*shubid*) was woven from a grass that had to be traded from afar. Both river nets were suspended between a pair of canoes working together, but the weir also included a wide pocket to contain the fish. Today, native fishers, protected by federal and treaty laws, rely on commercially manufactured nets and motor boats to accomplish the same tasks.

Of note, the plain straight net of the *shubid* was deployed effectively in the water, as well as in the air and on land. Set above the ground in strategic locals, it caught flocks of waterfowl as they rose in flight, while set across game trails it took deer and other mammals. Sometimes, as on Whidbey Island, these nets were once set up before communal deer drives.

In the very beginning, other beings already lived on the earth, including an underwater Wealth spirit, who took on the appearance of an ugly, pitiful young man or of a tiny baby. Using mind control (probably through *dicta*), he compelled the family of KeKedab to adopt him. The daughter who nursed him eventually became pregnant, and he married her in the guise of a handsome, hard-working man. Again using *dicta*, he enabled his wife and son to live underwater with their affines until the boy was old enough the quest for spirit power on land. The son fasted for a year and received "help" at both Sneatlum Point and the bottomless lake across from Greenbanks, a portage. Arriving outside of his own home, he sent his fasting cousin to tell his parents to "clean out" their home so he could publicly dance and sing his newly acquired powers. As he did so, the beach filled with fresh foods (Sally Snyder, Box 109, Folder 2, Pages 12-13, 39-40 AJ). Thereafter the Lower Skagits were known as a wealthy, powerful, and generous tribe. Those inheriting the name Kekedab managed all of the trade along the Skagit River through an upriver partner at Concrete who also inherited the very same name over deep time.

Descendants of the first founder, with bewildering sets of names, marry into nearby communities, beginning with the Swadabsh [true Swinomish] and Samish to beget seven named grandchildren. These in turn marry further away into Lummi and other villages. Since these sons are wealthy, they have many wives, all of whose children stand to inherit their own renowned names. The names of daughters are equally renowned and pass to females along bilateral lines. The only bar to sharing a name within the same kindred is proximity. Siblings and cousins who live far apart can share the same ancestral name as long as confusion about identities is kept to a minimum by distance. Though holding the same name, each is unlikely to appear at the same ritual events and have their name called out for gifts and speech making.[41] In time, these names passed to known historic personages, such as Goliah who signed the treaty. In the begats, the original name belonged to the son of a woman from Oak Harbor on Whidbey Island, married to a grandson of the founder KeKedab. Oak Harbor itself was founded by someone named *Xachded* (Sally Snyder, Box 108, Folder 2, page 96 AJ). Such ancestors might be preexisting beings, animals, or geological features changed into mere humans, and thereby in need of spiritual aid to be successful.

---

[41] Today, however, it is common for father and son, grandmother and granddaughter, and other cross-generation gender lines to share the same name, with the older person designed as "name X" #1, and the youngster as #2. With the death of the elder, the numbers are dropped and only the original name is used until another youngster is selected to share it at a family potlatch or invitational party.

Among the many descendants of *Kekedab* were famous standouts, such as the boy who was an endurance warrior, who trained by spitting on a rock, running around Sneatlum Point, and returning before it had dried (Sally Snyder, Box 108, Folder 2, Page 97 AJ). He easily outran deer, elk, cranes, and eagles. Much later, as part of US Coastal defenses, the strategic lookout used by this warrior eventually became fortified with concrete encasements as Fort Casey.

The heirs of *Kekedab* suffered through many crises, including the periodic destruction of the known world. Four major eras include 1) a primordial one of real or semi spiritual beings who marry humans to create descent lines, 2) lawless times when humans and dangerous spirits are punished for damaging general wellbeing, 3) Changers who prepare the world for present conditions, and, most recently, 4) the world as now known. The high god system for transferring power goes back to the beginning of the world.

Specific communities have traditions of particular disasters. Northern Lushootseeds tell about Glacier Peak in the North Cascades – a volcano that erupted 6700 years ago. A flood of its ash and debris formed Sauk Prairie and rerouted the Sauk River itself from the Stillaguamish into the Skagit (Vance 1957: 309).

For Skagits, the earliest Changers were four brothers, oldest to youngest, named Shield, Knife, Fire, and Baby. Each taught ancestors along the river important skills, such as defense, butchering, cooking, and child care. The immortals (spirits) system of power was another result.

Starchild and Diaper Boy created orderly time by becoming Moon and Sun, while their heirs formed chiefly families across the region, receiving the first *dicta*. Before they settled in the sky, they incinerated the whole world and used the ashes to more evenly scatter resources for use in the next era.

Lower Skagits share the story of Robe Boy, whose family survived the Flood in a canoe. The many victims of the Flood probably established the ghost system of power. As the scoured landscape slowly revived, Robe Boy and his dog hunted for the meat of tiny animals, sewing these pelts into his robe. Later, a voice from Above told him to gather up scattered animal bones and, using *dicta* while waving the robe, create new people. They arose dull and very cold, so he waved the robe over charcoal to recreate fire. Herring swarmed in the slough to feed them, and a mountain goat provided wool for warm clothing. They lacked sense until Robe Boy took up local dirt to make brains for them (Snyder ms, Tale 68 AJ). Eventually these dull humans wandered away, and Robe Boy discovered that his parents were alive and had taken refuge on Sneatlum Point where they were mourning for their children presumed to be dead.

Robe Boy married a human woman and had two sons, First Light and Daylight (*Lehalbid*). Much later when plague from the east threatened all the people, Lehalbid envisioned a protective song and dance. As a prophet, he led the community at La Conner in constant services until the pestilence passed over them. Holders of this name maintained at least four houses around Fidalgo Island – near the present Swinomish police station, in a fort on Sullivan Slough, on Pull And Be Damned Road along Martha's Bay, and at Snee-osh Point. They shifted by season to these "resorts" to benefit from local foods as these reached peak conditions for harvesting.

The founding of the Indian Shaker Church in 1882 provided the most recent system of power, which was linked with the universal one of Christianity. As such, it renewed the primordial power from the high god, closing the loop that began at creation.

namings

Conclusions

The very mention of King Arthur, Brunhilde, *El Inka de la Vega*, King Philip (*Matecom*), Jesus, *Malinche*, *Wovoka*, Fatima, *Panini*, Slocum, and so on identifies these famous names with a place and a time, as well as a gender. Each represents a moment in world history, with the understanding that namesakes partake of the qualities and personalities of their eponymus ancestor. Eskimos (Inuit) remain empathic on this concept.

Similarly, names, especially renowned ones, are at the very heart of Lushootseed culture. Regardless of the loss of language, of territory, and of community health, these names continue to be passed on to appropriate heirs. Associated with them are symbolic households, resource estates, art forms, and histories. Upholding these institutions on either side are the mainstays of "blood" and "mud". As a name serves to infuse a person with all the past, present, and future of prior namesakes, so Andrew "Span" Joe evoked the eternal fusion of mud and of blood when he said that Robe Boy made the "brains" of his revived people from the very earth of that place. Among Lushootseeds, as most other native peoples, the mind is located at the heart not the head of a person, at the very center of being, so these brains involved the core of a person.

Hereditary names have long been recognized as vital features of the complex matrilineal cultures of the North Pacific Coast, and regarded as distinct from the ambilateral and bilateral cultures to the south. Yet the regional elites consistently have intermarried, and continue to do so. The pedigrees established are based on the ownership of traditions based in hereditary names. Given this context, it is not at all surprising, in hindsight, that esteemed ancestors founding chiefly blood line on rich mud steeped in the past, were as crucial to the Salish as to their neighboring potential affines.

SAANICH 1935

At one time or another practically every sheltered bay and nook along the southeast coast of Vancouver Island, and on the small islands adjacent to it, carried a settlement of greater or less size; but at the coming of Europeans late in the 18th century, the Salish inhabitants of this area appear to have been divided into four main groups.[42] Around Victoria was the Songish ~ Songhee group whose main body wintered at Cadborough Bay and summered at a place called Xthapsam, just above the gorge at Victoria, while a lesser body occupied the territory around Sooke Basin. The second group inhabited the Saanich peninsula, extending down its east side as far as Cordova Bay. From about Mill Bay to Qualicum lived the Cowichan-Nanaimo group, and from Qualicum northward the fourth group, the Comox, who abutted on the Kwakiutl Indians about Campbell River and absorbed many of their customs.

This division into four groups is somewhat arbitrary, based more on geographical considerations than on differences in dialect or culture. There were such differences, it is true, but they were slight, in some cases, hardly greater than the differences between individual settlements within the same group. Society was organized on a family, not on a tribal basis, and since each family intermarried both within and without its group, the customs and dialects spoken even in individual villages were not always uniform, but reflected the marriage ties with other communities. Thus there could be two families in the same village which, though more or less closely related, practiced slightly different rites for ushering their sons into manhood.

Neighboring groups maintained friendly relations, only occasionally broken by personal feuds that did not involve whole villages. The principle enemies of the Vancouver Island Salish (and also of the Salish on the mainland) were the Kwakiutl Indians from the northern part of the island. The Comox group which, being nearest to the Kwakiutl Indians absorbed many of their customs, seems to have joined them occasionally in their raids on the Saanich, Songish, and Fraser River groups. At all events, the latter today bracket their Comox kinsmen with the Kwakiutl and the West Saanich natives attribute the destruction of their old village in Brentwood Bay about 1850 to either Comox or Kwakiutl Indians (they are uncertain which), who attacked the settlement at a time when nearly all its inhabitants were fishing on the opposite shore of Saanich inlet near Malahat and burned its three long, shed-roofed houses, as well as several smaller ones. One old Saanich woman stated that her grandfather, a Cowichan native, used to intercept the Comox war parties after they had raided the more southern Salish, ransom any persons of rank whom they had captured, and restore them to their people, collecting the ransom price with interest. Some natives of the Cowichan-Nanaimo group declared, on the other hand, that they were always friends with the Comox, in whose territory they rested during their periodic raids against the Kwakiutl. Since a few Saanich Indians accompanied them occasionally on these raids, it seems probable that the Comox did not actively make war on their southern kinsmen, but attached a few volunteers to Kwakiutl raiding parties. [p2 in original]

It was through fear of both the Comox and the Kwakiutl that the Songish retreated in summer above the gorge at Victoria, and the Saanich Indians sent their women and children to secluded spots in May and June, the usual season for raids, while the men maintained a nightly watch on the housetops. During the 19th century, indeed, the Saanich abandoned one of their

---

[42] Some Klallam Indians from Port Angeles settled in Beecher Bay during the 19th century (See Erna Gunther, Klallam Ethnography, UWPA 1 (5): 179, 1927).

villages near Sidney, on the east side of the peninsula, and moved to Patricia Bay, on the west side, where they were less exposed to attack.[43] The last fight between the Kwakiutl and the Salish took place in Maple Bay, near Cowichan, about 1860, when the Cowichan natives, assisted by the Saanich and Songish, annihilated a Kwakiutl war party and, travelling north in their enemies canoes, destroyed the village from which it had set out.

The present-day Salish seem to remember no conflicts with the Nootka Indians of the West Coast until the middle of the 19th century, when the penetration of the Nootka to Cowichan Lake occasioned some skirmishes. However, about 1860, with the consent of the Cowichan natives, the Nootka erected two houses beside the falls on the Cowichan River, and from that date, the two peoples mingled in harmony. Lummi and Samish Indians from what is now the state of Washington occasionally raided the Saanich Peninsula and perhaps northward, but so long ago that the details of their raids have practically faded from memory.

To determine either the population or the number of houses in an average Coast Salish village of pre-European times is no longer possible. The old kitchen-middens that accumulated in and around them vary in length from a few yards to many hundreds. One at Sidney, on the Saanich Peninsula, stretches for more than a mile, and varies in depth from six to nine feet. There may have been a score of houses on this site, but not necessarily contemporaneous. Moreover, the houses themselves varied greatly in size, so that even if one knew their number at any given time, it would give us little clue to the total population. In all cases, they formed one, two, three lines facing the water of the bay and the canoes drawn up on the sandy or gravelly beach. Behind them stretched the forest to which the inhabitants could flee for refuge in case of attack, and within a few hundred yards was a stream of fresh water.

The sheltered position of these settlements within bays offered many advantages that offset their exposure to sudden attack. In any case, raiders always came in canoes, giving villagers ample time to organize resistance or flight, unless, as sometimes happened, the attack occurred at night. Not always did they flee to the forest behind the houses. Occasionally they took refuge on rocky headlands impregnable on three sides, and protected on the fourth by a ditch and an artificial rampart of earth. Traces of such ramparts, originally surmounted by wooden palisades, are still visible in certain places, even on Beacon Hill within the city limits of Victoria. Most of them date from prehistoric times, but one at Khenipson, near Duncan, was constructed as lat as the middle of the 19th century. Menzies, who sailed with Vancouver, thus [3] described a fortified Coast Salish village near Homfray Channel, on the mainland side of the Strait of Georgia:

> "At the farther end of these islands we came to a small cove in the bottom of which the picturesque ruins of a deserted village placed on the summit of an elevated projecting rock excited our curiosity and induced us to land close to it to view its structure.
>
> This rock was inaccessible on every side except a narrow pass from the land by means of steps that admitted only one person to ascent at a time and which seemed to be well guarded in case of an attack, for right over it a large Maple Tree diffused its spreading branches in such an advantageous manner as to afford an easy and ready

---

43 The Sidney village was known as Sai'klam "clay", and Patricia Bay was called Klangan "salty place"; but when the Sidney inhabitants moved over to Patricia Bay they transferred the name "clay" to their new home. {Original Klangans moved to Tulalip, USA.}

access from the summit of the Rock to a concealed place amongst its branches, where a small party could watch unobserved and defend the Pass with great ease. We found the top of the Rock nearly level and wholly occupied with the skeletons of houses – irregularly arranged and very crouded {crowded}; in some places the space was enlarged by strong scaffolds projecting over the Rock and supporting Houses apparently well secur'd – These also acted as a defense by increasing the natural strength of the place and rendering it still more secure and inaccessible."[44]

By the end of the 19th century, the huge shed-like dwellings in which the Vancouver Island Salish were living at the time of their discovery had been abandoned or destroyed, and the Indians had built Houses of more modern form, not always on the same sites as the old ones. It had been necessary, indeed, in the interest of white settlement, to move one or two of their villages; thus one, inhabited by the Songish, which hindered the development of Victoria, was moved a few miles west of the city. Early in the 20th century the Canadian government appointed a Royal Commission to delimit the lands to which the Indians should be given legal rights, taking into consideration the villages they were occupying at the time, the places in which they buried their dead, and the streams on which they had plied their nets and built their fishing weirs. Thus were created the present-day reserves on which the Indians live, reserves that correspond in the main with the sites of some of their settlements in earlier years. In 1929, the entire Coast Salish population of Vancouver Island, to the number of 1892, was distributed among 26 reserves, arranged from north to south as follows, with their population in brackets:

Comox (35), Qualicum (2), Nanoose Bay (25), Nanaimo (222), two reserves near Ladysmith (Kulleets 79, Siccameen 44), Halalt reserve near Chemainus (23), Cowichan Lake (8), seven reserves around Duncan (Khenipson 45, Quamichan 245, Clemclemaluts 135, Koksilah 16, Comeaken 60, Somenos 170, Kilpaulus 10) Malakut in Mill Bay (24), four reserves on Saanich Peninsula (Pauquachen 53, Tsekum 25, Tsartlip 102, Tsawout 106), Songees reserve between Victoria and Esquimalt (90), Esquimalt (18), Beecher Bay (37), Sooke (28), and, off the coast of east Vancouver Island, Lyacksum reserve on Valdes Island (50) and Penelakut reserve on Kuper Island (240).

The accompanying sketch-map {AWOL} shows the positions of the four Saanich reserves, whose inhabitants are the main topic of this paper.

ECONOMIC CYCLE [4]

In the early 19th century, life in the Saanich communities followed a seasonal rhythm which varied slightly from village to village owing to slight variations in the economic and social environments. In the West Saanich village of Tsartlip, on Brentwood Bay, the cycle ran thus:

<u>Dec-Feb</u>: This was the season of the winter dances, when the population remained in the village. On fine days the men fished off shore for cod and grilse, or caught a few ducks, and the women

---

[44] Menzies' Journal of Vancouver's Voyages, edited by CF Newcombe, Victoria BC, 1923: 66.

gathered clams and a variety of seaweed, green with brown edges; but for the most part the people subsisted on the dried fish and berries they had gathered during the summer.

<u>March</u>: In this month seals and spring salmon supplemented cod, grilse and ducks. The regular winter dances ended, but the members of the secret Black Dance held their ceremonies.

<u>April</u>: On land, the men hunted deer and elk; at sea they fished for cod, grilse, spring salmon, halibut, and, particularly, herring, which spawned in this month.

<u>May</u>: While the men pursued the same activities as in March, the women gathered camass roots, wild carrots, and rushes for making mats.[45] The camass season lasted only about three weeks, but an energetic family could fill 10 or 12 bags with the roots during that period. If the weather was warm many of the people left the village and camped near their camass grounds on San Juan Island, using for shelter either a few boards taken from their houses, or rush mats.

<u>June</u>: Many of the villagers went out to the islands to fish for halibut in deep water. Others contented themselves with capturing cod, spring salmon, and grilse near the village. They paid many visits to neighboring villages, and occasionally held a potlatch, though the usual season for potlatches was later.

<u>July</u>: From the beginning of this month until the end of August, the village was deserted. Its inhabitants crossed to Point Roberts, on the mainland, to net the sockeye salmon which was their staple winter food, and the humpback salmon that succeeded it. In the intervals of salmon fishing, the men killed a few elk and deer, which were not in their prime. Throughout July and August, the women gathered berries, and also dried large quantities of the consumption plant seeds that they used for flavouring their meat and fish, and as an antidote against supernatural contagion.

<u>August</u>: Over and above the activities of the previous month, the men repaired their boats or made new ones, and one or two small parties, leaving their women behind, sometimes went into the mountains to hunt {mountain} goats. The women gathered and dried many Saskatoon, salal, and other berries that ripened in this month. [5]

<u>September-November</u>: Early in September the people returned to their village, where they set their houses and graveyards in order and laid in a stock of wood for the winter. Often three or four canoes manned by men only went out among the islands to hunt seals, sea-lions, and sea-

---

[45] Only the round variety of rush was gathered in May, when it was easily pulled out of the water; the bulrush, which required cutting, was usually gathered about July. After being thoroughly dried in the sun, the rushes were rolled into bundles and stored away until needed. Subsequently the woman steeped them in water, stripped off the outer edges for thread, and, spreading them in rows, stitched them together with a 24" or 30" needle of hardwood, usually <u>spireae</u> <u>discolor</u> {ocean spray}. Then she bound their edges with a grass (Phagmites sp) that flourishes in the Fraser River Valley, and flattened seams with a curiously grooved presser. In the 19th century the Vancouver Island Salish purchased many halibut from the Nootka Indians with rush mats.

otters. Other men fished near the village, or hunted deer, while the women gathered clams, made blankets and rush mats, and attended to other duties around the homes. Late in September appeared the dog-salmon, which the Tsartlip Indians caught as they approached the river at Goldstream. Both Sept and October were favorite months for potlatches, so that there was much going and coming between one village and another. November with its frosts and high winds checked this travelling. In that month the villagers settled down for the winter, and the women left their homes only to gather clams and fern-roots while the men made canoes, and hunted and fished in the immediate neighborhood.

Many East Saanich natives, the Songish, and those near Chemainus, followed practically the same routine as the West Saanich; they too abandoned their villages in the middle of the summer and netted sockeye and humpback on the mainland, but only over the waters immediately adjacent to their shore and around Mayne and Saltspring Islands ; so while many of them fished for herring, cod, and halibut off these two islands during the mid-summer months, living in rush huts on their shores, others preferred to remain the year round in their villages, where they were less exposed to enemy raiders coming down from the north. Food was always plentiful, even without the sockeye and humpbacked salmon, which did not enter the Cowichan River; for the steelhead salmon began to ascend this stream in January, increased in numbers during March, and continued until June, when blue-backs made their appearance in the weirs. The blue-backs lasted until August, and were followed by cohoe; and when the cohoe run ended in October, the dog-salmon entered the river and ran until Christmas. Both in Cowichan Bay and near Saltspring Island, herring spawned in great numbers during April; seals, too, frequented the waters near shore, and sea-lions a little farther out. Deer, elk, bear, and grouse abounded in the Cowichan woods and could be captured at every season of the year. There was no lack, too, of vegetable foods, since camass, fern and herring {berries} of every kind grew all about. Even rushes for mat-making were procurable in Quamichan Lake.

The Nanaimo Indians followed the Saanich custom of visiting the mainland in midsummer. There were five communities in the district: <u>Solachwan</u> ("swampy ground"), <u>Tewahlchin</u> ("village to the north"), <u>Anuweenis</u> ("village in the centre"), <u>Kwalsiarwahl</u> (meaning unknown), and <u>Ishihan</u> ("end village"); the first was within the present city of Nanaimo, the other four strung out along the Nanaimo River two or three miles away. These river villages were occupied only from about September till Christmas, when their inhabitants moved to Departure Bay to celebrate their winter dances, carrying with them the walls and roofs of their houses so that only the bare frames remained on the bank of the river. The Solachwan natives, however, occupied their village until about April, when they joined the others in moving out to False Narrows and Gabriola Island to fish for cod, grilse, and other species, to hunt seals and sea-lions, and to gather clams and camass: for every family had its own bed of camass on Gabriola island. In August all the Indians moved again to the mouth of the Fraser River for the sockeye and humpback salmon season, returning to Nanaimo in time for the dog-salmon. [6]

HUNTING

In addition to special regulations governing the pursuit of such animals as the whale and the sea-lion, the Saanich had one general rule: that a man should never hunt or fish on a full stomach, because the taint he acquired from eating would offend the game and keep it beyond his reach. The hunter or the fisherman therefore started out before daylight, and did not break his fast until he returned home. Even his wife and children in the village fasted and moved about quietly, lest some action on their part should militate against his success. Only if he had gone far away and would be absent for several days did they eat and behave as usual.

<u>Deer and elk</u>: These animals were caught in three ways: in pits, in nets, and by individual hunters with bows and arrows.

In many places the natives dug pits about 10 feet deep along the animal's trails, placing in the bottoms of some pits sharpened stakes and notched poles for ascending and descending. The pits trapped far more deer than elk, the latter being, of course, less numerous. A Duncan native stated that his father commonly trapped two deer a week.

The deer-net, made of plaited sinew, or, on the Fraser River, from a grass called <u>sakwats</u>, varied in length according to the number of hunters, each of whom brought his own section to join those of others along the line of stakes.[46] While some of them drove the deer towards the net, others concealed themselves behind it to kill the trapped animals. They then divided up the meat more or less evenly, but the man in whose section the deer was caught could claim its hide and sinew. A Saanich Indian said that his people never used dogs for driving the animals, having only the woolly-haired variety that was unsuitable for hunting; but a Westholme native said that in his district they did use the wooly-haired dog in deer-drives. The mainland natives along the Fraser River, in whose territory elk were unusually numerous, drove them, in historical times, at least, with a larger breed of dog.

Hunters who went out singly in pursuit of deer and elk often painted their faces with red ochre, or wore red caps; and they carried a pair of horns to plant on their heads in close stalking. To attract a buck elk they whistled with their mouths, to attract a female deer they whistled through a blade of grass. Generally, they threw away the head, filled the reticulum of the animal's stomach with its blood, and pushed the forefeet through incisions in the hind feet so that they could carry the carcass on their back without the necessity of a tump-line. At home they heated the blood in a wooden box and drank it.

The rituals connected with deer-hunting varied slightly in the different family groups. All agreed that a man should never mention by name the animal he intended to hunt, lest it hear him and keep out of his way.[47] All agreed, likewise, that he should purify himself beforehand and keep away from his wife for at least one night. A Tsawout (East Saanich) medicine-man said that he should keep away from his wife for [7] four nights, and pray night and morning to the shades of his dead relatives and ancestors. A Tsartlip (West Saanich) native denied this, asserting that only a priest (<u>theetha</u>) { ~ $\theta i\theta a$} or a medicine-man would dare to pray to the shades, and then only that he might spoil a hunter's luck by making the shades frighten the animals away. In his own family group, he added, the hunter hired a priest to paint his face with red ochre and teach him the incantation he should say in the woods the night before, and again in

---

[46] Fraser speaks of "a net … made of thread of the size of cod lines; the meshes were 16" wide and the net 8 fathoms long". (Journal of Simon Fraser in Masson, LF <u>Les Bourgeois de la Compagnie de Nord-Ouest</u>, I, p.192, 1889.)

[47] While I was talking to an old Tsartlip Indian one afternoon, a youth came up to borrow two cartridges, saying he intended to hunt for deer on the morrow. After he had gone, the old man said to me "He will not get any deer. He has let them know that he is going to hunt them and they will flee far away".

the early morning before he started out for the chase, an incantation that would check the deer from fleeing. Then when he shot an animal, he opened it up (taking care not to inhale any of the warm steam, which would cause his early death), sprinkled around a few handfuls of blood for any shades that might be near, both human and animal, and held up the heart to the sun as a thank-offering. Finally, on returning home, he scrupulously removed all blood from his clothes lest it prevent him from finding any more deer-tracks.

Another old Tsartlip Indian used to pray to Haylse (see p. {122?}) in the solitude of the woods in the morning, and again at evening, on the eve of the day before he went hunting. Then, during the night, he would dream where to find deer, and how many he would kill; he would dream, perhaps that he met two women and a man, who would ask him what he was seeking; and he knew by this that he would kill two does and a buck. Long before daylight, he would leave the house to search for them, and his family, finding him gone, would remain very quiet throughout the day lest the deer, which learns through dreams as man does, should hear their noise and flee far away. This man sprinkled on the ground some drops of blood from the first deer he shot after the close of winter, as a thank-offering to Haylse.

An old Tsekum (West Saanich) Indian observed the following rules: For three or four days in succession, he wandered into the woods about sunrise, bathed, scrubbed himself with branches, and prayed to the Sun "Bring what I wish into my path". The night before he actually went hunting, his soul (*smastimauch*) left his body and discovered the location of the deer, and learned also whether he would be successful. He left his house before daylight, fasting, since if he ate any food, the deer or elk would see steam issuing from his mouth and flee; and he carried with him a deer knucklebone to attract the game by its smell. As he walked along, he prayed his feet and the ground to cause no earth-movement that might warn the deer; and after he had shot the animal, he cupped up some of its blood in his two hands, raised it toward the Sun as a thank-offering and poured it on the ground.[48] [8]

Hunters kept their bows and arrows in deerskin cases to protect them from the rain. Most bows were made of yew, curved at each end by steaming inside a length of kelp; their strings were of elk hide or sea-lion gut. These bows are said to have lacked any backing, but from the mainland some of the Saanich Indians obtained bows of yellow cedar that were backed with twisted deer sinew set in a groove and then covered with sturgeon glue. One measurement for the weapon was the distance between the elbows when the finger knuckles were joined on the chest; but this excluded the horns, which were extra. Arrows were made of cedar, or, more rarely, of Saskatoon wood; and one measure for them was the distance from the tip of the middle finger to the middle of the chest. The Tsartlip native who gave these measurements said that arrows were winged, preferably with two golden eagle feathers lashed on with cherry bark, and

---

[48] The Quamichan (Duncan) natives observed similar rules: they bathed and separated from their wives one or more days before going out to hunt, avoided mentioning the name of the animal, and poured out a little of the blood for the shades of dead relatives. At Westholme, however, an old couple told me that their people never prayed to the Sun or to the shades for aid in hunting, and never made any blood-offerings.

The Vancouver Island Salish killed only those bears that they encountered accidentally, and in most cases paid no special respect to the {slain} animal; but the old Tsekum Indian mentioned above, following a custom which he claimed was restricted to his family, shouted *He* when the bear fell mortally wounded, then chanted a song to please its soul and check it from crying out in agony.

that they carried three kinds of points: a stone or musselshell point that disengaged when it struck, used for deer and for war; a bone point, rounded or knobbed to skip over the water, for ducks; and a point with two barbs, for other birds. This man used the primary release, and held the shaft of the arrow between the middle and third fingers of his left hand. A Tsawout native said that in his village the points were fastened with sturgeon glue as well as with cherry bark, and that while two feathers were usual for small game, three were preferred for large animals. The golden eagle feathers were purchased from mainland natives, since the bird does not frequent the south of Vancouver Island.[49] Toy arrows of the present day carry duck-feathers.

Goats: On the mainland, usually at the close of the salmon season, the Saanich killed a few mountain goats with their bows and arrows, but perhaps not before the 19th century. They may have trapped, too, a few beaver and musk-rats, which were present in the lower Fraser Valley, though absent on Vancouver Island; in any case, they were of little importance.

Waterfowl: Two men often paddled out at night to where waterfowl, principally ducks, were resting on the water, kindled a small fire in an earth-filled box to attract the birds, and speared or clubbed them when they drifted within reach. A Duncan native said that his people used a spear with two points, which seems to have been the usual type, but a Tsawout man of East Saanich stated that the spears of his family group had four points, three blackened, the fourth painted white for aiming. He described the procedure as follows:

Two men paddled out to a place where two currents met, for that was where the ducks slept. The man in front had a four-pointed spear that rested on a cross-beam and on some noiseless material set on the bow. The steersman sat a little forward of the stern, behind him a small fire burned in a wooden box filled with earth. When they drew near the ducks, the steersman muffled himself under a cape to resemble a stump and sat motionless, merely steering the canoe without raising his paddle. Then the man in front, paddling with as little noise as possible, speared the ducks, one after another, and drew them into the boat.

The Saanich natives disclaimed any use on Vancouver Island of the square net which their neighbors, the Lummi Indians of the south, sometimes threw over flocks of ducks that were resting on the water. Nevertheless, they did use two kinds of nets for waterfowl. Over the spawning [9] grounds of the herring, they occasionally stretched a net horizontally about three feet from the bottom of the sea to enmesh and drown the ducks that dived down to eat the spawn.[50] Again, in favorable localities, they erected two or more high poles at distances up to 100 feet apart, and stretched between them a long net to intercept the ducks as they flew to their feeding grounds at dawn, and returned from them at evening. In certain places, this net was stretched over water, in others (e.g. on the East Saanich reserve) over dry land; and some natives changed its height morning and evening. A Westholme Indian said that his people strung the net on a rope between two trees on opposite sides of a stream in such a way that it could be drawn from one side to the other. One man drove the ducks, one man was stationed in each tree, and the net-owner supervised the operations. Most ducks were caught by the net, but now and then

---

[49] The price of one golden eagle feather in the 2nd half of the 19th century was $1.

[50] In the shallow Sumas Lake, up the Fraser River, the Indians stretched out the net on the surface and floated a dead salmon below it, {then} when the ducks and geese that were attracted by the bait became caught in the meshes as they pushed their heads up to breathe.

one fell to the ground stunned. If only two or three birds were trapped, one of the men stationed in the trees pulled the net over and disengaged them; but if a number struck the net, the men in the trees released its ends simultaneously so that it dropped to the water, whereupon they paddled or waded out and wrung the bird's necks.[51]

Other birds: A few grouse and other birds were caught in nooses, a few swans and eagles shot with bow and arrows. None of them, however, played an important role in Saanich economy except the swan, and that not for its flesh but for its down, which the natives strewed over their heads in many of their ceremonies and dances. Hunters sometimes filled a swan with its down and sold it.

Seals and porpoises: Seals were hunted all along the coast, most commonly on moonlight nights. The harpoon of yew-wood, had two heads fit with stone or shell points set in bone or antler sockets, and the line was of twisted cedar twigs and bark, or, very rarely, of nettle. According to a Westholme native, the hunter did not attach the end of his line to a cedar-bark buoy, as for sea-lions, but retained it in his hand. Seal-hunting, like the porpoise-hunting conducted with the same weapons, was not regarded as an occupation requiring hereditary power or knowledge, and so was open to any native. Two men generally went out in a boat together.

The oil obtained from seals and porpoises was stored in the bladders of seals to eat with dried fish.

Sea-lions: The Saanich Indians killed very few sea-lions, which the present-day natives say were not plentiful off their shores, though common a little farther north. Harpooners of these animals inherited their profession, together with the songs that accompanied it; for the [10] natives believed that while other men might succeed in harpooning the animal, they could never bring it to shore unless a professional tamed it by his chants. Each canoe generally carried three weapons, a double-pointed harpoon for any seals that might be encountered, a single-pointed harpoon attached to a cedar buoy for sea-lions, and a stout wooden spear whose tip had been hardened in a fire for dispatching the wounded animal. While the crew of laymen paddled, the harpooner kept watch in the bow.

Every harpooner had to dissociate himself from women for three or four days before the sea-lion season, and while the boats were away the women of the village had to refrain from washing their hair. If either regulation were violated, a sea-lion would bite one of the harpooners and probably drown him.

The captured mammal was dragged ashore, cut into cross-sections, and divided among all the hunters. The flippers and the intestine were the special prerequisites of the harpooner, the intestine because, when slightly twisted and dried, it made a very stout cord suitable for a bow-string or a halibut troll.

Whaling: Whaling also was an inherited profession, practiced only by the Songish group of Coast Salish and by an occasional Saanich native.[52] Usually several canoes went out together,

---

[51]   Cf. illustration of 4 bird poles at Port Townsend in George Vancouver, A Voyage of Discovery to the North Pacific Ocean and Round the World, I: p234, London, 1798.

[52]   An East Saanich (Tsawout) man hunted whales in Saanich Arm during the 19th century. So heavy was his harpoon, it was said, that only he alone had the strength to wield it.

each of them carrying ten men. In the bow of the leading canoe sat its owner, the harpooner, a man of high rank in his community; besides the heavy yew harpoon with shell or stone point, he carried a bone club which had come to him, supposedly, from his guardian spirit and without which he dared not whale. The second man bore a long spear pointed with elk bone, for stabbing the exhausted whale behind the fore arm. The third took care of the bulky harpoon line, made of twisted cedar-twigs; and the fourth had charge of the three (one native said four) sealskin floats. The next five men merely paddled, and the tenth was the steersman.

Before the whaling season opened, the harpooner spent from ten days to a month in the woods, half-fasting, bathing, and praying to his guardian spirit. Certain restrictions were laid on the villagers while he was at sea, but I failed to discover them. A Tsartlip native stated that when the wounded whale towed the canoe along, the harpooner and crew chanted the following incantation in order that the animal might drag them towards some creek near the village where they could conveniently cut up its carcass:

"Turn to that mountain. Go quietly to the creek. There I shall meet you."

As the canoe approached the shore, they chanted again, and the villagers on the beach joined in, some of them beating drums:

"Whale spirit, do not desert me. Give me your protection for the future." [11]

The men drummed and danced and repeated the second chant, under the harpooner's leadership, after the whale had been cut up. The crews then divided the meat and oil according to certain rules, the harpooner, of course, receiving the largest share, and they invited the people of neighboring villages to join them in the feast.

FISHING [12]

Custom demanded that the bones of all fish, whatever their species, should be thrown into the water, when it was believed they reclothed themselves with flesh and became fish again.[53] Animal bones also were generally thrown into the water, not, however, to restore them to life, but to preserve them from molestation by dogs, which would annoy the animal's shades. It was forbidden to roast fish and meat at the same fire, under penalty of failure of fishing and hunting.

The Tsartlip natives threw back into the water every fish that was disfigured and begged forgiveness of the fish spirit Skwanaylets for catching it. They state that toward the end of the 19th century a young girl made fun of a disfigured fish and laughed when her mother reproved her, but that a few days later, her own face became contorted like that of the fish and she died. Other Coast Salish groups on Vancouver Island held similar beliefs.

<u>Cod</u>: The Saanich, and probably other groups, speared many cod by night, and not only cod, but salmon, perch, flounders, and soles. The fishermen generally went out alone, lit a fire in a box of sand at the bow of the canoe to illumine the water, and impaled the fish from the stern with a two-pointed spear. Some cod were speared also by day close to shore during the spawning season; for the Indians claimed, rightly or wrongly, that a few one- or two-year fish always

---

[53] There was a popular belief among the Saanich Indians that the moment the bones of the sockeye salmon touched the water they changed into a fish that leaped above the surface. If a bone were missing, it leaped only a little, thereupon the Indians searched for the missing part and threw that in. The salmon leaped high out of the water.

guarded the spawn from the depredations of other species, and that these guardian cod were so savage that they even attacked the spears of the fishermen. The latter, not wanting to deplete their ranks, speared two or three only and left the rest to keep watch.

The Saanich, like the other Coast Salish Indians, often used a peculiar two- or three-vane spinner of light cedar to attract cod to the surface; they thrust the spinner almost out of sight with the shaft of the spear, or else with a long pole, and when it came spinning upward, again stabbed the fish that darted after it.

More successful than the spear, perhaps, was the hook and line, the latter often made of kelp.

Halibut: For halibut the Saanich used a wooden hook bent into the shape of a horse-shoe and fitted with a bone barb. The wood was either a hemlock knot or a piece of straight-grained balsam bent into shape by steaming, then lashed until it dried. The favorite bait was octopus, and the line commonly of spruce-root.

Dog-Fish: Dog-fish were caught with the same tackle as halibut. The skin, peeled off with the fish was half-dry, served as sandpaper. The meat was generally squeezed into a pulp before it was eaten. [13]

Sturgeon: Sturgeon were common only in the Fraser River and in the lakes that drained into it, so that the Saanich Indians rarely saw this fish. The Fraser River Indians captured it at different seasons, but mainly in spring during the ookakan run when it seemed most plentiful. They caught it in three ways: with a bone (?) hook baited with oolakan or salmon roe attached to a line; with a bag-net woven from nettles (?) that was dragged between two canoes; and with a long two-pointed spear whose detachable bone points were fastened by a long line of ? to a float of light cedar. Often a man would drift downstream in his canoe and probe the bottom of the river with his spear, stabbing whenever it touched a fish. On Sumas Lake the Indians walked down a long weir and raked the bottom of the water with a detachable hook set on the end of a long pole and fastened to a line.

There is a story that long ago, when the Indians at the head of the Fraser Delta were suddenly attacked by enemies during the celebration of a ten-day festival, some of them jumped into the river and changed into sturgeon; whence the sturgeon still gather at this place every year for ten days.

Herring and Oolakan: The oolakan shoaled in the Fraser River in May, when the local Indians raked them in with long poles studded with spikes made from Saskatoon wood, and also caught them in dip-nets made from twisted nettle-fibers. The Saanich natives employed exactly the same methods for herring, which shoaled round the coast in April for about three weeks, on two high tides, the Indians say, after which they retreated into deep water.

While the herring were spawning, the fishermen suspended cedar-branches three or four feet above the mud bottom by means of wooden floats and stone sinkers, then drew them up with the spawn after the herring had departed and shook them out in their canoes. Unlike oolakan, herring do not consistently return each year to the same places to spawn, but change from one locality to another. The Saanich have frequently tried to establish them in convenient bays by transporting the roe, but without success. A Tsartlip woman many years ago carried some roe from Cole Bay to Brentwood Bay, hoping that the fish which hatched from them would return {here} the following season. When they failed to return she blamed, not the wandering habits of the herring, but a fellow-villager whom she accused of offending the fish by capturing some with his rake just after his wife had been initiated as a winter dancer.[54]

Both herring and oolakan were dried in the sun for about ten days, either strung on sticks or laid out on rocks; but the largest herring were smoke-dried, which in the eyes of some Indians improves their flavor.

Salmon: Salmon of one kind or another was the main food of the Saanich, as it was of all the other Coast Salish Indians. Wherever weirs could be built across rivers, they set basket traps to capture them; at other places on the rivers, they used dip-nets of nettle fibers or else willow-bark purse-nets drawn between two canoes. Many salmon were also impaled [14] on two-barbed bone points detachable from a long wooden handle while still remaining lashed to it. On the Cowichan and Chilliwack rivers three men in one canoe, and two in another, sometimes blocked the river with a long gill net made from willow-bark and drove the spring salmon into it. The Saanich also employed gill-nets for spring salmon nets that averaged about 10 fathoms long by 1½ feet deep; but for the sockeye and humpbacked species they used a larger purse-net called sgwala {$sg^w ala \sim s\underline{x}^w al\partial$'}. The top and bottom ropes of this net were generally made from twisted cedar-boughs, and meshes from willow, gathered in May or June, peeled, split into thin strands that were then twisted together to form a long rope; but the Westholme natives fashioned their purse-net from a flax-like plant that grows on the mainland. Stones made convenient sinkers, and blocks of light cedar served as floats.

A weir belonged to the five or six men who built it, each of whom commonly set against it three or four traps. It was understood, however, that other men in the same community might set their own traps at the weir as soon as the owners had satisfied their needs.

Most of the natives regarded the sockeye as the choicest of all fish, but not all of them possessed fishing rights over waters where the sockeye ran; for, like the humpbacked, it does not enter the streams of Vancouver Island. The Saanich had an immemorial claim to the fishing off Point Roberts, near the mouth of the Fraser River; and there, during July and August, they caught and stored for the winter large quantities of both sockeye and humpbacked. Similarly, the Westholme natives owned the fishing-rights at Cuwassim, and the Songhese at San Juan. The Duncan Indians, however, lacked any corresponding rights on the mainland, and for the most part disregarded the sockeye fishery, although they did catch a certain number of these salmon off Pender island.

Because one man alone could never make a purse net long enough for sockeye and humpbacked, several Saanich families cooperated by making sections that could be joined together at the fishing-grounds. The leader of the group then supervised the fishing, appointed one man to watch, with painted face and feathered head, which way the shoals were running, and apportioned the catch equally among the several families without regard to their social rank.

---

[54] This woman stated that in earlier times, the Indians sometimes squeezed the sperm of the male salmon over the roe of the female, packed it in a special kind of moss inside a cedar chest, and deposited the box under some cliff on a mountain face where the sun would shine on it all day, but no rain could penetrate. Before departing they chanted certain prayers to the spirit ruler of the fish, Sk^{w}anaylets. Years later, if for some reason the salmon failed to revisit their usual haunts, they retrieved the roe and placed it in the sea. Then not only salmon, but fish of other species appeared ther in large shoals. {p17 into text}

Each family then dried its share on its own rack. Not until all their requirements were satisfied did the leader provide for himself; but thereafter he appropriated the entire catch, which his followers cut up and dried for him.

At Point Roberts, each family dried its fish in the same spot year after year, and left there its stone net-sinkers; the same customs prevailed, probably, at other Coast Salish fishing-grounds. In distributing the salmon, the leader, or the man he assigned to the task, counted the fish in twos up to ten until he made the requisite number of heaps of ten pairs, when he started the count over again while two old men sat near to check his figures; from one good haul, each family might obtain as many of four lots of 10 pair, plus 5, i.e. 85 fish. Most of the Vancouver Island communities used the everyday numeral system for the count but the Tsartlip natives of West Saanich employed a special vocabulary derived, they claim, from the fish spirit that taught them to make the [15] purse-net.[55] This count ran, in pairs, thus:

tsέz (one pair) ; cέz (two pair) ; tl'xkwέ• msέł ; skɑtcέ•z ; tkaɷέz ; slokwέ•z ; tísέ•z ; tɑkwέux ; apé•n

The same strange tongue, they added, provided the vocabulary they employed when handling the net:

niłɑsit = "prepare to pull on the net"
sɛléu'kum = "lean back and pull hard"
kuntohwetcum = "pull"
lamat téheu' = "throw stones far out beyond the fish, to frighten them
        into the nets"
k'lest'autsil = "throw stones to the side of the net"[56]

The Saanich, in common with other Coast Salish groups, deeply reverenced the salmon, believing that they were human beings from some far-away land that transformed themselves into fish during the migration season. At this season, therefore, they never referred to any species by its common name, but called it selewa = "rich man" or ceas = "elder brother", and they allowed no dogs at their fishing-grounds. Furthermore, they honored the dead bodies of the fish by cutting them up on ferns, which they afterwards threw into the water; and when they dried the fish in a hut, they burned in it, day and night, the seeds of the consumption plant (Lomatium nudicaule Pursh), which was their specific against supernatural contagion. Every Salish group on Vancouver Island celebrated the first catch on the season with a special rite – the "First Salmon Ceremony"; but whereas the Songhese, Saanich and Westholme natives celebrated it over the sockeye and humpbacked, those around Duncan and Nanaimo celebrated it over the dog-salmon.

The Tsartlip, and I believe, other Saanich natives, related their ceremony only to the humpbacked because it was the one variety that young and old might eat at all times, fresh or

---

[55] For the legend, see Appendix. David Latess, who supplied this vocabulary and claimed that he was the last man to remember it, died in 1937, at the age of over 90.

[56] Tsawout (East Saanich) natives said that one man in each of the two canoes that worked the net streaked his face with red ochre and wore a hat trimmed with goat's wool, while a priest (theytha) on the shore chanted "tcala skwansilawa" = "look back and go into the net." {19}

dried; for even the sockeye, which ran and was captured with it, was forbidden to sick people lest it cause hemorrhages. When the men discovered the first humpbacked in their nets, therefore, all the children in the camp from the age of 5 or 6 years to puberty, bathed in the sea, painted their cheeks with red ochre, sprinkled bird down on their heads, and lined up in a row on the beach. The priest whose face was painted also, chanted a prayer over the fish,[57] then laid one in each child's arms as if it were a baby, with the head pointing towards the water. The children gripped the dorsal fins between their teeth and, marching in line, carried them to the fire-pit, where they laid them [16] on a pile of ferns, very gently, so that they would call on other salmon to follow them. After the priest had daubed each fish with ochre, the old women cleaned them, sprinkled them with the seeds of the consumption plant, and roasted them on the hot coals. The children lined up again as soon as they were ready and received each one a whole fish (if there were enough to go around), while the priest prayed to <u>Skwanaylets</u>, the spirit-lord of all edible fish, in words to the following effect:

"Oh, <u>Skwanaylets</u>, our children this day eat the first of the fish that you have sent us.

We thank you. We shall treat the fish carefully as we have always done."

He ordered the children to eat, and, marching behind them with a stick, forced them to swallow as much as they were able. When they could eat no more, the old women gathered up all the fragments and bones into baskets, and made the children empty them in the sea. A Tsawout native said (without being able to give any reason that the children were supposed to limp as they carried the fragments down).[58]

The Saanich celebrated also the close of the sockeye-humpbacked season, but with a purely secular entertainment. The women and children under the supervision of the priest, gathered up all the loose sticks and refuse on the beach and piled them in a heap. Then towards midnight everyone rose, lit the bonfire, and threw into the air little balls of mixed deer-fat, camas, and bird's down; one ball for each place in which they and their kinsmen were accustomed to net the sockeye and the humpbacked. As they threw away their balls, they shouted the names of these places: "Point Roberts, I feed you with this; Sooke, I feed you with this, etc." Then they scattered their fire, threw the burning brands in play at one another, and yelled and danced until daylight, when they packed up their belongings and returned to the Saanich Peninsula.

The eggs of the salmon, like its flesh, were dried in the smoke of the fire unless their envelopes were broken, in which case they were thrown into baskets and warmed over the fire. The heat then congealed the outside of the mass, leaving the eggs in the middle still raw, but so tightly enclosed that they kept fresh all winter. Before cooking them, the women washed them in cold water, when all dead eggs floated to the surface. Oil from salmon eggs was a regular ingredient in paints.

The Saanich sometimes buried their fresh salmon in the ground for ten days or more before boiling them in wooden boxes. The Indians around Sardis often boiled salmon (and also sturgeon) in a canoe, and with a wooden spoon skimmed off the fat into bags {made} of sturgeon or bear bladders.

---

[57] A Tsawout man said the prayer ran *tsam skwatsilawa* = "Come up out of the canoe". {21}

[58] For the "First Salmon Ceremony" in the other communities on Vancouver Island, see Appendix {B}.

<u>Clams</u>: The enormous quantities of clam shells in the kitchen middens along the coast indicates their importance in the diet. The women dug them out on the beaches with sharpened stakes and carried them home in baskets of cedar-bark and spruce-roots.

<u>Miscellaneous sea foods</u>: Sea-urchin eggs were gathered with light cedar bark nets, about the size and shape of a large bucket, fastened to long wooden handles; a few octopus were captured with the two-pointed spears; and some crabs in wicker traps. These and other sea foods gave variety to the diet, but did not play an important role in Saanich economy.

DWELLINGS [17]

Only the oldest Saanich Indians today recall the long shed-roofed dwellings which seem to have been the characteristic homes of all the Coast Salish at the beginning of the 19th century. The houses in the Songish village at Victoria, built after the establishment there of a Hudson's Bay Company fort and dismantled about 1880, were shed-roofed, and one persisted near Duncan until about the same time; but on the Saanich Peninsula itself dwellings of this type seem to have been replaced about the middle of the century by gable-roofed ones that combined both native and European characteristics.

Judging from the houses still standing on the Saanich Peninsula and near Duncan, this gable-roofed dwelling, whose frame is best revealed by the accompanying photography of an old Kwakiutl house at Campbell River (except that the Coast Salish ones often had a single ridge pole instead of two), averaged from 60' to 80' long by 35' to 40' wide, with the wall boards outside the posts running perpendicular, not horizontal as in the shed-roofed type, and with a roof of overlapping boards or shingles. There are usually two doors, one in a corner of a long side, the other at the opposite end of the house near the middle of the short side. The interior had no flooring and was not divided into compartments except by temporary mats, but around the four walls ran a low wide wooden platform on and under which the inmates stored some of their possessions, depositing the remainder, especially cedar-bark sacks filled with dried fish, on racks suspended from the rafters. They slept on the platform, lying feet to feet and head to head, on mattresses of rush mats and blankets made from goat's wool, or before goat's wool became plentiful, on blankets made from nettle-fibres spun with bird-down, or on cedar-bark mats interwoven with the same down.[59] These nettle and down mattresses were very strong and warm, but because they rapidly spoiled with dampness, the Saanich at least never used them in their summer camps where they slept on the bare ground, but substituted seal or sea-lion skins. Three or four families generally occupied a single house, and the women took turns in cooking for the entire household over one of the fireplaces in the middle of the floor.

Boas has published a plan of the older shed-roofed type of house,[60] and several of the early explorers have left us rather indefinite verbal descriptions. Some of them attained enormous lengths. One visited by Simon Fraser on the river that bears his name was

---

[59] A Katzie native said that on the lower Fraser some mattresses were woven from dog hair.

[60] Boas, Report of the 60th Meeting of the British Association for the Advancement of Science, pp. 563-4, London, 1891.

"six hundred and forty feet long by sixty broad, under one roof; the front is eighteen feet high, and the covering is slanting; all the apartments, which are separated by partitions, are square, except the chief's, which is ninety feet long. In this room, the posts or pillars are nearly three feet in diameter at the base and diminish gradually to the top. In one of these posts is an oval opening answering the purpose of a door through which one man may crawl in or out. Above, on the outside, are carved a human figure as large as life, with other figures in imitation of beasts and birds. These buildings have no flooring the fires are in the center and the smoke goes out by an opening in the top."[61] [18]

Fraser mentions no door except the oval opening in a carved post of the chief's room, which may have been a corner post, but is more likely to have been a centre-post, thus corresponding to the doorway in the northern type of house seen by Meares at Nootka, and common in the Queen Charlotte islands down to the second half of the 19th century. In Fraser's house there must have been other doors along the front leading into the different partitions or rooms, perhaps, too, one at the end opposite the chief's room and one at the back; but there were apparently no corridors or lane-ways from front to back separating the different rooms, as in the shed-roofed houses that Captain Cook visited at Nootka:

"The houses are disposed in three ranges or rows, rising gradually behind each other; the largest being that in front, and the others less; besides a few straggling, or single ones, at each end. These ranges are interrupted or disjointed at irregular distances, by narrow paths, or lanes, that pass upward; but those which run in the direction of the houses, between the rows, are much broader. Though there be some appearance of regularity in this disposition, there is none in the single houses; for each of the divisions, made by the paths, may be considered either as one house or as many; there being no regular or complete separation, either without or within, to distinguish them by. They are built of very long and broad planks, resting upon the edges of each other, fastened or tied by withes or pine bark, here and there; and have only slender posts, or rather poles, at considerable distances, on the outside, to which they are also tied; but within are some large poles placed aslant. The height of the sides and ends of these habitations, is seven or eight feet; but the back part is a little higher, by which means the planks, that compose the roof, slant forward, and are laid on loose, so as to be moved about; either to be put close, to exclude the rain; or, in fair weather, to be separated, to let in the light, and carry out the smoke. They are, however, upon the whole, miserable dwellings, and constructed with little care or ingenuity. For, though the side-planks be made to fit pretty closely in some places, in others they are quite open; and there are no regular doors into them; the only way of entrance being either by a hole, where the unequal length of the planks has accidentally left an opening; or, in some cases, the planks are made to pass a little beyond each other, or overlap, about two feet asunder; and the entrance is in this space. There are also holes, or windows in the sides of the houses to look out at; but without any regularity of shape of disposition; and these have bits of mat hung before them, to prevent the rain getting in.

---

[61]   Journal of Simon Fraser, in Masson, Vol. I: p197, Quebec, 1889.

On the inside, one may frequently see from one end to the other of these ranges of building without interruption. For, though, in general, there be rudiments, or rather vestiges, of separations on each side, for the accommodation of different families, they are such as do not intercept the sight; and often consist of no more than pieces of plank running from the side toward the middle of the house; so that, if they were complete, the whole might be compared to a long stable, with double range of stalls, and a broad passage in the middle. Close to the [19] sides, in each of these parts, is a little bench of boards, raised five or six inches higher than the rest of the floor, and covered with mats, on which the family eat and sleep. These benches are commonly seven or eight feet long, and four or five broad. In the middle of the floor, between them, is the fire-place, which has neither hearth nor chimney. In one house, which was in the end of a middle range, almost quite separated from the rest by a high close partition, and the most regular, as to design, of any that I saw, there were four of these benches; each of which held a single family, at a corner, but without any separation by boards; and the middle part of the house appeared common to all."[62]

It appears from Cook's description that the Nootka built rows of small, shed-roofed dwellings that might be called either compartments (rooms), because all in each row were joined together by a common roof, or houses, because, though joined by this common roof, each was separated from its neighbors by a narrow corridor. Seeing that there were no fixed walls between them, but, in some cases at least, mere pieces of wood, easily removable, that ran out towards the middle, the term compartment might seem more applicable.[63]

An exactly similar building plan appears in a photograph taken at Nanaimo in 1858 (Fig. 00), which shows the back of a row of shed-roofed compartments or dwellings with lanes or corridors separating most or all of them, and, on the extreme left, two single, shed-roofed houses corresponding to the straggling ones present at Nootka. In one respect these Nanaimo dwellings differ from the Nootka ones; their roofs slope downward toward the back, not upward, so that the highest portions are the fronts. Higher in front also are the two dwellings or compartments (one of them stripped of its wall-boards) shown in another early photograph taken at some unrecorded place within the territory of the Coast Salish (Fig. 00), and the Songish houses at Victoria painted by Paul Kane.[64] In neither of these did any lanes or corridors separate the compartments, though Fig. 00 shows a low door near their junction. They correspond in this respect to two houses near Duncan described to me by two old Indians who were familiar with them in childhood.

The first house stood about 1870 at Quamichan, where it sheltered all the families of that community. It was from 700 to 800 feet long, very similar, apparently, to the house seen by Simon Fraser except that it lacked the special compartment for the chief. There were three entrances, all rectangular, one in each of the two short ends and one in the middle of the long side facing the Cowichan River. The interior was divided into rooms on each side by fixed wooden partitions, leaving a wide aisle down the middle, the entire length of the building, in which the villagers celebrated their dances; and every room had two [20] rows of benches, the lower of seats, the upper for sleeping. Each family had its own fire-place, but quite often one

---

[62]   James Cook, <u>A Voyage To The Pacific Ocean</u>, II: p 314-5, London, 2nd, 1795.
[63]   Paul Kane's painting of the interior of a Songish house at Victoria shows similar removable partitions, See National Museum of Canada, B 65: p140, 19xx.
[64]   National Museum of Canada, B 65, p93, 19xx.

cooked for all the rest, in which case the men ate together, and the women and children afterwards. There was no palisade around this house, because its distance from the sea sheltered it from sudden attack.

The other house also stood near Duncan, but its exact locality I did not ascertain. Although only about 100 feet long, much smaller than the Qualmichan house, 12 families occupied it, six married brothers and their six married sisters. Each family had its own compartment or room, separated one from another, however, not by fixed partitions, but by rush mats that were removed at potlatches, leaving the whole house open. As usual, the walls were lined with rush mats, but the position of the doors, and whether there were two rows of benches or only one, I failed to enquire.[65]

We find still a third pattern of settlement near the mouth of the Fraser River (Musqueam?), where, in a row facing the water, the natives seem to have built a number of small, single-roomed dwelling so far apart that it was impossible to unite them under a single roof (Fig 00 {??}). It was a village of this type, apparently, but of rather large houses, that Menzies inspected at Boundary Bay:

> "A large deserted village capable of containing a least 4 or 500 inhabitants, tho it was now in perfect ruins – nothing but the skeletons of the houses remained, these however were sufficient to shew their general form, structure, and position. Each house appeared distinct and capacious of the form of an oblong square, & they were arranged in three separate rows of considerable length: The Beams consisted of huge long pieces of Timber placed in Notches on the top of supporters 14 feet from the ground, but by what mechanical power the natives had raised these bulky beams to the height they could not conjecture. Three supporters stood at each end for the longitudinal beams, & an equal number were arranged on each side for the support of smaller cross beams in each house."[66]

These varying descriptions and photographs leave little doubt that the Coast Salish did not build their houses to a single pattern, but modified them as circumstances required. Such is the opinion of Mr WA Newcombe, to whom I am indebted for two of the above {AWOL} photographs. He writes:

> "As you are aware from your visits to many of the 'old middens' in the Coast Salish area, few of the localities permitted the continuous structures for many hundreds of feet as stated by some of the early writers: the rising and falling of the ground level, local streams, points, etc., caused a break in the structural line .... As far as interior arrangement is concerned, the area occupied by a family was governed by its size. This practice was retained until quite recent times in the barn-like gabled houses of which you saw a number of examples. The individual [21] groups were arranged along both walls. There were one or two doors, sometimes at the ends, in other cases, on the sides, depending on which was the most convenient to the canoe

---

[65]   Taken from TT Waterman, North American Indian Dwellings, Smithsonian Institution Annual Report, 1924: plate 8.

[66]   Menzies, Journal of Vancouver's Voyage, edited by CF Newcombe, Archives of Britsh Columbia, Victoria, 1923 Memoir V: 60.

landing. What I remember of my earlier visits to these gabled houses is an apparent jumble. It was hard to distinguish a dividing line in the interior of the house between two families other than the matting partitions in the sleeping quarters. The belongings hanging from the house beams and those on the ground towards the centre of the house did not appear in any particular section to have any relation to the sleeping quarters. Some sort of order was made of this jumble, no doubt, when the house was to be used for ceremonial purposes, but otherwise the Indian was similar to many whites today, leaving things scattered about ready for the next meal or for whatever the items were used for."

It would have been impossible for the Indians to build houses of this character without metal tools had they not been surrounded with magnificent stands of soft red cedar trees, which tower to a height of 50 or 100 feet without a single {intervening} branch. To fell them, the Saanich hacked all round the trunk with a stone chisel set in bone or antler, using a heavy hand-hammer also fashioned from stone. A number of these stone chisels and hammers have been found in cedar swamps. Two old men stated that instead of a chisel of stone, they sometimes used one made from the sharpened leg-bone or antler of the elk, but they disagreed as to whether or not it was necessary to char the trunk in such cases.[67] After the tree had fallen, they split the straight-grained log with wooden wedges, and dressed the rough planks with small hand-adzes. Thus they obtained posts and rafters for the frames of their houses, and planks for the walls and roofs, as well as for the boxes and chests that held their food and household possessions. {T}he house-planks required no further dressing, but those used for chests and boxes were smoothed with dog-fish skin. Incidentally, it was with the same four tools (chisel, hammer, wedge, and adze) that they hollowed out the trunk of the cedar to make their canoes. Some of them opened out the hollowed log by heating water inside it and spreading it with cross-bars; but an East Saanich native said that his people did not soften the wood with water, but warmed it by building fires along the outside. After finishing the inside of the canoe the maker turned it over and charred and trimmed the outside, giving it a final smoothing with hemlock and other branches, since dog-fish skin was too scarce to use on so large a surface.

An old Indian on the Koksilah reserve near Duncan describe how the people of his district handled the heavy pillars and rafters of their houses in the middle of the 19th century, and his description probably holds true of the other Salish natives. At that period, a notable warrior named Tsuhaylem decided to settle on the then-uninhabited Khenipson reserve, at the mouth of the Cowichan River, and to build for himself and his retainers one of the later-type, low-gabled [22] houses. Higher up the river, for its ridge-pole, they felled a cedar-tree with a trunk about 4 {feet} in diameter, cut holes at regular intervals along its length, and inserted stout poles in the holes. Three or four men then lifted {up} on each pole and carried the log to the river, where they dropped it into the water and let it float down to the sea.

At the chosen site in Khenipson, they dug a deep hole for each of the two pillars on which the ridge-pole would rest, and laid a broad plank against the back of the hole so that the bottom of the pillar would slid down it. Then, with poles beneath, they lifted the top end of the pillar until it was high enough to be caught in a V formed by two struts that were notched into

---

[67] A Sardis native said that when using the elk-horn chisel alone, it was necessary to char the tree, but that an elk-horn chisel was often used in conjunction with the stone chisel to knock off the loosened chips, in which case charring was necessary.

each other and lashed in such a way that they opened and closed like shears. By using a number of such struts and gradually closing them at the bottom, they succeeded in raising each pillar high enough to slide into its hole and stand vertically. Then they tamped it in place, and braced it with posts and anchor ropes until it was firm enough to receive the ridge-pole.

Men from all the villages around Duncan gathered to help with the ridge-pole. First they lifted one end by means of poles, and the holes, resting it on poles of various lengths until it was high enough to receive the struts, which also were of different lengths. Then, with their struts, they raised it a trifle higher than its pillar, but its weight was so tremendous that to lower it again, even a very little, they had to dig under the struts before they would open. Raising the other end of the ridge-pole from the ground was even more difficult, though they finally accomplished that also in the same way. Tzuhaylem made only one door into this house, in the middle of one of the shorter sides; and, for still greater protection, he surrounded it with a mound and a palisade pierced by a gate that was guarded by a sentry. He did not subdivide the interior into rooms, though at one time he is said to have kept in it ten women, beside numerous retainers and slaves.

It was the custom of the Saanich, along with other Coast Salish Indians, to remove the wall-boards of their houses in summer and use them for temporary shelters at fishing and other camps where they intended to stay for several weeks. That explains why in many places, early navigators saw only the frames of houses, and imagined the settlements had been abandoned – as, indeed, they were, though only for two or three months. On brief journeys, when it was not convenient to freight heavy house-planks, the Indians contented themselves with a few rush mats thrown over some cross-poles. Slaves commonly lived in the same houses as their masters, sleeping wherever they were assigned places, since each family arranged its space to suit its needs; but if their masters died and left them without homes, they too made dwellings for themselves of poles and rush mats, in which they lived winter and summer alike.

Neither the Saanich nor the Cowichan Indians gave names to their houses. The carvings on their house-posts did not represent crests, as in the gabled dwellings of northern British Columbia, but dream spirits of their owners, or in one case at least, of the man who was hired to carve them.[68] On the Fraser River a house-post carved with human [23] and animal figures served also as a door, like the posts in the gabled form of house. (See quotation from Fraser, p32). The Songish, Saanich, Cowichan, and Nanaimo natives seemed to have no recollection of this feature in their dwellings. The carving was invariable naturalistic, not conventionalized, though in recent times some conventionalized carvings of northern type have appeared at Chemainus and other places farther south in Coast Salish territory.

The 'furniture' in the houses, apart from the bedding and the rush mats, consisted mainly of rectangular boxes and chests of various sizes, all made from cedar. Some, fitted with lids,

---

[68] This was in a house on the Quamichan reserve near Duncan, whose pillars were carved by a Vancouver (Musqueam) native. Actually, it is not the pillars themselves that are carved, but the heavy false boards nailed to their fronts. The four boards on one side depict fisher (see), those on the other a fanciful creature believed to fly through the air and to prey on two-headed snakes. They were carved for a house on the neighboring Somenos reserve; when that fell, the nephew of the original owner removed them to the newer house at Quamichan, which later passed to another nephew, the present owner. The same Musqueam artist carved four fishers and a two-headed snake on his own coffin, which was later transferred from the Musqueam reserve to the National Museum in Ottawa (See photo in National Museum of Canada, Bulletin 65: p349).

held spare clothing, paraphernalia used in ceremonies, fishing tackle, or miscellaneous tools and weapons; others, without lids, were cooking vessels, water-buckets, or trays for serving up meats and fish. Few if any of these boxes bore animal carvings such as were common further north. Food was generally stored in cedar-bark bags and baskets, but some also found its way into these wooden chests.

Every village appointed some old man to go from house to house at dawn, greet the inmates, see that the boys had gone down to the sea for their morning plunge and that the slave-women were tending to their cooking. There were no regular meal-hours when the men were at home, but the Saanich usually ate twice, once in the morning and again towards night. The morning meal commonly consisted or dried fish dipped in some kind of oil, generally seal or porpoise oil, and fern roots baked in the ashes of the fire. Most families served up their oil in large horseclam shells, but natives sometimes used the highly-prized haliotis shells. The main dish of the evening meal was roasted or boiled fish, but supplementing it were dried berries, wild carrots, or some other vegetable food. After Europeans introduced potatoes into British Columbia, the Saanich Indians often bought them from the mainland natives, paying as much as one goat's wool blanket for a small basketful.

When camping alone, all the members of the family ate together, but in the big village houses, as we have seen, it was quite common for the women to cook in turn for the whole household, and the men then ate first, the women and children afterwards. Occasionally a man invited some friend from another house to dine with him, or was himself invited out, in which case again the men ate alone and each guest received some extra food to carry home with him. Polygamists had to provide each wife with a separate compartment or room, in which she kept her own stock of dried fish and berries. Slaves usually ate after the women and children, but occasionally with them. Under ordinary circumstances, food was so plentiful that no one ever went hungry. [24]

To light a fire, the Saanich struck together two lumps of pyrite and caught the resultant spark in crushed, dry cedar bark; or else, commonly perhaps, they 'drilled' a stick of cedar into a log of cedar, when the friction ignited the powder at the base of the drill.[69] Both methods were troublesome, especially in rainy weather, so in their settlements, natives lit a cedar-bark torch in another house if their own fire went out, and when they were travelling, they enclosed some live coals in large shells.

They prepared their fish and meat in one of three ways. When cooking for a few people only, they generally roasted it before a fire on sticks, but when cooking for many, they boiled it by dropping hot stones into a wooden box half-filled with water. The ordinary cooking-box required six stones, but the exact number naturally varied with the size of the box. The third method was to bake the meat or fish on a bed of stones that had been brought to a moderate heat by a fire kindled on top of it. The charcoal and ashes were swept away with branches, the meat laid directly on the bare stones, surrounded with moss, and covered with old rush mats that were then buried under clean sand or gravel.

Camass roots were cooked by the third method, on hot stones, which were covered with kelp, and the kelp first with bark[70] that had been pierced in numerous places, then with salal and

---

[69]   A Sardis Indian said that his people used a hearth and drill of very dry cottonwood root, placing shredded cedar bark under the hearth to catch the spark.

[70]   One old Tsartlip woman said arbutus bark, but whether this bark was large and thick enough seems doubtful.

blackberry bushes. {Any} roots were piled on the bushes, and water poured through a hole in the centre of the pile, creating a column of steam. Everything was then buried under a layer of fern and other leaves and covered with about three inches of sand. Finally, a great fire was built over the heap and the camass left to steam for from 24 to 36 hours. A favorite dish was camass whipped up with soapberries.

Fern-roots (Pteris aquilina) were roasted over a fire, stripped of their outer integuments and pounded with a stick to release the fibre. Dipped in seal or porpoise oil that had been previously warmed in a horse clam shell, they were a popular after-meat course.

The usual beverage was cold water, but the Indians enjoyed the broth from boiled fish or meat; with the broth from meat, they sometimes mixed the animal's blood. They made, too, infusions from various plants but these were primarily medicinal. [25]

CLOTHING

So mild is the climate in the south of BC that among the Saanich Indians, as in other Coast Salish groups, men often wore no clothing at all in the summer, and women only a diaper (stikwaelak) {loincloth} woven from cedar-bark or dog's hair. The women, however, generally covered their diaper with a short cedar-bark skirt (sqallitch)[71] that was tied around the waist, reached to about the knees, and sometimes at least, was laced down the thigh. A Katzie Indian said that on the lower Fraser River men always wore loin-cloths of either cedar-bark or tanned deer-skin; but on the Saanich Peninsula these loin-cloths, together with the deer-skin shirts (smeluk), sleeved or sleeveless, that both sexes put on in cold weather, came into use, apparently, only in the first half of the 19th century. At that period a few men also wore moccasins and even leggings, whereas in earlier times, both sexes went barefoot, or else covered their feet with strips of deer or elk skin tied around the ankles.

To protect themselves against flies the natives rubbed grease and ochre over their bodies. In rainy weather, they wore a hat of woven cedar-bark or spruce-roots (sqaas), and also a mat of woven cedar-bark (lapus), either square so that it could be thrown over the shoulders and tied at the neck with sinew, or rectangular and with a hole through the middle like a poncho so that it could be drawn over the head. Similar ponchos or capes, fringed round the bottom occasionally with sea-otter fur and with the down of water-birds woven in with the cedar-bark to make them warmer, were worn also in winter, according to a Tsartlip woman of West Saanich ; but at that season most of the natives wrapped goat's wool blankets (sorqual)[72] around their shoulders, or, if they lacked wool blankets, robes of deer- or elk-hide (spetsatsan), seal, sea-lion, or sea-otter skins. In cold weather, too, a few of them replaced the rain-hat with a cap of raccoon or other fur.

Such was the general costume of the Saanich Indians, in common with other south Vancouver Island natives and with those of the lower Fraser River ; but differences in rank occasioned differences in details. Thus only poor or slave women wore diapers of cedar-bark;

---

[71]   The Indians preferred the bark of the yellow cedar for clothing, the bark of the red cedar for mats and baskets.

[72]   When this blanket bore colored designs, the Katzie Indians called it hoksalwit.

women of higher rank wove their diapers, and occasionally also their skirts, from dog's hair,[73] which the Saanich beat with diatomaceous earth and spun with fireweed fibre before working up into garments.[74] In [26] pre-European times, again, goat's wool blankets were rather scarce, especially on Vancouver Island, because the natives killed comparatively few goats prior to the introduction of firearms. Consequently the majority of the Indians wore fur robes in winter; but while the leading men and women paraded in sea-otter and other rich furs, the slaves, who were always scantily clad, were fortunate if they could secure a common deer-skin. Rain-capes of woven cedar-bark, and rain hats of cedar-bark or spruce-root, generally indicated prosperity and high standing; the poorer people and the slaves wore rush mats (snowas) woven along the top edge and either tied round the neck like capes or worn as hoods so that they would cover the head and trail far down the back. Most hats were made of cedar-bark, not of spruce-root; occasionally a little goat's wool was woven in with the bark. Some bore animal designs painted on their surfaces; whether any designs were also woven into the hats, as at Nootka I did not discover. A West Saanich woman said that the designs were heraldic, referring to some episode in the family history; but I obtained no confirmation of her statement.[75]

The Vancouver Island communities obtained practically all their goat's wool and goat's wool blankets from the mainland natives in exchange for rush mats, woven hats, the skins of deer, seal, and sea-lion, and, in the 19th century, potatoes. Apparently they never mixed the wool with cedar-bark, dog's hair,[76] bird down or any other material, though they sometimes dyed it brownish red with alder bark, brown or dark red with hemlock bark, and grey with willow bark.[77]

---

[73] The dogs that supplied this hair belonged to a small breed now extinct, though very numerous before the introduction of trade blankets destroyed their utility. During the sockeye and humpbacked salmon season, the Indians commonly abandoned them on islands with whatever dried fish remained over from the winter; then they recovered them in the autumn and sheared them with mussel-shell knives. In 1936 I noticed an old-creamy-white dog on the East Saanich reserve which seemed to carry some of the old {hair}. Its owner sheared it every autumn and sold the hair to a relative on the mainland, who knitted it into mittens. See further, F.W. Howay, The Dog Hair Blanket of the Coast Salish, Washington Historical Quarterly IX: p ?? .

[74] A Katzie native said that his people made diapers of cedar-bark only not from dog's hair, which they used solely for bed-blankets; further [26] that they beat it with diatomaceous earth and fine swan's down before spinning, and did not use fireweed fibre.

[75] Two Katzie natives said that the woven hat characteristic of the Fraser River area, and also south Vancouver Island, had no brim in front, but a very wide one behind to protect the shoulders. Moreover, it was pointed on top, or slightly knobbed, not rounded like some hats made in recent times by the North Vancouver (Capilano) natives, who had copied, they claim, a more northern style.

[76] A Sardis native asserted that on the Fraser River the Indians added to the goat's wool some dog hair, crushed cedar-bark and bird's feathers, and beat them all together with two sticks before spinning and weaving. The warp was either nettle fibre, or, preferably, a certain species of grass.

[77] Other dyes used by the Saanich, but for basketry rather than woolen blankets, were: a brown from balsam bark, a black from swamp water, a slatey blue from a certain mud, a pink by combing ochre and white balsam bark, a yellow from Oregon grape (Berberis aquifolum) or else from a moss (Leucolepis acanthoneura (Schur.) Lindb.).

Like the dog's hair, it was cleaned by pounding diatomaceous earth into it, then spun on a distaff and woven on a crude loom.[78] Most of the blankets were pure white, but during the 19th century the Indians often introduced into their wefts, at wide intervals, bands of brightly colored stroud {cloth}; the designs on the decorated blankets, that utilized colored yarns, were invariably geometric. The garment was sometimes thrown over both shoulders [27] and pinned at the neck; more often, it passed over one shoulder(commonly the left) and under the other so that it left an arm free, and was fastened in front with a wooden or bone pin, or else held in by a belt.

The tanning of the deer- and elk-hides devolved on the hunter, not on his wife. If he wished to retain the fur, he scraped away all of the fat and flesh from the underside with a stone or bone scraper, rubbed it with the brains of the animal,[79] and after letting the brains soak in for a few days, dried the hide in the sun. Skins for dehairing, he first soaked in water for from four to five days, when the hair could be readily scraped off with a bone or wooden knife. These hairless skins were not usually dried in the sun, but in the smoke of a fire.[80]

Since their clothing was not tailored, the Saanich had comparatively little use for thread. The back-sinew of the deer supplied such as they did require, and a wooden or bone awl took the place of a needle.

ADORNMENT [28]

In pre-European times, women commonly wore necklaces made from arbutus berries or from the dried fruits of the wild rose; occasionally also strings of small stone beads. Whether they also had armlets, and anklets, and of what kind, I could not discover. Haliotis and dentalium shells were extremely rare before the 19th century; the former served not only for ear and nose pendant, but to decorate the front of a nobleman's war-hat or cedar-chest. In the early years of that century shells of various kinds became quite common, together with metal ornaments and glass beads, although the Saanich have never regarded beads with much favour.

What they lacked in ornaments, Saanich made up for in paint. On every important occasion, they streaked their faces with ochre or with a black pigment obtained by mixing fat with the charcoal from burned devil's club. They often laid on these paints in definite patterns to represent their guardian spirits or to convey some other religious meaning and, to heighten the effect, sprinkled on top a layer of glistening mica. Very rarely they used also a white paint from diatomaceous earth, but only to banish some fancied infection of supernatural origin.

Men seldom resorted to tattooing, and when they did, they merely marked on their arms some design that commemorated an adventure, real or imaginary, of some ancestor.[81] About the age of puberty, however, all girls (except perhaps slaves) were tattooed by some skillful relative

---

[78] See ML Kissell, A New Type of Spinning in North America, <u>American Anthropologist</u> 18: 204-270 1916; Organized Salish Blanket Pattern, <u>American Anthropologist</u> 31: 85-88 1929.

[79] At Sardis, and perhaps elsewhere on the Fraser River, boiled salmon heads were substituted occasionally for animal brains.

[80] A Westholme native said that his people never used a stone scraper for removing the fat, but a tool made from the deer's leg-bone, split and sharpened along one edge. Duncan natives (and probably others) commonly used the shoulder-blade of deer to scrape away the hair.

[81] An old Tsartlip man bore on his left forearm a heart, tattooed with needle and thread by his mother when he was a small boy, for what purpose he did not know.

on the faces and wrists, sometimes too on the backs of the hands, the legs, and the bosom. The usual marks, according to an old Tsartlip woman, were four parallel lines across each cheek and two or three short ones on the chin, parallel lines all or part-way round the wrists, and rows of W- and V-shaped lines on the back of the hands.[82] The skin, she said, was first punctured with a sharp bone awl and the wounds rubbed with a mixture of fat and charcoal obtained by burning devil's club, giving a bluish-black coloration. The same woman declared that they produced red tattoo-marks through the use of a red powder obtained by burning together cedar, alder, and a fungus that grows on hemlock trees. Dawson has reported red tattooing among the Haida Indians of the Queen Charlotte Islands.[83]

Boas states[84] that the Songish women tattooed themselves by introducing charcoal from bulrushes under the skin with a needle held horizontally. An old woman on the Quamichan reserve near Duncan bore on the back of one hand several parallel lines made by running a nettle fibre under the skin with a fine needle of hardwood.

SOCIAL ORGANIZATION [29]

Every Saanich (and indeed almost every Coast Salish) village (<u>auhwulmuk</u>) was a unit by itself, linked by economic and cultural ties, and by intermarriage, with neighboring villages, but politically quite distinct. During the first half of the 18th century the old village near Sidney that has since disappeared contained six and probably more big houses, each of which sheltered several families, while some single families occupied smaller huts; and there were at least two big houses in each of the other Saanich villages. Just as the villages lacked all political cohesion, so also did the big houses in the villages, even though they were separated from one another by only a few yards. Thus the enemies of one house could be the friends of another in the same village; and one house would send out a party to trade or raid without consulting or notifying the others. Faced with a common danger, as from war-parties of Comox or Kwakiutl Indians, all the houses in a village united in self-defense; and they collaborated at certain feasts and ceremonies ; but as soon as the emergency or special occasion passed they immediately dissolved this temporary union and lapsed into their customary independence.

The real political unit was therefore not the village, but the big house occupied by a number of kinsfolk – an enlarged or genealogical 'family' to which the Saanich applied the term <u>hunit's'lakum</u>, and we in speaking of similar European nobility {use} the term House. Each Saanich House, as we may call it then, possessed its own long shed-roofed dwelling,[85] its own camas beds on Galiano and neighboring islands, its own set of ancestral names or titles, and its own stock of legends, songs, and medicinal remedies. Other Indians knew some of those songs and legends but might not recite them in public or depict them on any carving or painting, any

---

[82] Cf. illustrations in F Boas, Sixth report of the committee on the northwest tribes of Canada, BAAS, p574, 1890.

[83] GM Dawson, Report on the Queen Charlotte Islands, Geological Survey of Canada, Report of Progress, 1878-9, part B, p108, Montreal, 1880.

[84] Boas, <u>op</u> <u>cit</u>, p 575, 1890.

[85] The extremely long houses reported from two or three places in Coast Salish territory must have sheltered more than one house and its dependents.

more than they might usurp one of the titles.[86] Whether the Saanich set up weirs in any places I did not discover; if so, they too were almost certainly the property of individual Houses, or of certain members of individual Houses, as they were around Duncan, where one stood in front of every large dwelling facing the Cowichan River, not blocking the stream completely, of course, but with gaps through which the salmon could ascend beyond. On the other hand, the sea near the villages, the hunting grounds and berry patches round about, were common property; any villager, whatever his station in life, might fish and hunt wherever he wished within the village territory.

In one or two rare instances a House seems to have comprised merely a group of brothers with their married sons and grandchildren; but because mortality was high and many of the Houses very large, the group commonly included first and second cousins and relatives even more remote. Each married family in this group occupied one segment or room in the dwelling; it owned the wall and roof boards of that segment, either through inheritance or through having cooperated in the building; and it might remove these boards whenever it wished, leaving that portion [30] of the common home wide open.[87] Within its segment or room were its individual fireplace and racks for storing food and other possessions; but the families seldom confined themselves strictly to their own space or maintained any great semblance of orderliness.

Not all the inmates of a House possessed equal standing. Those who had acquired ancestral names at potlatches were addressed by the honorific title <u>see-am</u>, whereas those who lacked such names because they could not afford the expense of potlatches ranked as 'undistinguished people' or 'commoners' (<u>sas musteemuch</u>).[88] Theoretically, not only did all Houses enjoy perfect equality, but all the see-am or nobles in each house, since they claimed a common ancestry and attached little or no importance to primogeniture. No village and no house, therefore, recognized any one officially as its chief. Nevertheless, nobles did differ from one another in prestige and influence, partly through their personal characters and achievements, partly through the varying prestige attached to their titles, which depended to some extent on the prestige of previous incumbents. Generally, therefore, one noble exerted so much influence in his House that he became its leader (<u>salweans</u>) in fact if not in theory; and if his House was numerically the strongest in the village, he was recognized as the principal man in the community.[89]

Each House had its stock of names or titles that it handed down from one generation to another and guarded as jealously as the nobles of Europe guard their titles. Some of them dated

---

[86] Almost any departure from established custom might become the privilege of a House, heritable by later generations, and by them alone, provided the public had ratified it ; and the public ratified it when during some potlatch it heard the statement of claim without demur and accepted the gifts that followed the statement. All such privileges or rights, however, hinged upon proof of lineal descent, and the most obvious indication of such descent was the possession of an ancestral title.

[87] As a rule a family only removed its wall and roof boards for temporary shelter in a spring or summer camp; but occasionally (e.g. in the event of a quarrel), it removed them permanently and used them for the construction of a new home. See Photo 85742 {AWOL} for an illustration of a house with some of the boards removed.

[88] Another word, <u>sweeawilas</u>, was used sometimes, but meant strictly any person even the young child of a see-em, who had not yet received an ancestral name.

[89] Less often, two or three men competed for the leadership.

back, in theory, to a 'golden age' when the world was very different; and they had descended in the same family line, century after century. In theory, too, the families had dwelt in the same localities from time immemorial, so that the names were inseparably linked with certain villages. The Saanich villages, it is true, were so near one another, and so closely related by intermarriage, that the titles current in any one of them received recognition in them all; but in other districts, even in Victoria and Duncan, they had no official standing. Inheritance of titles or of property, however, was not entirely restricted to the male line. A man acquired a title from his father's House, as a rule, because women commonly went to live with their husbands, and a child was raised in his father's community; if for any reason he was raised in his mother's village, or even if he visited it for any length of time, he received a title from her House that made him a full member of her community. The Saanich intermarried with so many of the surrounding Coast Salish groups that a man could find relatives nearly everywhere, and assume or be given a different name or title in each group. Yet there were two restrictions on multiplicity of titles; first, some, through their historic or legendary associations carried greater significance than others, even in neighboring groups, and a man naturally preferred to be known by an important title rather than by an insignificant one; and, secondly, every title required confirmation by the House and community that claimed it, and this confirmation was obtainable only at a potlatch, when the recipient [31] or his sponsors had to disburse large amounts of food and property.

At the present day, the Saanich, like other Coast Salish, have adopted European names by which they are known in ordinary life, and they use their old titles only on ceremonial occasions, mainly at the winter dances. Many, indeed, neither know or trouble to acquire any titles to which their descent may entitle them, especially since potlatches are now prohibited and titles have lost their social significance. Even before potlatches had been prohibited an old Tsartlip woman, Mrs. David, whose parents had died when she was a little girl failed to receive any title, and consequently bore only her childhood name, until she was 32 years old, when a sister whom she happened to visit during a potlatch at her old home near Duncan conferred on her two titles, one her mother's Lateetlia, to be used at Duncan, the other her Saanich grandmother's (mother's mother's) title Swateesia, for use on the Saanich peninsula. The sister merely invited all the principal women attending the potlatch to her house, and Mrs. David, mounting a high platform in front of it, threw them down strips of a goat's wool blanket to confirm acceptance of the titles.

As the modern incident suggests, each House possessed two sets of titles, one for women only, the other for men. Every bearer of a title, man or woman, was a <u>see-am</u>, a noble, and the children of nobles normally became nobles also in due course; the parents, or, if they were dead, the grandparents or near kinsfolk, gave a potlatch for each child and invested it with a title before or about the time it attained puberty.[90] Occasionally, however, a few children were passed over, either because their parents and kinsfolk had fallen on evil days and could not afford the expense of a potlatch, or because some calamity had left the children without near kinsfolk who were able or willing to take an interest in their welfare.[91] Unless through their own effort later they succeeded in gathering together enough food and property for a potlatch, these children never

---

[90] Since the term <u>see-am</u> carried an implication of mature years, these children were designated <u>see-abl</u>, not <u>see-am</u>; they became <u>see-am</u> only in later years, generally after they had given potlatches on their own account.

[91] There must have been numerous instances of this kind after the terrible smallpox epidemic that ravaged the population in the lat 18th century.

acquired titles, never attained the dignity of nobles, despite their birth, but swelled the ranks of the common people who attached themselves to various Houses for protection.

Contact with Europeans in the 19th century brought about a great change in the status of nobles. Previously no native unsupported by a considerable body of kinsmen and relatives could gather enough food and presents to hold a potlatch and entertain many guests for two or three days. It was therefore hopeless for a commoner to aspire to noble rank unless his skill as a hunter or fisherman, and his prowess in war, combined with a talent for leadership, attracted a body of retainers who were willing to work for his advancement and to support his right to some title, whether that right was real or fictitious. Such cases must have been comparatively rare; it was far easier to descend in the social scale than to ascend. But when Europeans abolished slavery, furnished a labour market as open to the ex-slave and commoner as to the noble, and enabled one man to purchase with his year's wages as much food and goods as a whole village could have gathered previously in one year, then commoners and even ex-slaves began to rival the nobles in the number and magnificence of their potlatches, and to assume titles to which they had no legitimate claim. This inevitably led to much friction and jealousy, but the helpless nobles could no longer uphold their [32] old authority or stem the new economic and social currents that swirled around their doors. Before the end of the century, every Indian, as an old man sadly stated, could assume a title and become a noble, if he wished, even though ancient prejudice still lingered and the upstart might be ridiculed behind his back.

Just as the manor lords of the Middle Ages upheld their state with a body of freemen and villeins, so the Houses of the Saanich Indians required the services of many commoners and slaves. It is almost impossible at this late date to calculate the numerical proportions of the three classes, nobles, commoners, and slaves, but a rough guess would made the ratio 3:7:2. The slaves, who were at no time numerous, were either captives taken in raids or the descendants of such captives; but the origin of the commoners, who seem to have made up more than half of the population, is less clear. The Saanich themselves account for them by the following legend:

"Haylse, the great creator and transformer, created human beings in various places from some kind of earth, but he fashioned the stomachs of the women from bands of cherry bark so that they might expand during pregnancy. At Duncan he created a man named Hayletha; at Sooke another man named Yayakarmat, with a wife, a daughter, and a maid for the daughter. The girl and her maid walked from Sooke up to Duncan, where they spied on Hayletha as he talked with a female image he had made from rotten cedar; for Hayletha was lonely, and whenever he left his home to hunt or fish he would leave his distaff and the wool he spun on it in the hands of the image, as though it could spin for him. After he had gone, the girls slipped into the house, spun the wool, and hid in some bushes before he returned. Hayletha was delighted at the industry of his image, and the next time he left out more wool for it to spin; but this time the girls spun his wool and burned the image. He was sorely puzzled when he found only its ashes, but called out at last, 'I don't know who you are but come out and let me see you'. The girls came out from their hiding-place, and Hayletha married Tayakarmat's daughter. From their children sprang the groups of Indians around Duncan, while the Sooke Indians are descendants of Tayakarmat's other children. Later Haylse created at Malahat a man named Hwanam and his wife, and from this last couple came the Malahat and Saanich Indians. In the earliest times all alike ranked as nobles, but after they began to raid and enslave one another some of the nobles married their slaves, and the offspring of the mixed marriages became commoners."

Whether, as this myth suggests, they were the offspring of nobles and captives, or of nobles who had been unable to keep up their stations, or of refugees and settlers from other districts – and it is probably that their numbers were recruited from all three – the commoners relied for security in their daily life on the protection of the nobles, and therefore attached themselves more or less closely to the different Houses. In many cases they seem not to have been assigned rooms or space in the longhouses where the nobles dwelt, but to have erected [33] small dwellings of their own a few yards away. While they might regulate their lives very much as they pleased, they were expected to man the canoes of nobles, to assist in the netting of deer and salmon, in the felling of trees and construction of dwellings, and generally to support {their} Houses their {sic} both in peace and in war. In return their Houses protected them from enslavement by other villages, and aided them in times of need.

Below the commoners were the slaves (skwaias), who slept in the same houses as their noble masters and were distinguished only by their poorer dress and greater activity. Men slaves did most of the hunting and fishing, gathered the firewood, helped in the felling of trees and making of canoes, and paddled their masters' canoes on ordinary excursions, but not on ceremonial occasions or in war. Women slaves, who were valued as highly as men slaves, prepared and cooked the food, gathered clams, roots, and berries,[92] collected large quantities of cedar-bark and rushes, and made from them clothing, baskets, and mats.

Some slaves were the children of slave parents; others were captives taken in raids. The latter, when they lost their freedom, lost also their earlier names and were given new ones, occasionally derisive,[93] but more often terms taken from their places of capture or slaves names current in the Houses of their captors. They might be addressed by these names, or by expressions such as silaywa or kokwa-anuk; but a nobleman generally called his man slave "my younger brother", and a noblewoman called her female slave "my younger sister".

Slaves belonged to the individual nobles who had captured, purchased, or inherited them, but were subject to orders from other members of their owners' houses, particularly from its leading man. Though absolutely in the power of their masters, they were seldom ill-treated or even punished, their owners preferring to sell them to other villages if they were lazy or incorrigible. A certain noblemen on Mayne Island, who was killed later by a Saanich Indian, is said to have often bruised and lacerated his slaves by launching his canoe over their bodies; but this was exceptional and widely condemned. Generally speaking, they had the status of servants, and were often highly trusted and esteemed. They ate from the same dishes as their masters, shared many of the same pastimes, even obtained guardian spirits in infancy like those of other Indians, and their children played with their master's children, boys with boys, girls with girls.

Nobles rarely married slave women until the 19th century when the social system was breaking down. A woman commoner who married a slave became a slave herself; but a woman slave who married a commoner was regarded as free (and her children free), though it did not necessarily improve her lot. A slave might become free, too, through the death of his master, but his freedom was so precarious that he often preferred to attach himself to another member of the

---

[92]   Their mistresses helped them to gather berries, since this was an enjoyable pastime.

[93]   A famous Saanich warrior named one of his slave women "Worm" and afterwards married her.

same House rather than incur the danger of being enslaved by some other house. Slaves captured in raids soon received husbands and wives to make them more content with [34] their fate.[94] In most cases, perhaps, they were content, or at least resigned, for they often fought bravely beside their masters when their villages were attacked. There was indeed no place to which they could flee without being enslaved again or returned to their masters, unless by good fortune they reached their earlier homes:[95] consequently, they seldom even tried to run away, though they had many opportunities, being allowed to fish and hunt alone.

> "Two slave girls belonging to my grandfather once tried to escape. The household was camping on one of the San Juan Islands, the men engaging in halibut-fishing, the women in gathering camas. One of the girls said to my grandmother, 'My companion's back is aching terribly. She wants me to stay home and rub her.' My grandmother consented, but when everyone had gone, the girls launched a small canoe and fled. The next day my grandfather saw them on the beach of a neighboring island, crying, for they had taken no food with them. He sent my grandmother to bring them back. 'Why are you staying here?' she asked them. 'Why don't you come home?' The girls had been afraid to return home, though they were not punished in any way."

WARFARE [35]

In villages thus organized without definite chiefs, the nobles were able to settle quarrels among the commoners and slaves, but quarrels among themselves could be composed only by consultations and the pressure of public opinion. A disgruntled man could always take up his residence in some other village where he had close kinsmen. Quarrels between nobles of different villages, not only on the Saanich Peninsula but from Duncan on the north to Victoria in the south, were likewise patched up through the intervention of common kinsmen, and seldom resulted in open feuds. With Salish communities a little more remote, the Saanich did have feuds, but they were feuds between individual nobles, as a rule, in which the villages as a whole played the part of spectators only. One noble would challenge another to approach his village and settle their quarrel by single combat; or he would send word through a messenger that he would attack his enemy in his own home. The principles then fought out their duel on the beach,

---

[94]   This was the case also at Nootka, apparently, for Jewett received a wife soon after his capture. See (John R Jewett, The Adventures and Sufferings of John R Jewett, Edinburgh, 1924).

[95]   A few did escape. An old Saanich man of 90 remembered seeing in his boyhood another old man, also a native of Saanich, who had been carried off and enslaved by some Indians north of Comox. The slave had appeared so reconciled to his fate that he became his master's sole companion on several hunting trips. On one occasion when they were setting out to hunt, he asked his mistress to put an extra amount of food in the cedar-bark bag because they would be absent longer than usual. Then, the first night they were away, he killed his master and fled south, paddling by night instead of by day. After making good progress for two or three days, he became careless and while paddling before dark was captured and enslaved by the people of another village. There, too, however, he worked the same stratagem and succeeded in regaining his home on the Saanich Peninsula.

while their retainers stood by to guard against treachery. The victor might kill one or two of his enemy's nearest kinsmen, and carry away a few of his slaves, but the conflict seldom became general because it was a strictly personal quarrel between the two men, and all the Salish groups accepted the rule that no one should interfere in a duel. The only weapons permissible were the spear and the club; bows and arrows were reserved for hereditary enemies like the Kwakiutl. Many natives even frowned on the wearing of elk-hide armour; and all condemned the decapitation of a fallen duelist because he belonged to the same people as his conqueror.[96]

Some feuds arose from mere jealousy. More often they flared up through the high-handed action of one side or the other, and a refusal to pay compensation. A party from one village, perhaps, had encroached on the fishing grounds of another, or had robbed and carried away a slave or other member. The victimized House then took up the quarrel; if the offenders were Salish from Vancouver Island or from the mouth of the Fraser River its leader demanded redress or settled the affair with a duel; but if they came from other parts of the mainland, or from north of Campbell River, it organized a retaliatory raid. One or more nobles belonging to the House manned a canoe of volunteers, mostly commoners, set an ambush for some unsuspecting party of their adversaries that was fishing or gathering berries, and either killed them or carried them off into slavery. This naturally led to a counter-raid, and the feud continued until one side or the other made overtures for a settlement, usually by marrying a noble girl of one village to a noble man of the other. The chief victims of such raids, however, were the slaves [36] and commoners who did most of the fishing and berry-picking, and who, if not killed, merely exchanged one master and House for another.

When a noble was taken prisoner, his captors nearly always sent word through another village, and his kinsmen immediately took steps to ransom him. He thus avoided slavery and retained his noble rank‚ though not without some loss, for even the briefest captivity produced a blot on his record that nothing he did afterwards could entirely erase. Girls of noble rank who were taken prisoners, however, could escape any loss of prestige even without being ransomed, through their people arranging for their marriage to some noble man among their captors.

"Two East Saanich men who had been hunting seals near the mainland put in at an island to boil an octopus, but just when their meal was ready, four natives from Sechelt approached them in a canoe. One of the Saanich men would have let them pass, but his companion invited the strangers to share the octopus. They accepted, but carried their guns ashore with them, which so alarmed the first Saanich man that he quietly moved away along the beach. His suspicions were justified, for his companion, while dishing up the meat, was shot in the back and killed. The survivor fled into the woods and eluded pursuit by climbing a high tree; but the Seechelt natives carried away his seals and canoe, leaving him marooned."

---

[96] "Their spears, which are of horn, have often wooden handles of great length" (Simon Fraser, in Masson LF <u>Les Bourgeois de la Compagnie du Nord-Oeste</u>, I: p195, Quebec, 1889). The Saanich spear had a single barbed point, for unlike the Klallam Indians south of them, they never used the two-pointed seal-spear for fighting. The club was made from bone or elk-horn, sharpened on the edges; the armour from two layers of elk-hide quilted to hold flat stones between them. I know of no evidence for helmets. A Sardis native said that his people sometimes sewed a round stone in leather, fastened it to the wrist by a thong, and used it as a club in close combat.

Three days later, he sighted another canoe manned by men and women whom he recognized from their speech as Victoria natives. At his hail, they took him on board and conveyed him to Saanich, where the murdered man's widow organized a war-party to seek revenge.

Three canoes set out. In one was a Saanich medicine-woman, in another a medicine-man from Malahat; it was their duty to capture the souls of some Seechelt natives and make their bodies follow, thus delivering them into the hands of the Saanich. Actually, near Seechelt they did sight a canoe occupied by a man and his son, and, hastily putting ashore, left the medicine-man and medicine-woman on the beach as decoys, while they hid in the woods with their guns. When the Seechelt natives paddled close to shore the Saanich shot them dead.

The Seechelt then organized a counter-raid that resulted in the death of a Saanich man; and the feud continued for several years. Finally a Saanich Indian married a Seechelt girl who happened to be visiting some relatives at Nanaimo, and the two groups composed their quarrel at the wedding celebration."

"Many years ago when the Nanaimo natives were raiding a certain place, they captured a Saanich girl who was a distant relative of my husband's family. His uncle decided to ransom her; as the affair, however, seemed comparatively trivial, he did not go to Nanaimo himself, but sent two young kinsmen with a slave crew, an elderly slave woman, one or two guns, some goat's wool blankets, and some baskets of camas roots. The girl's captor, who knew the young man, entertained them hospitably, and when they announced their mission said, "I cannot refuse you, but you must compensate [37] me with another slave." They offered him the elderly woman, and though he protested that she was rather old, he consented to take her if they would add a certain amount of goods. Then they brought up their guns, blankets, and camas roots. This satisfied him, and he let them take the girl to Saanich, where she married soon afterwards the son of a notable warrior. Her kinsmen repaid the ransom price, with interest, at the wedding."

In the national Museum of Canada is a carved wooden coffin depicting a man's guardian spirit flanked by two wolves. It is the coffin of a famous Saanich warrior Kwalarhunzit { ~ Kwalahunzit = No /r/}, who was born a commoner in the 18th century and died a noble in the early years of the 19th. Like other nobles he had several wives, two of them nobles, the other slaves; and even today there is secret friction on the Saanich reserves because the descendants of his slave wives claim the right to noble rank. Kwalarhunzit's life story gives a fairly clear picture of the raiding and dueling that was taking place at the time Europeans first penetrated into this region.

"When Kwalarhunzit was only 13 years old, some Kwakiutl Indians carried away his father, leaving the boy and his mother dependent on the other members of the Tsawout community of East Saanich. One day his mother caught him stealing food. She thrashed him with her wool-beater, told him that such conduct would never make him a warrior, and drove him out of the village. The boy wandered into the hills on the western side of the Peninsula and, when it grew dark, crawled into the hollow base of a giant cedar tree, drawing in some moss to keep himself warm. That night snow fell, and for ten days kept him imprisoned. Finally snow turned to slush, and, faint from hunger, he set out for his home, barefoot. Just as evening fell, a man discovered him crawling on hands and knees on the outskirts of the village and carried him into his mother's home.

After recovering from the ordeal Kwalarhunzit made himself bow and arrows, club and spear, so that he might train to be a warrior; for a terrible epidemic of smallpox had just decimated the Saanich Indians and crippled their resistance to the raids of their enemies.[97] His first fight was against some southern Indians who were visiting relatives at the big settlement near Sidney. He and a friend attacked and killed them at sea, then upset their canoe so that their relatives would think they had drowned."

A few years later, he visited with his people some notorious raiders on Mayne Island. The Mayne Islanders invited their visitors to participate in a deer-hunt, but Kwalarhunzit noticed that they were bathing in the sea, blackening their faces, and rubbing their bodies and hair with deer-fat, which indicated that they were really preparing for a battle. He warned his companions, and while the hunters were setting up the deer-net [38], he and his people fell on them, killed most of the men, and carried away all the women and girls whom they had enslaved.

This exploit carried his reputation far and wide. It reached the Comox Indians, who challenged him several times to single combat. Every time he accepted one of their challenges, he returned victorious.

A Mayne Island Indian once sent him this challenge: "I am ready to fight you. If you are not afraid of me, come." Kwalarhunzit mustered his followers and paddled north. As they drew near the island they saw his challenger strutting up and down the beach, brandishing his spear, and the villagers lined up behind him. Kwalarhunzit shouted "I'll fight you single-handed." And the man accepted, expecting to stab him as he disembarked from the canoe. Kwalarhunzit, however, leaped into the water and reached the beach before his enemy could strike him. Both parties drummed and sang to encourage their companions, who began to fence with their spears. Gradually Kwalarhunzit gained the upper hand, and step by step, forced his enemy back. The man's father then rushed into his House to seize a spear, and Kwalarhunzit's own warriors dashed ashore to protect their leader from a treacherous attack in the rear. Before anyone could interfere, however, Kwalarhunzit killed his adversary, after which he and his warriors slew the father and several other men in the village.

The Cowichan natives once sought his help to settle a score with the Indians of Port Angeles after the latter had massacred some Cowichan visitors during a squabble over a gambling game, *lehal*. Four Cowichan canoes from four different villages, each manned by about ten men, put in at Deep Cove, where many Saanich Indians had collected to gather clams; and they invited Kwalarhunzit, together with another Saanich warrior who had married a Cowichan woman, to join their party as volunteers. Kwalarhunzit consulted his uncle, who advised him to accept if he wished to uphold his reputation, and promised to go with him. So, after bathing in the sea, and oiling his head and body, Kwalarhunzit tried on his elk-skin armour, and

---

[97] An epidemic of smallpox swept this coast about 1780 {1782}.

his friends drummed and sang to kindle his fighting spirit.   Afterwards, they drummed for the other Saanich warrior, who strutted up and down the beach in his armour, catching at the arrows his people shot at him. The Saanich contingent then embarked in a canoe and paddled with the Cowichan natives to Sooke, where they all rested a night before crossing over to Port Angeles.

When the Port Angeles natives observed the canoes approaching, they mounted with drums to the roofs of their houses while their champion, a man named Skaiyus, marched down to the beach in full war panoply to repel the invaders. Kwalarhunzit kept his canoe in the background so that the Cowichans could begin the combat. While both sides drummed and sang, the leader of each Cowichan canoe sprang ashore in turn and engaged Skaiyus, who repelled them, one after another, and drove them back into their canoes. Then Kwalarhunzit drew near, standing on the front cross-bar and leading his crew in a war-song. He leaped into the water, which [39] swirled up around his waist, parried Skaiyus's spear-thrust and gained the beach. There he countered thrust with thrust until his opponent gave ground and turned to flee, when he speared him and cut off his head with a knife.[98] Immediately villagers jumped down from the roofs and sought refuge in the woods, but the Cowichan natives killed several before they could escape. The Vancouver Islanders did not carry away any women and children, however, because they were their own kindred.

After becoming very old and totally blind, Kwalarhunzit met his end at the hands of the Comox Indians. One of his sons, with a slave man and some women, were taking him to the fishing ground at Point Roberts when they sighted a Comox canoe bearing down on them. They paddled hurriedly to shore and the women, leaving the old man in the canoe as a decoy, fled into the woods while the son and slave hid behind a tree. At this period, the Indians had obtained muzzle-loading guns. The Comox fired several shots at Kwalarhunzit, but his son fired back at them and apparently hit one man, for as they paddled away they tilted their canoe on its side for protection. After they had gone, Kwalarhunzit's party joined other Saanich Indians, who, however, refused to stay ashore after it became dark, but kept watch in their canoe. About midnight, they heard footsteps and saw dark figures moving along the beach toward the Saanich camp, whereupon they shouted and fired two or three warning shots. The Saanich fled into the woods – all but Kwalarhunzit, who was decapitated by a Comox Indian while still struggling to put on his coat. His son shot three of the Comox before receiving a bullet in his side, and split the skull of a fourth enemy when the latter stooped over him, chanting, to cut off his head.[99] However, he too died the next day.

---

[98] The victor carried home the head as a trophy and planted it on a stick or hung it from a cross-pole, generally near the graveyard some distance from his village to avoid being disturbed by the ghost. The prestige of a warrior depended on the number of heads he could boast, reckoning women's and children's as well as men's; but as a rule, the Coast Salish slew men only, and carried away the women and children as slaves.

[99] The Saanich say that only the Comox and Kwakiult, not their own people, chant a prayer before decapitating their enemies.

CHILDHOOD [40]

During the first few weeks of life, before its bones had time to harden, a baby lay continuously in a wooden cradle lined with shredded cedar-bark, and a cedar-bark pad pressed heavily on its brow to flatten the head: For the Saanich, like their neighbors, considered a head of natural form unshapely. Parents attached neither toys nor charms to the cradle and they discouraged precocity in talking and walking, believing that a too precocious child would not survive. Yet they rejoiced if it smiled and laughed aloud while alone, because then it was presumably playing with some spirit (saila). As the weeks passed by and its forehead hardened into shape, the mother often took it out of the cradle and let it play on the bed-mats. She called it simply "baby" {q̲eq̲, ♂ wəy'qə' ♀ łeni'} at this period, or a pet name that carried no significance. Only after it began to talk and walk did it receive a real name taken from some dead member of its family. This name might last throughout life, but the child of noble parents discarded it later for a family title if his (or her) parents could afford the necessary potlatch; and so also did the man who won riches and renown through his own efforts.

Invariably if a baby died, and often when it did not, the Saanich discarded its cradle as soon as it was no longer needed, conceiving that it had become too unhealthy to use for another child. They deposited it therefore on a ledge high up on some cliff (Malahat Mountain was a favorite place), where the Sun-spirit would gaze on it each morning and impart some of its strength to the child.[100] Similarly any hair that they clipped away, whether from a child or an adult, they inserted in a cleft or notch of a tree, and covered with mark or moss so that the tree would absorb it into its own life; and they took care to choose only a healthy tree, since if it fell soon afterwards, the owner of the hair would die. Nails wore down from use; to them they paid no attention; but when a milk tooth fell out the child threw it into the sea and called to the spirit of the porpoise, the beaver, the seal, or some other animal that has strong teeth to replace the lost tooth with a strong firm one.

Very little children ran naked, but as they grew older, they received clothes similar to those of their parents. Girls, like their mothers, bound their hair in two braids which they anointed with fat (usually mixed with certain herbs) and wrapped with cedar-bark, but boys and men let their hair hang loose or tied it in a knob at the back of the head. Some female relative unostentatiously pierced a child's ears and nose before it reached its teens, and inserted feathers in the holes until they healed; later, the feathers were replaced with shell pendants according to the means of the parents. No charms were worn, these being permitted to hunters only. Little children were discouraged from talking too much to their elders lest they become chatterboxes all their days, and disobedience was punished with a stick.

As soon as they were old enough boys and girls had to take an early morning plunge in the sea, winter and summer, and harden their bodies by rubbing them with yew branches after the bath. Each village appointed [41] an elderly man to stir the boys out of bed and drive them down to the water, if necessary with a switch; he seldom troubled about the girls, who bathed at their own section of the beach under the supervision of an elderly female. A boy occasionally fooled his mentor by bathing unusually early and returning to his bed. On very cold mornings, too, a kindly grandmother might drench him, inside or outside the house, with a basin of luke-warm water, so that he would already be drying himself beside the fire when his mentor entered to

---

[100] New dancers (see p. ??, added to edit later from fieldnotes) deposited their trappings in similar places, for the same reason.

rouse him for his bath. Parents tried in many ways to make their children strong and hardy; thus during a heavy thunderstorm, one mother made her little boy run naked through the woods in the hope that, just as he safely sped through the storm, so in later life he would emerge safely from every sickness.

The Saanich strictly regulated the diet of their children. They forbade them fatty foods such as seal-meat, the belly of salmon, and the marrow from the bones of deer and elk; or else they permitted these foods but seldom. Even the flesh of the spring and of the sockeye salmon was considered too strong until a child reached its teens; the sockeye might cause nightmares, the Indians thought, whence some parents smeared their children with consumption plant seeds the first time allowed them to eat this fish. Crab-apples, wild goose-berries, and hot water supposedly spoiled the teeth (if not also the digestion); and cold water should be drunk sitting down, not standing up. The child who ate the leg muscle of an animal would develop cramps in his own legs; if he ate the heart of any creature, but especially of a duck, he would become a coward. Even the liver had its place in the list of forbidden foods: only old people, in fact, ate either heart or liver. Because ducks swell up when they are roasted before a fire, a child should avoid eating them lest his own stomach swell up in middle life; likewise, he should avoid eating the red cod that, when hooked, rises quickly to the surface and twists itself round the line, because his own stomach might become twisted and cause vomiting. On the other hand, he should eat as much dog-fish gullet as possible, because its unusual length would make him long-winded.

Once they reached their teens, girls of good families gave considerable attention to their appearance. They removed all down from their cheeks by coating their faces with a reddish paint obtained from the hemlock, all hair from their armpits by scrubbing with yew branches, and they evened their eyebrows by pulling out the longer hairs. From now on they never went out of doors unless accompanied by some female relative,[101] and, instead of playing, they spent their days in beating and spinning wool, making small canoe mats on which their fathers and uncles might sit and kneel, stringing seed necklaces, cleaning fish, and training for all the other duties that would fall to their lot in later years. During the winters, therefore, they seldom left their homes; but on the Saanich Peninsula winter lasts less than three months; and the pleasantly warm days of spring and summer brought them many outdoor excursions for [42] berries, roots, and bark. Boys, of course, spent most of their days out of doors, not in pastimes only, but learning to paddle the canoes, to fish, to hunt, to adze and steam planks, weave nets, and perform a hundred other useful tasks. Parents feasted their kinsmen on the first deer their sons shot, and on the first seal they harpooned; the lads themselves ate other food at these feasts.

At the approach of adolescence both boys and girls tried to attune themselves for contact with the world of spirits. Instead of eating twice a day as usual, they often ate in the mornings

---

[101] There is a story that long ago a young girl would not work in the house at her baskets, but insisted on taking them out of doors. As the days passed by, she wandered with them farther and farther into the woods until at length she was roaming about like a wolf. Then the wolves came and took her away, as her parents discovered when they found her baskets and tracks of wolves all around. For a long time, they attempted to rescue her, but without success. On one occasion, hey sighted her gathering clams on a beach, unclad, and covered with a thick coat of hair; but when they tried to encircle her, she fled with the speed of a wolf. Subsequently she gave birth to many wolf pups that were able to understand human speech.

only and went to bed fasting. Parents encouraged their boys to wander alone. One family on stormy days used to anoint the young son with deer-fat and send him out in a canoe by himself to woo the favor of some medicine-spirit.

It was when their children neared adolescence that parents of noble rank conferred on them ancestral titles or names. A man {David Latasse}, who died in 1936, at the age of over 90 had received a grand-uncle's name {*q'alekwalt'an*} when he was 12 years old, and another name {*sxwa'wał* ~ whirlwind}, his great-grandfather's, two years later when he was 14. He was known by this second name until he was about 50 years of age, when he assumed a third name {st'e'ełum}, borne previously by his mother's father. The third name served him at potlatches and other ceremonies until his death; like other Indians, he used an English one in ordinary life.

Another old man received his name when he was 14 years old and never changed it, although he occasionally contemplated bestowing it on some grandson or grand-nephew and taking a new one for himself. It had belonged to his maternal grandfather, who was more distinguished than any member of his father's line; and his father had bestowed it on him in a special potlatch at which he was made to stand on a high platform inside the house and throw down blankets to the assembled crowd. Poor people, of course, could not afford to hold such potlatches and give away many presents, consequently their children retained the names that were given to them during infancy.

ADOLESCENCE

Parents watched their children closely for the first signs of adolescence, and warned them at that period to keep away from fires, lest their lower eyelids droop and redden in after years. When a boy's voice appeared to be changing, they kept him quiet inside the house for four days and gave him very little to eat or drink. Each day his mother or some female relative chanted a prayer over him and rubbed his chest (sometimes also his mouth) with a hard stone. On the fifth day she sent him to bathe, and either going or returning made him jump four times over bushes or perform some corresponding ritual. The details varied from family to family, but no well-born lad passed through his adolescence without undergoing some rite. Poor people, however, paid little heed to their sons during this transition period but focused their attention on the daughters.

Some old men narrated these details of their own adolescence:

"When my voice began to change I was {kept} four days inside the house and my head and neck encircled with bands of cedar-bark. Each morning about 4am my aunt aroused me, and shaking the family rattle (a [43] copper globe with a wooden handle trimmed with goat's wool pendants), chanted over me four times a wordless prayer to Haylse. I ate and slept very little during those four days, from time to time, I expectorated on a boulder so that I might become as hard as the stone. My aunt gave me, too, a small black pebble and told me to rub it on my mouth and breasts so that my teeth would grow straight and even and my chest hard. On the fifth morning, she sent me into the woods to bathe, and on my way back to the house made me jump over a number of small bushes in my path, to strengthen my soul (smastimaux).

"I stayed in the house four days. My parents allowed me to walk around, but not to play with other children or go outside. On the fifth morning my aunt, who was a seer

(<u>siowa</u>), painted my face and the top of my head with red ochre, crowned my head with cedar-bark and feathers, and led me to a creek not far from the house. As we passed through the woods, the feathers and cedar-bark were knocked off by the bushes or blew away. Near the creek I pulled down a branch of a fir tree, and, sitting stride it, facing the rising sun, rubbed the ochre from my face with its needles, while my aunt chanted a prayer; the bough, when I slipped off it, carried the prayer high into the air. Four boughs I bestrode this way before bathing in the creek. Then my aunt said to me, "You have finished, my child. You will have a long life. But take this black stone and rub your breasts with it every time you bathe. It will prevent any swelling of your nipples." She did not make me jump over any bushes, because there was no idea of my becoming a medicine-man.[102] [44]

"During the four days I remained in the house I expectorated frequently on a big black stone. On the fifth morning, an aunt painted my face with red ochre and sent me into the woods for the day; then in the evening when I returned, she told me to wash off the paint in the sea. Three times I walked into the water up to my knees and walked out again; the fourth time I sat down in the water and washed.

"During the four days I was kept in the house my aunt, who was a medicine-woman, chanted over me, morning and evening, praying that Haylse would make me strong. Since she wished me to become a medicine-men , she placed blackberry bushes under my sleeping-mats (not ferns, as some people do), made me lie on my back most of the time, and forbade me to talk. On the fifth morning, she led me outdoors, told me to strip, and pointing to a blackberry bush, said "Jump over that bush and back four times." I jumped over the bush and back four times, while she drummed and chanted a prayer; had I fallen, she would have known that I would not live long. She then sent me to bathe in the sea, where a male relative scrubbed me with blackberry bushes after my bath."

---

[102]   The Songhese around Victoria generally paid little attention to adolescent boys, but an elderly man on their reserve underwent a similar ritual during a visit to the Indians of San Juan Islands when he was about 7 years old. One morning while he was there, an old medicine-woman painted his face and chanted a prayer over him, shaking her rattle, and she repeated the chant in the evening. Following her instructions, the boy left the village early the next morning, accompanied by his father, and ascended a mountain. Near its summit, he climbed up the sunny side of a tree as high as he dared, and rubbed the paint from his face with its branches, saying as he let them fly upward again, "Thank you, <u>siem</u>". He left on this tree the cedar-bark towels with which the woman had painted his face, and climbing a small tree in the grove, swung from tree to tree, Tarzan like, until he was exhausted and had to rest on the ground. Next he and his father sat astride some small saplings and let them swish skyward up their backs; then, with his arms shielding his face, he ran as fast as he could through the thick brush until he fell. After thus carrying out all the old woman's instructions, they bathed and returned to the village which they reached at dusk. Next morning she seated the boy, his father, his mother, and his sister, on a bench, and, shaking her rattle and chanting, announced to his parents, "The soul of your son has climbed very high. He will therefore live to a ripe old age."

A girl's four-day confinement differed in no essential respect from a boy's, except that her seclusion was more rigid and the prohibition against her eating and drinking enforced more strictly. If her mouth became too dry, she might moisten it with water drawn up through a tube, but not swallow any of the liquid. She passed the long hours spinning wool or making baskets, forbidden in some cases even to lie down at night, though she might rest against a post. Her mother, and aunt, or, if the family could afford it, one or perhaps two medicine-women painted her face each day and prayed to Haylse to grant her health and long life; or occasionally they painted it on the fifth day only, and made her rub off the paint with cedar boughs as she went through the woods to the bathing-place. After her bath, too, they scrubbed her body with yew-boughs (or with blackberry bushes if she was to become a medicine-women), and rubbed it with a smooth black stone to preserve its shapeliness. Then the girl deposited at some sacred rock (i.e. a rock that legend said had once been a human being), or in some other place designated by her attendants, the fern-leaves on which she had sat in the water, and the yew-boughs or blackberry bushes with which she had been scrubbed.

Every girl, even one of slave parentage, underwent the ceremonies outlined above, though the details varied slightly in almost every case. As in more civilized lands, too, families of high rank announced their daughters' coming of age with special entertainments, partly to enhance the family prestige and partly to improve the girls's chances in the marriage market. Some even postponed the most striking entertainment for weeks and even months after the first seclusion, so that it might coincide with some potlatch or other public function that would bring together a large crowd. Below is a description of such an entertainment, held toward the end of the 19th century in Cowichan Bay, though it might have occurred equally well on the Saanich Peninsula. [45]

"The debutante's family partitioned off two corners of the house with goat's wool blankets. One room concealed the girl, the other served as a dressing-room for the four medicine-men who had been hired to stage a performance. At the entrance to their room, two watchmen with painted faces stood guard to announce when they would emerge. Along the side of the house opposite the rooms were benches crowded with spectators, women with sticks in the front row and a mixed audience behind.

The leading medicine-man began to chant from his room, and the audience became silent. He stopped suddenly, and recommenced; then, as the women in the foremost row beat their sticks on planks in front of them, the four medicine-men filed out, each carrying a forked stick, shuffled round the open arena in the middle of the house, and retired to their room. An old man whom they had stationed in the audience immediately announced what the show would be, and drew attention to four long, narrow stones that had been place in the middle of the floor. Hardly had he finished speaking when the watchmen again called on the women to beat their sticks, the medicine-men re-emerged, and, shuffling forward, one behind the other, picked up each stone (after the usually three feints) in the fork of the stick. Amid deep silence the leader then leaped about and sang while his three companions walked around him. As soon as he stopped all four began to leap and sing, and the women pounded their sticks again and joined in the chant: "The stone is my toy. I am going to play with it". This act ended after a few minutes, and the four men retired with the stones to their room.

Presently the watchmen signaled the women for the second act. The medicine-men shuffled out, their leader hiding a black stone against his breast. He hurled it to the floor, recovered it, and retreated with his companions to his room.

At a command from the old man in the audience, two swift runners dashed out to the middle of the floor, leaped about to the beating of the women's sticks, and sped through the doorway to seek a certain shrub in the woods. The audience relaxed as soon as they disappeared, but became silent and attentive again when the beating of the sticks heralded their return. Each leaped through the doorway with a shrub in his hand and a wreath of fir boughs round his head. While they stood in the middle of the house adjusting their wreaths, two women led forth the girl from her room and seated her on a pile of goat's wool blankets. The runners then 'swept' her with their shrubs and retreated into the room of the medicine-men.

Again, the watchmen called the audience to attention, the sticks resumed their pounding, and the medicine-men reappeared, their leader carrying his stone and each of the other three a basket of water, which he laid on the floor after shuffling round the arena. Their leader then planted his stone beside the baskets, and, as the sticks became silent, 'drilled' a feather into it. The stone screeched with his drilling, and the feather stood firmly upright. When he threw the stone into one of the baskets, it floated on the water, while the feather rocked slowly like a sail. He threw it into the second [46] basket, and the third; each time it floated as if it were a boat. Then he gathered it up, his companions recovered their baskets, and the four men retired to their room.

For the fourth time, the watchmen gave the signal. Two women went forward and sat down, one on each side of the girl. The medicine-men approached, wearing blankets round their shoulders, and their leader laid a mink-skin on the round in front of her. As he held it by the tail, the skin (worked presumably by hidden strings) crawled toward her as if alive; but when the two women beat it with fir branches the man hid it under his blanket again and returned to his room.

Once more they came out, each carrying in his hand a hard, dried fish. The leader held out his fish to the girl, who bit off a small piece and dropped it into the hand of one of the women. The second medicine-men offered his fish, then third, and fourth. Each time she bit off a fragment, the mink under the blanket of the leader emitted a loud squeal. Thus the drama ended, and the medicine-men retired from the scene.

The old speaker in the audience now arose and, after thanking the people for their attendance, called out the name of a certain noble who was to receive one of the blankets on which the girl had been sitting, the blanket in this case being a token of a canoe which would be handed over later. He named also other old men who were to receive blankets. The girl gave them their presents, then mounted a high platform that had been erected at one end of the house. From there she threw a huge pile of blankets to the floor, and the men and boys in the audience scrambled for their possession."[103]

From the time of her 'coming out' no girl or woman might enter a man's fishing or hunting canoe, or a canoe that was used in warfare. Neither might she walk on any fish-weir, or

---

[103] <u>See</u> Appendix {D}.

touch any tools or weapons used in fishing, hunting, and war. Periodically each month, and throughout pregnancy, she refrained from eating halibut and black cod, foods which were forbidden all sick people; and she avoided also the meat of seal, bear, certain waterfowl, flounders, and all varieties of salmon except the humpbacked.

Parents occasionally married off their daughters within a few days of their 'coming out'. More often they waited a year or longer until the girl became more mature and their own finances less straightened; for both the 'coming out' ceremony and the marriage often involved considerable expense. During the interval maidens remained in semi-seclusion, weaving wool, making rush mats, and busying themselves with other house-wifely duties, but never leaving the house unless accompanied by some female relative.

Youths likewise intensified their training in all of many pursuits. Not only did they hunt and fish with their elders, but they learned to fence with spears and clubs, so that they might defend their villages from attack and take part in raids and forays. They were expected to gain 'warrior' spirit-guardians whose war-songs they might chant when [47] dancing at the winter festivals, and also when going into battle; and, to seek other spirits which would preserve them from sickness and rescue them from sudden dangers. Since these spirits revealed themselves only in solitude, parents encouraged their sons to wander much alone, and even sent them out to isolated places in the woods or on the mountains, where by fasting and purifying themselves for two or three days, they would qualify for a supernatural visitation.

"When I was about 12 years old, my grandfather said to me: "You see Mt Newton yonder. If you act aright you will find something near its summit. Follow a small creek up its slopes until you reach a pond near which are some circles of stones.[104] The Thunderbird dwells in a deep cave within the high bluff behind the pond. Bathe in the pond, rub your right side with a bundle of yew bough and place them under one of the stones. Rub your left side with another bundle, and place it under the next stone. Rub your right shoulder, your left shoulder, your right arm, your left arm, your right leg, your left leg, and your back, until bundles of yew underlie all the stones in a half-circle. When you have done this, lie down and sleep; but next morning, bathe again and complete the circle."

I carried out his instructions, noticing as I placed my bundles under the stones, {there were} fragments of other yew branches which my own grandfather probably had deposited there some fifty years before. As I looked round after my second bath, I heard a loud whirring above my head, and many leaves floated down to the ground at my feet. Looking up, I saw a giant bird – the Thunderbird itself – soaring out of sight in the sky. Alarmed, I hurried home, but that night, as I slept in my bed, the Thunderbird entered me and taught me two songs. The first I sing before I begin my dance at the winter festivals, the second while I am dancing. Neither has any significant words.

A few months later, again, at my grandfather's bidding, I climbed up the slope of Malahat Mountain, bathed in a pond and slept. About midnight I awoke, and feeling very thirsty, groped my way in the darkness to drink from the pond. Just as I was dipping up the water in my cupped hands, a loud cry echoed near me and made my

---

[104]   On a rocky flat in the interior of Saltspring Island are several stone circles that may have been set up by Indians fasting. Present-day natives seem to know nothing of their origin.

hair stand on end; and as I drank, the cry echoed a second time. I returned to my fire and lay down again; and while I slept two songs, both wordless, came to me, though I do not know to this day what spirit entered me. These songs too I have sung at the winter festivals."

MARRIAGE

A youth might marry any girl of his own or other village provided she was not his sister, his first cousin, or his second cousin;[105] but to avoid marrying beneath his social level his parents generally arranged his match themselves and the youth merely fell in with their wishes. They combed the list of the eligible girls in the neighborhood, and, selecting the one that seemed most suitable, sounded out her parents, [48] to discover whether their son was acceptable; when assured in that regard, they sent him to announce his suit publicly by fasting just inside the door of her house until such time as her people invited him in to eat. If the latter highly approved of the match, they usually invited him in after a few hours; but if the suitor was unexpected or unwelcome (for occasionally a youth acted on his own initiative, or his parents sent him out without making preliminary inquiries), they ignored him for two or three days, then quietly advised him, through some kinsman, to go home; or else they kept him in suspense for a still longer period before they finally accepted him.[106] In one or two rare instances, an unwelcome but obstinate youth succeeded in winning his suit by fasting so long at the doorway that the girls' parents became alarmed lest he should die and make them liable to heavy compensation. Once he had been formally accepted, that is to say, invited inside the house and fed, the youth hurried home to notify his parents, and returned with his kinsmen a few days later to claim his bride.

On the Saanich Peninsula, as in other, perhaps all, Coast Salish districts, custom demanded that the bridegroom should travel for his bride by canoe, even though she lived in the same village. The youth and his kinsmen, therefore, loaded two or three canoes with blankets and other goods and paddled to the bride's home. As they approached the shore, the head of the house, if a nobleman, stood up in the foremost canoe and chanted the family marriage song.[107] Disembarking, they marched up to the girl's house, where the bride and bridegroom sat side by side on a pile of blankets while elderly kinsmen of both families gave them wise counsel. All then sat down to the wedding feast, after which the bridegroom's people brought up their blankets and other goods for the bride's father to distribute among his kin.

The bridegroom and his people seldom departed immediately after the feast, but remained a day or two in the village enjoying the hospitality of relatives and friends. When the time came for them to return home, the bride's father sometimes led his daughter down to the canoe, wearing a wooden face-mask (if he owned one) and shaking a rattle, an honor to his son-in-law that called for liberal payment. The young couple took their places in the middle of the canoe on a pile of blankets provided by the bride's father , and behind them sat the slave girl whom he often sent along to be her maid. Then the bridal party paddled away, chanting a song.

A year or so later, the bride's kinsmen, travelling in two or three canoes, paid a visit to her home, bringing presents for the young couple, or, more correctly, repaying the bride-price

---

[105] For a list of the terms of relationship, see Appendix {G}.

[106] One man said that his father has fasted ten day inside the door of the girl's home.

[107] In one family it ran "This world is going to be mine".

132

they had received at her wedding. Families always tried to balance these payments so that there would be no financial loss on either side, and consequently no loss of prestige. Hence they kept strict account of their obligations, even though years might pass before they succeeded in liquidating them all.

"When I was about 18 years of age my kinsmen sent an aunt to Victoria to arrange a match for me with a Songhese girl. She approached the girl's parents, who consulted [49] their relatives first and then gave their consent. As soon as my aunt returned with this news, four of my uncles launched their canoes and took me to Victoria, where three of them stayed in different houses while the fourth kept me company just inside[108] the girl's doorway for two days and nights. During that period, we neither ate nor drank, but quietly sat there, wrapped in our blankets until darkness fell, when we lay on the ground and slept. In the late afternoon of the second day, the girl's father told my uncles that I had fasted long enough, whereupon two of them led me right inside and brought me some food. My bride and I were then seated side by side on two piles of blankets her people had provided, and four old men preached to us, telling us now that we were married we should be faithful to one another and live in harmony all our days. After these sermons, my kinsmen brought in the bride-price – 40 sacks of flour, a large number of blankets and other things. We stayed there that night, but early the next morning the blankets on which we were seated during the wedding were carried down to my canoe, and my father-in-law led my wife down, shaking his rattle and chanting a song. My own people, who had already embarked, chanted their two marriage songs: "I come down from the mountain" and "The nobleman begins to sing as my wife stepped into the canoe. We paddled away to their singing".

"When I was old enough to marry, my parents, who lived then at Komiakin on the Cowichan River, sent four relatives with a present of food to the house of a girl in Clemclemalets, three miles away and asked them to propose a marriage. The girl's parents silently laid the food at the back of the house and consulted their relatives, after which they fed the four envoys and let them depart without a message. We knew, however, that they had agreed to the match, because they did not offer to pay for the food. A few days later, therefore, I myself poled up to her house taking three goat's-wool blankets, one to sit on, and two to wrap around my shoulders. For four days and four nights I sat or lay just within the entrance. Then four old men led me right inside, and transferred my blankets to the shoulders of two old kinsmen of my bride. At the same time, they sent word to my parents that my probation had ended, and invited them to attend the wedding.

---

[108] An old Songhese Indian said that among his people the youth generally sat just outside the door, which was shut against him to test the sincerity of his suit; and that whenever anyone came out he would beg "Open the door for me". If he became cold or very tired, he might take shelter in another house provided some one temporarily took his place, because if it remained vacant his suit was canceled. After two, three, or four days, he was invited to sit just inside the door, and the girl's people began to prepare for the wedding. He watched them for a time, then returned home to make his own preparations.

"My parents sent two men ahead to lead me into the portion of the house occupied by the girl's immediate family and followed in their canoe with a number of relatives. I was conducted to a bench at the side of the room, while my bride sat on a pile of blankets in the middle of the floor. Ten of her relatives came in: Eight of them carried her blankets, the other two led her by the hands and seated her beside me. My own people arranged themselves behind us, and my parents, stepping forward, paid these ten relatives and handed over the bride-price. They paid 100 goat's-wool blankets and 100 Hudson's Bay blankets, besides other [50] things, all of which were distributed among my bride's relatives. The latter then carried down to my canoe the blankets and other things which she was to take with her, and my people poled us down to Komiakin.

"Next day my parents-in-law came down in two canoes to our house, bringing a quantity of food, and I invited all my neighbors to come in and share it the day following. Several of my relatives during this feast made speeches, thanking my parents-in-law for the food and expressing approval of the match.

"Our marriage occurred shortly before the end of the winter, and my wife became a dancer just at the beginning of that season. It was therefore dangerous for her to marry before it closed, but by {my} chewing consumption plant seeds and rubbing them on her body after each morning bath, she escaped unharmed."

In both these instances, the bridegrooms were of noble rank. Below is a commoner's account of his marriage:

"When I was a young man and found a girl to my liking, I did not ask any of my relatives to arrange the match for me, but just went over to her house and sat in the middle of the floor. Her parents were annoyed and told me to go home, but I refused, and sat there fasting for four days and four nights, afraid to leave lest they should lock the door against me. On the evening of the fourth day, they gave in; they led me to the fire, cooked some food, brought the girl to eat with me, and sent me home. The next day, my people gathered all the goat's-wool blankets they possessed, piled them into a canoe, and escorted me to the house to bring away my bride. Neither going nor returning did they chant any songs, nor did her father escort her to my canoe; for we were commoners, and did not possess any rattles, face-masks, or marriage-songs. Instead, my people simply carried the blankets into her house and brought her away, with her sack of potatoes and bag of dried fish as soon as her father told her to leave. However, a few days later her people brought a lot of food and blankets to my home and feasted all my relatives.

After my first wife died, I sought the hand of my present one. Neither she nor her parents wanted me, so when I began to fast in her house, they smuggled her away to Victoria and told me she might never return. She did return, however, some time later, and I sued for her hand again. Her parents locked the door against me, but I waited outside all one night and when they opened the door in the morning, slipped in and sat down against a post in the middle of the floor. The girl took refuge in her uncle's corner of the big house, but after two days her parents yielded and fed me until she consented to marry me."

As is evident from the above accounts, marriage was patrilocal, the young husband took his wife to his father's home and was there allotted a room for himself. Though there was no real courtship prior to marriage and the young couple might never have seen each other before their wedding, the lack of privacy in a big house and the numerous inmates were [51] in some measure a safeguard; for a man could not abuse his wife, nor she neglect her duties, without incurring the condemnation of the whole household. Always in the background, too, was her family, which would certainly resent any ill-treatment, and in the last resort, might offer her an asylum and marry her to someone else. The social code enjoined strict chastity both before and after marriage, and the great majority of the Saanich lived up to this code. If a woman proved unfaithful, her husband might cut off her nose and mutilate the soles of her feet without interference from her kin, or he might divorce her by sending her back to her people; and he might kill her paramour without starting a blood-feud, if he had the courage to attack him. Such provocation, however, seldom arose. Only the principal nobles could afford more than one wife, and their wives came from different districts and occupied separate rooms.[109] Even slave women and girls received the same protection as others. A mistress who could overrule her lord might conceivably ill treat them, though the community would certainly condemn her; but masters were too jealous of their own prestige to consort with slave women or to permit their molestation by any outsider.

CHILDBIRTH

Since a childless marriage was considered a calamity, the birth of the first child occasioned great rejoicing. The expectant mother kept away from all fires as much as possible, though she might cook for her husband if it was absolutely necessary. Women often tried to diagnose the sex of the still unborn child. A girl, they thought, lay more quietly in the womb than a boy, made the left breast swell a little larger than the right, and the mother a little more prominent behind than before. Those that wanted boy babies deposited boys' toys in certain creeks and drank the water, chewed wild gooseberry leaves and certain other plants and permitted intercourse only during the first twelve days after the oestrous period. To facilitate delivery, they chewed various herbs, and drank decoctions from a certain moss that grows on rotten wood or from a fungus of the order *Claveriacea.*

A mother often delivered herself, all alone, in some corner of the house, screened off by mats. In every village, however, there was at least one woman who was prepared to serve as midwife. She knelt either in front of the kneeling mother (who generally grasped a stick) and held her head, or else she kneeled behind her and pressed downward on the womb. If labour was prolonged, a medicine-man might be summoned to pour warm oil on the mother's head and whisper "You shall give birth. You shall complete the act for which you were prepared in the beginning of time." The midwife cut the cord of the new-born babe with a shell knife, bound it with sinew and buried the afterbirth. After washing the baby with warm water, she rubbed it all over with fat and oil, wrapped it in sphagnum moss or shredded cedar-bark and laid it in the cradle, with a cedar-bark pad pressing heavily on its forehead. Then she washed the mother in warm water, squeezed the liquid from her breasts, and, if the milk was slow in flowing, applied a

---

[109] I {DJ} failed to enquire whether they were expected to fast inside the doorway for each wife, but consider it very improbable.

hot poultice of yarrow leaves (<u>Achilles millefolim</u>).[110] The mother rested from four to six days, after which she was free to bathe and resume her house hold duties. [52]

A mother oiled her baby's navel string until it dropped off, when she carefully wrapped it and concealed it where it would never be shaken or disturbed, believing that any disturbance would make the child restless and perhaps insane. It the first child died, the parents called in a priest, who faced, with the parents, the rising sun, and, raising the baby three times in his arms, placed it in the arms of the mother, shook his rattle over her and prayed to the Sun-spirit to let her next child survive. Taking the dead baby in his arms again, he repeated the rite over the father and then buried the child. Some of the Saanich thought that the soul of the dead infant was reborn in the next child, but others would not commit themselves definitely on this point.

Twins aroused a feeling of superstitious dread for which no explanation was forthcoming. Their hair was never cut short lest they sicken and die. For several months the parents were prohibited from embarking in a canoe lest they offend the spirits of the fish and mammals in the sea, and they had to live apart from their fellow-men, preferably in some lonely spot where the rising sun would shine on their cabin each morning. During these months, the father hunted land animals to support himself and his family; but he also spent much time in bathing and purifying himself, so that in the end he often became an influential medicine-man.

Women who wished to bear no more children interred the afterbirth from the latest child just outside the door where people would step over it; or they buried it at the water-line on the beach. A few, in desperation, stood in cold water up to the arm-pits immediately after delivery. Some tried to make themselves sterile by drinking a decoction from a yellow moss that grows on fir trees, or to induce an early menopause by drying on the sunny face of a mountain a tube of kelp that contained a little of their blood.

FUNERALS

Just as childhood and marriage ceremonies varied slightly from family to family, so there were variations, too in the funeral rites, although the ideas behind them remained essentially uniform.

However beloved a man had been during his lifetime, from the moment he ceased to breathe, he became an object of fear, because his shade or ghost was credited with power to inflict paralysis on anyone with whom it came into contact. A mysterious contagion attached itself to the man who made the coffin, to the 'undertakers' who handled the corpse, to the mourners who attended the funeral, to the house and bed in which the deceased had breathed his last, and, most of all, to the widow he left behind him. The ghost had to be expelled from the neighborhood of living beings, and everyone and everything that had been associated with the corpse had to undergo purification. At Westholme, 20 miles north of the Saanich Peninsula, the Indians burned all of the dead man's tools and weapons, even his canoe; but the Saanich were content to burn only a few of his movable possessions, to leave others beside the grave, and to

---

[110] The Saanich denied the use among themselves of the elderberry-rind poultices reported by Hill-Tout among the Squamish.

divide the rest among his sons and mourners.[111] They made no distinction between a dead nobleman and a dead slave except that they sometimes avoided the expense of a coffin for a slave by wrapping the body in a mat.

Families had their own cemeteries, some of them on small rocky islands a short distance from shore. There the Saanich deposited the coffins without regard to their direction, on the bare rock, or on horizontal logs and weighted them down with stones. Elsewhere they sometimes set them in trees, or on top of low posts carved and painted with red ochre. [53] Nobles of high rank were buried occasionally, not in boxes, but in canoes, which then became the repositories of other members of the same family until the canoe rotted. In the 19th century the Saanich, like other Coast Salish, built a few grave-houses, roofed usually with cedar-bark, in which they piled the coffins one on top of another; but they claimed that this custom and also burial in the ground, were post-European. They seemed to have no recollection of cairn burials, although a few cairns have been found on the Peninsula.

"When my first wife died, a cousin made a coffin for her while some of my female relatives dressed her in her best clothes. A priest chanted a wordless prayer to Haylse before they laid her in the coffin with her knees bent up close to her chin; then, while he prayed again, I leaped four times over the foot of the coffin, turning counter-clockwise after each leap, so that the ghost of my deceased wife might not follow me and bring swift death to any woman I might marry later. With other mourners I followed the procession to the graveyard, where the priest prayed again and all who had taken an active part in the funeral rites chewed some plant he had given them to ward off infection. Afterwards we returned to my house, but I was instructed to keep away from the others and to sit in a corner by myself. The priest dried some salal and Oregon-grape bushes before the fire, and, when darkness fell, set them ablaze, swishing them over the heads of the mourners and round the walls of the house, and hurled them outdoors, banishing my wife's ghost with them. The others then ate and drank as usual, but I received from the priest only a dried salmon. He made me bite off and drop into his hand four morsels, which he afterward threw on top of the roof for the crows; and he told me to turn my back on the people before eating the remainder, because if I ate facing them I might draw away the souls of some of the children and cause their death. He then placed blackberry, thistle, and other sharp plants under my sleeping mat to ward off any sorcery, and cautioned my to lie on my back, not on my side, to spit, not on the floor, but on a black stone he had planted close to the fire, and to remain in the house for four days.

"Early the next morning the same priest painted the faces of all the mourners except me and led us down to the beach, where he stationed me about twenty yards away from the rest. Softly chanting a prayer, he trimmed each person's hair and burned it in a fire, whereupon each of the mourners bound round his head a chaplet of salal, blackberry, or Oregon grape. Finally the priest lined them all up, and, chanting his prayer, marched them to the water's edge and back four times before commanding them to throw away their chaplets and plunge in. They were then free to go about

---

[111]   The Songhese and probably other Coast Salish Indians, occasionally reserved some of the property to burn and give away at some future potlatch, when they also chanted one of the dead man's songs to honor his memory. {p76 #8}

their usual occupations; but I, whom he forbade to bathe, confined myself to my house.

"Four days after the funeral the priest painted my face also with red ochre, prayed over me, and sent me into the woods to bestride four fir branches and rub my face with them. Next I sought out four moss-covered stones and rubbed the moss off with my cheeks. Then I bathed in a creek on the mountain side and returned home before night, since it was dangerous for me to be outside after dark. [54]

"On the following morning, he led me outside and made me strike with my axe four times, then cut four times with my knife; after each stroke, he chanted a prayer. Finally he led me to the beach and, after four feints, each followed by a prayer, made me enter the water. Thus he freed me from all contagion. Thenceforth I could hunt and fish and perform all my usual tasks, although for several weeks longer he would not allow me to talk to any children or to eat in company unless I turned my back; and for a whole year, he forbade me to eat seal, octopus, ducks, sockeye salmon, and cod. About ten days after the funeral he carried into the woods the black stone on which I had been expectorating, and left it beside some pool that had been a bathing-place of medicine-man long ago."

In most communities, there was not only a professional coffin-maker, but also a priest who specialized in marriage and funeral rites, and, with the assistance of his wife, acted as undertaker. Every priest was free to vary the ritual with in certain limits, so that the funeral just described was different from any others. Some priests inserted spoken words into their prayers, and addressed them to a vague sky-god, not to Halse, whom many regarded as primarily a spirit of the sea; some burned consumption plant seeds in the house-fire for several evenings to drive away the ghost, and kept the widow or widower in confinement for eight days instead of only four. All or almost all, insisted that the corpse should be carried feet foremost out of the house, through a window or hole in the wall, but not through the door, lest the souls of the survivors follow after it.

A very old priest on the Tsartlip reserve adopted the following procedure. He and his wife washed and dressed the corpse, and before laying it in the coffin, raised it four times while he prayed to Haylse to "receive his child". He invited various people to attend the funeral as mourners, and arranged for them to receive certain presents later as payment, since most Indians avoided funeral through fear of the ghost; and he painted the head, face, and blanket of the deceased, carried the coffin with cedar ropes to the family cemetery, where they laid it on the ground or set it on low posts. The priest chanted again his prayer to Haylse, burned beside the coffin some of the deceased's favorite foods or some possessions he had especially prized, deposited near by a few of his tools, and sent all the mourners away to bathe and scrub their bodies with yew branches.

At evening, he drove the ghost from the house by 'sweeping' its walls and inmates with burning twigs of fir, salal, and arbutus, and arranged a new bed for the widow(er), placing spruce boughs covered in diatomaceous earth under the sleeping-mat of a widow, and black berry bushes under the mat of a widower. For the latter, he prescribed also a chaplet of blackberry branches. He instructed them not to approach the fire or touch any tools or utensils for four days, to eat nothing but dried fish or dried clams, and to remain very quiet in a corner of the house, except once a day they should go into the woods and bathe in some fresh-water pool. On the fourth day, he assembled all the household, prayed over them, and singed their hair to mitigate their grief. He then led the widower and sons to their bathing place on the beach (his wife substituted for him with a widow and her daughters) and made them dive into the sea while he chanted his prayer. The widower's chaplet floated away on the water. Henceforth, he was free to go out in his canoe and resume his everyday life, though counselled to keep very much to himself for some weeks. The old priest said that if [55] the widower (or widow) bathed in the sea or entered his canoe before this ceremonial bath, painful lumps would develop on the inside of his legs. For their own protection, the priest and his wife, the maker of the coffin, and the men who carried it to the cemetery, all slept over blackberry bushes for four days.[112]

The Saanich often gave a feast to the dead, but it was neither obligatory nor was it held at any definite time. When given two or three days after the funeral, it was a very minor affair intended mainly to comfort the relatives. More often it was held some months later, a favorite time being the autumn after the close of the salmon season; and then the consolation of the relatives was subordinated to the actual feeding and propitiation of the dead man's ghost and of all his friends in the world of ghosts. The family hired a priest to light a fire within the house and burn ceremonially some food to which the deceased had been partial during his lifetime. One old woman whose husband had often officiated at this rite said that the priest should burn first some fish, whose crackling would summon the ghosts, then a little food for the person recently deceased, and finally some food for all deceased members of the community. He should not burn all the food lest another member of the family die soon afterwards; and he should warn away little children and ailing persons lest their souls be abstracted from their bodies and they too perish.[113]

A widower sometimes remarried within a year of his first wife's decease, but even if his second wife was a widow, he had to lay suit to her publically by fasting inside her door. A widow, after a lapse of about two years, tried usually to marry a kinsman of her first husband, who would be interested in the welfare of her children; if there were no kinsmen she returned to her parental village, taking her children and property with her.

POTLATCHES [56]

There was very little privacy in the life of a Coast Salish Indian; even the room he occupied in the big house was not closed off from public view. He spoke and acted as a member of a group that observed his every movement, and he sought the approval and backing of the group on every notable occasion. Tradition had established for him a definite mode of obtaining this approval; he gave a public feast or potlatch at which he distributed 'gifts' corresponding in number and value to his own rank and wealth, and to the importance of the event that he was celebrating. For a minor event, such as the naming of a child, even a noble might invite only the people of his own village and distribute a score or more goat's-wool blankets, a very insignificant outlay; but if he were celebrating the erection of a new house, or assuming a new title, he invited quests from villages all around and distributed not only most of his own goods, but others borrowed from friends and kinsmen. It was by holding a big potlatch lasting several days and attended by hundreds of people that a man established his fame and reputation along the coast. Such a potlatch differed very little, except in its elaborateness, from a feast that lasted

---

[112] For funeral rites in some other Coast Salish districts, see Appendix {E}.

[113] See further, Appendix {F}.

three or four hours only, and was attended by fellow villagers alone. The latter could be given by any man, commoner and noble alike, but it neither increased the giver's prestige nor raised his status in his own and surrounding communities; rather, if he were a commoner, it exposed him to ridicule for imitating men of higher rank. The Indian therefore never regarded these intra-village feasts as true potlatches, but only such as brought in guests from all around, and through their magnificence and lavish outlays enhanced the fame and honor both of their sponsors, and of the villages that supported them. With rare exceptions, none but the highest nobles could sponsor them in pre-European times, because they alone could amass the necessary food and goods; but when European settlement opened up new avenues to wealth, commoners, and even ex-slaves began to rival the nobles and even outstrip them in the lavishness of their feasts.

The potlatch was really a many-sided institution. It was a public assembly that ratified and celebrated important events such as marriages and conclusion of peace. It was also a social gathering at which people feasted and indulged in various games and pastimes. Again, it played the role of a commercial exchange; not only did it facilitate the ordinary bartering of goods, but it provided a field for investment, because the Salish Indian who 'gave away' his blankets and other articles merely placed them out on credit, confidently anticipating the reimbursement of his capital at some future date. Finally it furnished a public stage for the achievements of fame and honor, thus stimulating ambition and rescuing the community from stagnation.

Though the potlatch was organized by a single noble, its expense actually made it a cooperative undertaking, since kinsmen and friends were expected to help with considerable contributions. The organizer himself contributed the largest amount of food and goods, fixed the date for the celebration, issued the invitations and arranged in broad outline the program; but before committing himself to the undertaking, he shrewdly canvassed his kinsmen to find out how far they would back him and then calculated in minute detail the amount of his own 'capital' and indebtedness. He had to make certain of enough food to entertain all his guests for several days, or enough blankets, canoes, and other goods to liquidate old debts, to pay for the services of 'hired entertainers', and to disburse among the more prominent of his visitors what were conventionally called 'gifts', but in reality were interest-free loans.[114] [57] If, as was generally the case, he had himself contributed to the expense of earlier potlatches, he might discreetly solicit the return of those loans in order to augment his resources.

Walkem has described how a Saanich noble issued his invitations about the middle of the 19th century:

> "A chief, having decided upon the giving of a potlatch, selects the most prominent and trustworthy, as well as respected, young men of his tribe, and after giving them instructions as to which of the neighbor tribes he wishes to invite, provides them with an adequate number of blankets, to be used as I will presently describe. Choosing the largest of their war canoes, which, as is well known, are handsome models of sea-going canoes, and manning it with the very best 'paddlers' of the tribe, they set out for the various Indian settlements. As they approach the first village, the visitors strike up a song. When opposite, and close to the landing place of the first

---

[114]   The Saanich and their neighbors demanded only the equivalent for their contributions and gifts, without addition of interest; and they sought no return at all for gifts made to the aged and infirm, to whom they generally showed much charity. {p48 #19}

village, this chorus ceases, and one of the crew, arising, commences to sing another song in a loud, moaning tone – sadness itself. The method of approaching a village for the purpose of extending an invitation to a potlatch, is so well known to every tribe on the North Pacific coast, that few, if any, of the tribe run down to welcome the visitors, it not being considered the proper thing to do. On landing from the canoe, the last singer calls out the name of the chief's heir, or, if he has no son, his next of kin. The chief sends down one of his young men, and to him is given as a present for the chief, although his name is never mentioned, for the parent is always sheltered behind the heir. After sending a blanket as a present for the chief, another is given as a present for the second chief, and so on, until six chiefs are the recipients of presents. The visitors, or ambassadors, or whatever name you may call them, are then invited to the Rancheria, and properly entertained. Then they take their leave and proceed to the village of the next tribe on the invitation list, and the same present-making is gone through."[115] [58]

The older Saanich, and also the natives around Duncan, claimed that this method of inviting guests came to them from the Nootka Indians of the west coast of Vancouver Island , and that in earlier times, no Coast Salish Indian who was giving an important potlatch would delegate a kinsman to invite his guests, but would travel round himself, accompanied usually by a son or nephew, and carrying with him small bunches of cedar sticks, each about half as long as a lead pencil, one bunch for each village. He sat in the middle of his canoe, with paddlers in front and behind, and whenever they drew near a village he stood up and led his crew in a potlatch song. The villagers, recognizing him and understanding the significance of his song, quietly watched him disembark, and one of their nobles nearly always invited him into his home. Whether invited nor not, he entered the house of some noble and handed him an invitation stick,[116] while his son or nephew made a short explanatory speech. The noble then offered him some food, and often contributed a blanket towards the potlatch before letting him depart to deliver his next invitation. On rare occasions, the wife of the potlatch-giver travelled with her husband and delivered invitation sticks on her own account to the wives of his guests.

The Indians had no day-to-day calendar, so that any time set for a potlatch was approximate only. Some of the guests often arrived a day or more early, others a day or more late. Each party chanted a song as it approached the shore to indicate that it came in friendship, and hastily erected temporary shelters in the place the host had set aside for them. Whatever the hour of their arrival, it was his duty – carried out by his assistants – to light their fires and provide a cooked meal. Thereafter the visitors cooked their own meals, but their host furnished all the food and once or twice invited them to join his own people in a common feast. For this

---

[115] WW Walkem, Stories of Early British Columbia, Vancouver, pp.114-5, 1914.

[116] Some, apparently, gave the stick into the noble's hand, others threw it at his feet. A Westholme native said that his family used the sticks as tallies only, and threw them away one by one after delivering the invitation by word of mouth.

In more recent times, invitations to potlatches were less formal. The potlatch giver shouted out his invitations from his canoe and proceeded to the next village without even landing. An old Cowichan Indian who gave a potlatch that lasted two weeks and was attended by Indians from Saanich, Chemainus Bay, and Nanaimo as well as from Cowichan, travelled in a buggy to invite his guests.

feast, his assistants cooked an immense quantity of fish and camass in a long trench, dished them up into a wooden trough, and served each portion into a smaller dish. Whatever a guest could not eat on the spot, he carried back to his camp.

The program naturally differed with every occasion, but the organizer of the potlatch took pains to vary the entertainment as much as possible and to plan some activity for every hour of the day. He arranged ball contests and gambling games between the people of different villages, and sometimes hired a professional clown (*keenia*) to circulate among the guests and keep them in a state of merriment. If his daughter was of marriageable age, he might fasten a swing of goat's wool blankets from a rafter inside his house and invite the sons of nobles to swing her, paying each youth with a blanket, and, at the end, dividing among them the blankets that had formed the swing;[117] or he might honor his young son by having relatives carry the boy on their shoulders inside a painted box while they chanted some of the family songs. [59]

> "When I was a boy my father cooperated with his kinsmen in giving a big potlatch. At one stage in the proceedings, they made me stand in a box seven or eight feet long and about 12 inches wide, bearing on the outside a painting of the Sun. My kinsmen crowned their heads with chaplets of Oregon grape, and raising the box on poles, carried me out into the crowd, where everyone joined in singing two of our family songs, the same two that were chanted later at my wedding. Why they did not give me a new title at this potlatch I do not know."

Often the potlatch –giver held a 'memorial service' for a man who had died not long before. He hired two or, more commonly, four masked dancers – men who had inherited the privilege of wearing face-masks (swaiswai ~ *swaysway*) – set up a dressing-room for them in a corner of the house, and called in all his male relatives to chant the song his son had been accustomed to sing at the winter ceremonies, while the masked dancers waved sticks over them to allay their grief.[118]

It was at potlatches that men commonly assumed new titles, for only at such times could they be sure to have them ratified by all the leading nobles of the district. A man who could not afford to give a potlatch for this purpose himself sometimes waited until a relative was organizing one, and requested a place on the program in return for bearing part of the expense.

In early times no man could afford to give a potlatch unaided. All his kinsmen in the village cooperated with him and outside the village he often obtained support from a prosperous son-in-law. The son-in-law might arrive with several loaded canoes and camp over to one side of the village. Then one morning, when the potlatch was already in full swing, he would put out to sea, stand up in the middle of his canoe and lead all his crew in song. His father-in-law would go down to the beach to meet him, and 'anchor' the canoe to the shore by placing a goat's-wool blanket across it. After a few blankets and other objects had been thrown into the water so that onlookers might dive for them, the rest of the contributions would be carried up and pile on the floor of the potlatch house. There the son-in-law, with a dance and a song, would formally present them to his father-in-law, and the father-in-law expressed his thanks in a similar manner.

---

[117] The youths gave them to their mothers, who unraveled any that were mere strips and wove the wool into new blankets.

[118] If a daughter had recently died, the wife of the potlatch-giver presided at the memorial service and called the women relatives only.

The duration of the potlatch depended on the quantity of food provided by its giver and his fellow-villagers, and on the number of guests. As soon as the food supply began to run low, the celebration was brought to a close. All the people gathered round a platform in front of the potlatch house, the potlatch-giver mounted the platform, and, calling out the name of one guest after another, threw down his present. At the same time, he discharged his own debts from previous years, and paid the Indians [60] he had hired for various duties on the present occasion. This event usually took place during an afternoon. The following morning the guests loaded up their canes and departed for their homes.

Many Saanich Indians kept tallies of sticks to record their potlatch debts. To ease the accumulation of perishable goods in their homes and to prevent their debts from pyramiding, they frequently discharged their obligations at minor feasts to which they invited very few outsiders, except their creditors.

GAMES

Abundant leisure gave the Saanich opportunity for many games. Restricted to girls was battledore and shuttlecock (<u>sekkwoiya</u>), played with a wooden bat and a shuttle of light cedar-wood trimmed with three feathers. Girls played also with dolls, and boys with tops, but these, together with the games 'blindman's bluff' and 'hide and seek', may have been introduced by Europeans. Of native origin was a game in which a number of children crouched under a blanket and the 'out' person distinguished them by their legs. In another game the children squatted in two rows and planted a stick in front of one of their number; the child opposite had then to walk across and carry back the stick with unsmiling face, in spite of the funny grimaces, accompanied by the chanted words <u>taakchenum</u> <u>hwehwechiem</u> (their meaning is unknown), with which the line of children tried to break down his gravity.

String figures were more popular with children than with adults; I have described two in the Appendix. There was also a juvenile version of the men's gambling game *lehal* or 'hide the stick {bones}'. The children lined up in a long row with hands clasped on their stomachs and a captain stationed at each end; one captain, walking along the line, stealthily slipped a pebble into a child's hand and the other guessed who held it.

Boys and young men naturally preferred more athletic pastimes such as football and hockey. The football (<u>keektomas</u>) was a lump of wood, described by one native as 'the hard lump of wood that grows on the outside of the balsam'; and the goals were mere lines on the beach or at opposite ends of an open field. The players threw the ball to each other and tried to carry it over their opponent's goal. Hockey (<u>kwokkwokis</u>) resembled football in being played on bare ground with two lines as goals, but the curved sticks served more often to trip the players than to propel the ball. In 'ring and spear' (<u>sesaylam</u>) one man bowled along the ground a hoop of woven reeds or a perforated stone disk, which his opponent tried to stop with an arrow; while in 'ball and hook' (<u>cnilkem</u>) he rolled a wooden ball for his opponent to catch, like a salmon, on a hooked stick. 'Tug of war!' was identical with the European game except that a long pole took the place of a rope; if there were only two boys or men they dispensed with the stick and merely interlocked their fingers. Less strenuous was <u>hukkwim</u>, which resembled quoits, but was played with a piece of kelp and a number of stick tallies. Two boys took up positions two or three yards apart, and each planted a sharpened stake in the ground. [61] One threw the kelp, trying to impale it on his opponent's stake; if he succeeded, he won a tally, if he failed his opponent threw in turn. Whoever first stripped his opponent of all his tallies won the game.

Boys were also fond of war games. They shot at marks with their bows and arrows, and also with slings, though the sling was seldom if ever used in actual warfare. In one game, they selected a victim and lightly squeezed his jugular vein until he toppled over. In another they lined up in opposing ranks and attacked one another; the victors then knotted their prisoners' hair on the crown, bound their legs and pretended to carry them off as slaves.

At potlatches attended by natives from other villages the principal recreation was gambling. Women used sets of four dice (smetali) made from beaver teeth and marked on one side only. Men scorned to play with dice, but gambled away their possessions on two other games forbidden to women, *lehal* and slehaylem. *Lehal* was the familiar 'hide the stick' known in one form or another over the greater part of Canada. The Saanich used two bones or wooden sticks, one banded and the other not, which they concealed in their hands beneath a mat. The gambler had to guess which player held the banded stick, and in which hand.

Lehal may not have reached the Saanich until the 19th century, for their folk-tales seem to mention only the other game slehaylem, in which a number of painted disks or counters (usually ten) were rolled upon a mat.[119]

---

[119] For a full description of the game, see Erna Gunter, Klallam Ethnography, UWPA 1 (5), Seattle 1927.

NATURE AND MAN

The earth seemed to the Saanich a flat expanse of land and sea over which brooded the sky, which was just another land like this one, possessing water and trees, and supporting animals and human-like beings. The river that flowed through sky-land was the Milky Way, the northern lights were ice flows that drifted in the water and were lit up by the departing sun, and the sinking stars were the light of people's eyes. The Indians have names to many of the stars; they called the Big Dipper, the elk; the Little Dipper, the bullhead; the Morning Star, the day-bringer; and Orion's belt, which they imagined were six men in two canoes hunting ducks, was papayahtiL. Two girls once married stars, the legend ran, and they told the Indians about the sky-world after they returned to earth. The most powerful human-like beings in that land were the Sun, which was female, and the moon, which was male. A very old Saanich (Tsartlip) Indian affirmed that now and then the Sun caught an extra large cod, and only by desperate struggle succeeded in killing it. During the struggle, the sun was eclipsed by the cod passing in front of it, whereupon he and his family summoned to its aid the swiftest of all birds, the humming-bird, chanting "Go up, hummingbird, Go up hummingbird".[120] What caused an eclipse of the Moon he did not know, nor did he concern himself greatly with the [62] event because the Moon was definitely less powerful and less important than the Sun. However, another Saanich Indian (from Tsekum) flatly rejected this explanation of a solar eclipse. To him it denoted the impending death of some nobleman whose soul was already darkening the Sun's face, while a round light near the sun (a sun-dog) signified that the Comox Indians were approaching and would shortly cut off some people's heads. Under this earth, some of the Saanich thought, was another land about which, however, they could say little because it was more shadowy and vague than the sky-land above.

Between earth and sky roamed a giant eagle-like bird whose flapping wings created the thunder and whose blinking eyes the lightning flashes. Chain and forked lighting, however, marked the movements of a dangerous snake. Rain and wind were produced by certain of the superhuman beings or spirits in which this earth abounded. The winters grew more severe until they reached a maximum, then became milder, following a weather cycle whose length the Indians confessed themselves unable to determine.

Each object on this earth, even things that Europeans class as inanimate, consisted of a soul (smasteemauh) enclosed within a corporeal frame. Man was unable to change his frame, but this was not the case with many things; a deer, for example, might conceivably transform itself into a stump, or a fish into a stone.

"Once when my uncle was fishing for spring salmon in Cowichan Bay, he felt a fish tug strongly on his line. It struggled all the way to the surface, then suddenly changed into an apparently lifeless stone, which he kept, and thereby became a wonderfully successfully fisherman. I myself had a similar experience in the same bay. My salmon too changed into a stone with the result that I caught over 100 fish in that one night. But instead of leaving the stone in the boat, as I should have done, I wrapped it in a sack and concealed it in a hole in a bank. When I searched for it

---

[120]   Johnson, a Quamichan Indian from near Duncan, said that the cod was eating the Sun but that his people paid little attention.

later, it had disappeared, having reverted, no doubt to a fish and returned to the water."

"On Salt Spring island, a hunter shot a buck which fell on its back with it four legs in the air. When he walked up to it, however, he found only a stump pierced by his shot. A few weeks later, when he returned to the same place, the stump had disappeared, having changed back into a deer."

In the dawn of the world, all animals and birds (and fish?) were human beings, but a powerful being named Haylse transformed their outward shapes without depriving them of their souls. Whether or not there were trees in those earliest days, the Saanich could not say, but trees, too, they believed, possessed souls, and even wept whenever one of them was blown down by the wind. In far-away lands, fish and perhaps other creatures reverted to their human forms and lived in villages similar to those of Indians; thus the salmon were fish during the migration season but human beings all the rest of the year. An old Saanich woman said that there is a mother fish, larger than the usual one, in every species, and likewise a mother animal and a mother tree; that Indians travelling far from land have occasionally seen the mother cod and the mother salmon near some mysterious islands. She state also that there are male and female specimens of every plant, that the male grows straighter, taller, and with fewer branches; the female being stubby and round, and that only the male plant should be used for medicines. Whether her ideas prevailed [63] generally or not, I did not discover. No Saanich denied to the sea a soul, or hesitated to appease it in storm weather by a prayer.

In addition to a soul and a corporeal body, all creatures, including man, possessed a shadow or reflection (<u>kayahenettan</u>) visible in sunlight or moonlight, and as some thought also, in clear water. Naturally, this shadow or reflection resembled in form the body. So too did the soul, according to an old Tsartlip woman, who stated that it was very small and transparent, and that it normally dwelt in the heart. She and her aged husband thought that human beings (and perhaps other living creatures) must possess two souls, one of which remained constantly inside the body, giving it vitality or life, while the other, responsible apparently for thought and consciousness, sometimes wandered away, e.g. in dreams. This wandering soul was visible only to medicine-men. She herself saw one occasionally, and then she knew that she would receive a visitor the next day, an Indian if the soul appeared red, a white person if it appeared green. At death, this old couple concluded, the body and the shadow perished, but the soul that gave rise to thought or consciousness lingered near the grave and wandered abroad by night to hunt and feast. It was no longer a soul, but a ghost (<u>spalkweetha</u>) which fed on the souls of food, travelled in the souls of canoes, and generally passed {"lived"} a ghostly replica of its former existence inside the body. Instead of partaking of its principal meal in the late afternoon, it dined now two or three hours before daybreak. Not infrequently it assumed the form of the small owl which the old couple called <u>spalkweetha</u>; and because this owl frequently haunted their settlements, and ghosts were dangerous to living beings, their people would carefully close the roof-boards of their houses as soon as darkness fell, and burn in their fires the seeds of the consumption plant to drive away the ghosts. They were convinced, however, that many a ghost or disembodied soul was reborn in the same family, explaining in this way the frequent likeness of a child to some ancestor.

The next-door neighbor and kinsman of this old Tsartlip couple did not agree with them concerning the afterlife. Man, he thought, had one soul only, which at death commonly assumed the form of the larger owl <u>seetenuch</u>. It was the shadow that became the small owl which sometimes flew inside the Indian houses to talk with medicine-men.

Different again was the belief of another old Saanich Indian who lived on the Tsekum reserve in Union Bay. He postulated a shadow, a soul that resided in the heart and was visible in water or a mirror, and a mind (<u>shalli</u>). At death, the mind became the little owl, the shadow became a ghost, while the soul haunted the spot where the dead man had fasted and obtained a guardian spirit. There it lingered until it was reborn in another child of the same family. Each family had its individual stock of souls, which were not transferable; hence the total number of souls was limited.[121] [64]

There was not an Indian who did not dread meeting a ghost or shade believing that the mere touch of one induced partial paralysis. Indeed, if one credited all the tales of their adventures, a large percentage of the Saanich should have shown signs of paralysis. Ghosts, they said, live happily by themselves and wander abroad only at night, walking with a slight stoop and with their faces concealed or averted. They do not like living beings to discuss them, and a man should never mention them before starting out to fish or hunt lest they keep all fish and game away from him. Now and again they have helped an individual Indian; there was an old man, for example, who would merely draw his canoe up on the beach at nightfall and walk around while the ghosts of his dead relatives filled the boat with firewood for him. But their presence in the vicinity was always dangerous, and the mere touch of one occasioned a sudden cramp, causing paralysis to set in unless the victim had recourse to a medicine-man.

A medicine-man who was summoned to treat a sick girl announced that the ghost of her father had passed along the road outside and looked at her longingly, wishing to take her away with him. Her face was already becoming paralyzed, but the medicine-man rubbed it with fat every day and cured her.

---

[121] There was a similar disagreement among other Coast Salish natives (See Jenness 196f. {??}) An old man from the Quamichan reserve near Duncan who held that the soul generally went to dwell in a shadowy land very much like its old home, and only rarely underwent reincarnation, told the following story to substantiate his belief:

A man whose wife had died refused to return to his house, but mourned beneath her grave for four days and four nights. On the fourth night, he saw her alight from her coffin, adjust her blanket, and walk away from the grave. He tried to seize her in his arms, but she eluded his grasp, and glided along in front of him until they reached a lake. Without hesitation, she walked across on its surface, and he followed safely in her footsteps. Beyond the lake, he lost her in a crowd of people who were rejoicing and playing games. Someone came up to him and said, "What are you doing here? You are not dead." And he answered, "I followed my wife." Two messengers brought his wife to him, and the people gathered around, said "Since you love her so dearly, you may take her back again. But you must not touch her for four days and nights." The man and his wife returned to their earthly home and for two days he kept away from her. On the third day, however, he crept beneath her blanket. Then she arose, adjusted the blanket and glided away far in front of him; despite his utmost effort, he could not keep up with her. She crossed the lake to the other side, but when he tried to follow her, he sank beneath the surface and drowned.

APPENDIX {A}

<u>Origin of the Willow Fishnet</u> [65] {*sg^wale*}

A Saanich couple and their marriageable daughter joined some relatives on a fishing excursion to Blaine, in the state of Washington. There the girl used to wander outside the rush wigwam, and sit by herself at night while her parents were sleeping. One night someone approached her, and, before leaving arranged to meet her again the next night. Therefore they met night after night.

Shortly afterwards some strange youths began to join the girl's brothers and cousins as they played around the camp, and she wondered whether one of them might not be her nightly visitor. Towards evening, therefore, she smeared red ochre on her hands, and when her suitor joined her, playfully rubbed them on the back of his clothing. The next day, she noticed in the crowd of players a youth who seemed more serious than the others, and when he turned his back to her it was red.

When night came her suitor urged her to go away with him, but she refused unless he first spoke to her parents. He was afraid that if he spoke to them they might be angry and send him away, and suggested that it would safer if she herself told them. She did so, and her father consented to their marriage if they remained for a time with her family. So she married the youth, who thereafter ceased to play with the other young men and occupied himself with serious matters about the camp.

Soon afterwards fish became very scarce, and the community was threatened with famine. The youth then said to his young wife, "Tell your father and his people to bring me a lot of <u>sgwale</u>." No one knew what he meant by <u>sgwale</u>; all the names, indeed, that he gave to the various plants and land animals were strange. They brought him bundles of one plant after another, but he rejected them all until they brought him bunches of willow. From its bark he made a net <u>sgwale</u>, showed them how to use it, and taught them the expressions that should accompany its handling. Then they were able to catch plenty of fish again."

Now that they were prosperous once more he proposed to his wife that they go to his home. With the consent of her parents, the two of them embarked in a canoe, taking with them a large number of mats. Instead of heading, however, for some point or island in the distance where one might expect a village, he steered the canoe toward a very deep place in the sea not far from shore, where it vanished from view. Not many days later the girl reappeared above the surface of the water, showed herself to her people, and vanished again. They knew who it was from her singed hair, for along with other women of the camp, she had been mourning the death of a relative. But she never returned to them, because she married the fish-spirit <u>sgwala</u>. [66]

APPENDIX {B}

<u>First Salmon Ceremonies</u>

The Halalt ~ Westholme ceremony performed over the first sockeye of the season differed in no essential detail from the Saanich.

The Songhese also celebrated over the sockeye, which they netted at San Juan. They considered their net to represent a human being with head, body, arms, and legs, and they believed that unless it was set in a certain definite way, the leading sockeye would turn back disapprovingly and warn those behind. Since only a few priests knew how to set it, one always superintended the fishing, apportioned the catch, and directed the ceremonies. In their ceremony over the first salmon that were brought in, women and girls, not boys and girls, carried up the fish; men and women, as well as children, ate them, and the boys and girls who gathered up the bones lined up along the beach before marching into the water at a given signal and dropping them. They dried their second haul of fish on logs, the third and subsequent ones on stagings. There was a ceremony at the first utilization of the stagings. All the people lined up, with painted faces and feathered heads, and, after the priest had chanted a prayer, made three feints at hanging up their fish before completing the operation. Again, at the ceremony that closed the season's fishing, the priest chanted a prayer and threw consumption plant seeds into the flames while the people piled all the refuse into the bonfire, after which the older natives chatted and sang while the children played nearby. Thus in numerous small details the Songhese rituals seem to have differed from those of the Saanich; but I suspect that these differences were more apparent than real, since probably no two priests ever directed the ceremonies in exactly the same way.

The Indians around Duncan, unlike the Saanich, allowed salmon bones to be thrown anywhere, even to the dogs. Only one species they excepted, the spring salmon, which they caught with a net, whereas all other species they caught with spears or long hooks. Yet it was not the spring salmon that they honored with religious rites, but the dog salmon. When the season arrived for this species to ascend the Cowichan River, a man who claimed it as his guardian spirit (<u>saila</u>), painted two male and two female dog salmon on a board and carried it down to the mouth of the river. There, in the presence of his fellow-villagers, he dipped it into the water, and prayed that the shoals would be large and numerous. Then the first dog-salmon they caught, they split so that the heads remained attached to the backbone and tails, and they cooked the heads on the fire while the meat was hung overhead to dry. A few consumption plant seeds thrown into the flames fed the shades of the fish. As soon as the heads were cooked, the people gathered and ate them, while three or four old men chanted a song nearby and drummed on a board with sticks.

It was the run of the dog-salmon that the Nanaimo Indians celebrated also. At Jack Point, close to the city of Nanaimo, is a petroglyph, carved so long ago that no one remembers the artist. It represents a dog-salmon, a cohoe, a spring salmon, a humpbacked salmon, and a flounder. Each year before the dog-salmon season opened a priest covered the designs with red ochre, lit a fire in front of them, and threw various kinds of food into the flames to feed the souls (<u>smasteeuch</u>) of the dog-salmon. Present-day natives claim that the custom originated with a priest whose daughter in ages long past married a dog-salmon; and that it was probably this priest who carved the petroglyph. The legend is as follows: [67]

An old priest who lived in Solachwan village, Nanaimo, with his wife and daughter, went up to where the highway bridge now crosses the river and caught there a fish that he had never seen before, a dog-salmon. He placed it in his canoe, paddled home, and asked his wife if she would cook it for him; and when she undertook to cook it, he sent his daughter down to the canoe to bring the fish into the house. The girl lit a bundle of cedar sticks to light her path, and, when she reached the canoe, put her hand down to take up the salmon; but it changed at her touch into a young man, who seized her wrist and said: "You cannot go back. You must come home with me and be my wife."

Her father and mother wondered why she did not return and the old man went down to the canoe to look for her. He found the canoe where he had left it, but no trace of either the girl or the fish. The next morning he called in several seers (siowa) to discover what happened, but not one could find out. Finally one of them announced that the salmon had carried her away. At first the old man refused to believe the seer, but he was finally convinced when his daughter sent word to him some way that she was safe in the home of the dog-salmon and would visit him at a certain time of the year.

At the appointed time, the dog-salmon brought the girl back to Nanaimo and waited for her in the water while she went up to the house and visited her parents. She stayed with them only a little while, then went down to the river again, leaped in, and returned with her husband to their home.

When spring came, her father paddled away in his canoe to search for her. After travelling a long distance he reached the home of the humpbacked salmon, who told him that his daughter lived farther on. From the humpbacked salmon, he continued to the home of the cohoe salmon, who told him that his daughter lived in the next village. There he found her, and remained with her for some time. When he was on the point of returning, she said to him, "My husband and I with many of his people will visit you in the fall. Tell my aunts and uncles not to harm either my husband or myself. We will leap out of the water, side by side, so that they may know us."

In the fall, many dog-salmon entered the Nanaimo River, among them two that leaped side by side. These two the Indians did not touch, but of the others, they caught great numbers."

For the first salmon ceremony at Katzie, on the Fraser River, see Jenness, "Faith". Farther up the river, the Chilliwack Indians also held a ceremony over the first sockeye of the season, but the details are forgotten. These Chilliwack natives disregarded what happened to the bones of all fish except the spring salmon and the sturgeon; they alone had to be thrown back into the water. Long ago they refrained from eating oolakan, believing hem to be transformed women; more recently they have eaten them, but immediately afterwards wipe their hands and face with nettles to keep away sickness. Rubbing oolakan grease on the head, they claim, induces madness. [68]

APPENDIX {C}

<u>Puberty</u>

Just as the boy's ritual varied slightly from family to family, even on the Saanich Peninsula, so undoubtedly did the girl's, quite independently of their status or rank.

Similar rituals occurred in neighboring Coast Salish communities. Those current among the Katzie Indians on the lower Fraser River, I have described in my ms.: "The Faith of a Coast Salish Indian". Farther up the same river, at Sardis, there was no ritual for adolescent boys, but girls were confined to the house for four days. Each morning a priest prayed over her and painted her face with red ochre and white earth. On the fourth day, she wiped away the paint with fir branches and bathed.

APPENDIX {D}

<u>Songhees Puberty</u>

The Songhese round Victoria kept the girl indoors for four days, and, if they could afford it, screened her behind goat's wool blankets and hired two professional women attendants. Each morning these women sat, one at the foot of her bed, the other at the head, shook their rattles over her and prayed to Haylse to grant her happiness and long life, after which they rubbed her breasts with a pebble and painted her face, making the patterns different each day of her seclusion. At evening they prayed over her again and left her. On the fifth morning, they repainted her face for the last time, removed the curtain, and summoned the people for whatever ceremony the parents had arranged. When this ceremony ended, the girl carried into the woods all the cedar-bark towels with which her attendants had wiped away the paint each morning, and hung them up high in some tree, climbing only up their sunny sides. Then she drew down a branch, rubbed her face with it once, and sent it swishing upward. Descending, she climbed a second tree and did likewise, then a third and a fourth, until the two or three girls who had followed her announced that her face was clean again. The Indians believed that if one of the branches snapped off, or if she allowed the paint to harden on her face, she would die young. Finally she bathed in the sea or in some pool and returned home.

An old Westholme woman who had been a professional attendant of girls at their 'coming of age' ritual described the ceremony in her district for high-born girls as follows:

The girls fasted in the house for four days, working at anything she wished, but forbidden to lie down either by day or by night. Two women attendants crowned her with a goat's wool head-dress, tied a belt of red-dyed cedar-bark round her waist, and painted her face each morning with red ochre. They did not rub her body with a pebble, however, or make her expectorate on a stone. All through the day, they remained with her, but at night they slept in their own homes.

Early on the morning of the fifth day, they repainted her face and prepared her bath, which was in either a water-tight basket or a canoe; sometimes, especially for a canoe-bath, they screened off a special room. When everything was ready, they led her, shaking their rattles, into the main part of the house and seated her on some blankets, [69] themselves sitting on either side. The villagers trooped in and took their places, and, to the accompaniment of stick-pounding and singing, four boys danced back and forth towards the girl, each pretending to offer some object. The first boy pretended to offer her a forked stick, the second a shell, the third a stone, and the last a basket. Their dance usually lasted two or three hours, after which the two attendants singing and shaking their rattles, conducted her to her bath and the people dispersed.

During the bath, the attendants dipped a cedar-bark doll in the water and lightly beat the girl, to make her unafraid when suitors sought her hand. After washing all the paint from her face they led her back to her seat and sent a messenger to summon the villagers again. The girl's father shouted "Scramble for the blankets" (that screened off the bathroom), and the men, sometimes boys also, tore the blankets into sections and divided them up.

As soon as this turmoil had ended, the two attendants began to sing and shake their rattles while the audience beat time with sticks; then, taking a special comb, with four preliminary feints, they combed her hair and plaited it into two braids. Occasionally some family would tell their son to go and sit near her, thus silently proclaiming himself her suitor; but no one at this time paid any attention to him, least of all the girl.

Two young boys now advanced, each carrying a male dog-salmon painted red and, with the usual preliminary feints, extended them towards her mouth. With each corner of her mouth, she bit off a fragment and dropped it to the floor; and the boys gathered up these fragments and deposited them on the roof of the house for the crows.

This ritual feeding of the girl marked the end of the ceremonies. Her father paid the women attendants, the six boys and any others who had played a part in them. If he was wealthy, he feasted all the villagers; if not, they quietly dispersed to their homes. The girl broke her fast after her family had eaten, and was freed from further confinement. The first time she went out in a canoe again, however, the two women attendants had to go with her." [70]

APPENDIX {E}

<u>Funerals</u>

An old man on the Koksileh reserve, near Cowichan, listed these funeral peculiarities of his group:

1. Three or four people in the community were hereditary undertakers, three or four others inherited the knowledge of the ritual for widow(er)s, and still others the ritual for the feast to the dead. They received small payments for their services.
2. Prayers were addressed to the shade or ghost of the dead, not to any deity.
3. If a man slipped and fell when helping to carry a coffin he would die within a year.
4. Widow(er) had to keep away from the Cowichan River for eight days through fear of spoiling the run of salmon.
5. The widower, but not the widow, rubbed the ochre from his face with saplings.
6. No one might stand or sit in front of the widow, or speak to her, for eight days.

An old nobleman on the neighboring reserve at Quamichan also distinguished the professional undertakers (<u>shusowoiath</u>) who dressed the corpse and sometimes also carried it feet foremost to the grave, from the priests (<u>qoqweals</u>) who purified the house and the mourners. Nobles, he said, hired two priests to shake their rattles and chant a prayer ("You came from a woman's womb. Return now to your home.") before the corpse was carried from the house, to lead the procession to the cemetery and to chant another prayer at the grave. There the mourners deposited all the dead man's property, burned his bedding and broke up his canoe. Only his face-mask and rattle, if he possessed any, were kept back for his eldest son, who inherited also his share of the house and weir. The dead man's name was dropped for about two generations. After the funeral all the mourners returned to the house and waited outside while five or six priests swept the interior with burning branches of Oregon grape, when they too entered and were purified in the same way while they pounded boards in front of their benches to drive away the ghost. The widow(er) whose hair was cut at the nape of the neck, remained in his room eight days, wrapped in ochre-sprinkled blanket, sleeping over some prickly plant such as Oregon grape, and eating only small quantities of dried fish with his back turned to the wall; and the first time he ate a priest made him bite off four fragments to be thrown on the roof for the crows. At the end of eight days, the undertakers brought a tub of water into the house and bathed him, after which he was free to assume his ordinary life. Common people and slaves, the old man added, were buried in the same way, but with less ceremony.

An old man and his wife at Westholme, __ miles farther north, described their funeral rites as follows: Both, it should be noted, were commoners.

"The nearest of kin painted the face of the dead man (or woman), wrapped him first in a goat's-wool blanket, then in a rush mat, and carried him out, head foremost, through the door (only in more recent times through a hole in the wall) to an island near the village, where they laid him on the ground and burned his [71] property, even his canoe. No chants were sung, no prayers recited. On returning to their homes, all the mourners washed the paint from their faces with heated urine.

The next morning before daylight, the mourners went to the dead man's house so that the priest (<u>theetha</u>) might clip off their hair at the nape of the neck. Then they bound chaplets of blackberry vines and feathers round their heads, and, marching to the beach, lined up in a row with the priest on their right. While the latter intoned a brief chant, they marched into the sea and back again, still facing the water. The second time he chanted, they shouted as they entered the water; the third time, they washed the paint from their faces; the fourth time they dashed right in, threw away their chaplets, and, turning around, raced for their homes without looking back. Some then gathered branches of the Oregon grape to dry beside the fire in the dead man's house, and in the evening all the mourners gathered to sweep the house with the flaming boughs, burning in the fire at the same time, some seeds of the consumption plant.

The widow(er, for both followed the same regime) was considered impure for eight days. He slept on the floor, on a bed of blackberry vines and other prickly bushes from which the thorns had been removed. His pillow was a stone with feathers strewn round its edges, and beside it was another stone on which he expectorated. Anyone who spoke to him addressed him from behind. Each morning he wandered away and bathed in every suitable pool, but not in the sea. If he came upon a stone like the one on which he expectorated, he carefully stepped over it; but he avoided stepping over any solid log because then his next wife would die soon. Before returning home at evening, he rubbed the paint from his face with fir branches, and the priest, chanting a prayer, repainted his face when he entered the house.

During the first four days he neither ate nor drank. On the fifth, the priest offered him dried dog-salmon sprinkled with red ochre. He bit off four fragments to be thrown to the crows, and ate the rest, with his back turned to the inmates of the house. During the next three day, he ate only dried fish.

On the eighth day, his temporary bed was thrown out, and the priest instructed him, with the customary three feints, to use his knife and axe again. This ended his period of mourning.

Little children wore bracelets and anklets of goat's wool for a time after a parent died, but underwent no other restrictions."

For the funeral rites of Katzie, on the lower Fraser River, see D Jenness, The Faith of a Coast Salish Indian, 1955. [72]

APPENDIX {F}

<u>Funeral Feast</u>

An old man on the Koksileh reserve at Cowichan thought it was preferable to hold the feast on the fifth day after death, the day after the ghost, which at first wandered aimlessly near its former home, joined the host of ghosts.

Some Coast Salish priests used indifferently any kind of wood for the fire provided it was thoroughly dry, but a Quamichan woman at Cowichan thought it should always be cedar, because its loud crackling served to summon the ghosts. In her community, the priest was always a woman who had inherited the right (rite) from her predecessor. She lit the ceremonial fire and walked around it, summoning the dead person by name to come and eat. After allowing due time for it to arrive she took up a bowl, and, walking half-way round the food (which was commonly laid out on boards), poured water on the ground for the ghost to drink; then, after another brief interval, she threw half of the food into the flames; the remaining food she carried home to share with relatives and friends. The ghost naturally invited all its friends in the ghost world to share the feast, just as the deceased during his lifetime would have called in his neighbors.

At Westholme the feast was usually held two or three months after the funeral. The priest held up some of the food, silently offering it to the ghost of the deceased, and laid it on the pile of wood. He deposited a second offering for the ghosts of deceased relatives, and a third for the ghosts of all the dead. When he finally lit the fire, all the spectators turned their backs and hastened away.

For the funeral rites of Katzie, on the lower Fraser River, see D Jenness, The Faith of a Coast Salish Indian, ms.[122] [73]

---

[122] {Published by the British Columbia Provincial Museum in Victoria as *Faith of a Coast Salish Indian*, Anthropology in British Columbia, Memoir 3: 1-92 1955.}

APPENDIX {G}
<u>Terms of Relationship</u>

	Saanich	Quamichan (Cowichan)
<u>Same Generation</u>		
Siblings or cousins		oqwetql F , salokwa M
Older brother or sister	sceɛɬ	sceɛɬ
Younger brother or sister	sɛ'ɛtcɛn	
Half brother or sister		hansoyaxtal
Husband or wife	st'alis	st'alis
Fellow co-wife	saiya	caiya
Husband's younger sister / Woman's older brother's wife		cwelic
Younger brother's wife / Husband's younger brother	cnɛtkun ?	mituxtun sinsawak
Husband's brother's wife / Husband's sister's husband		
Wife's brother or sister / Husbands' brother or sister		kwiθlu
Wife's brother's wife / Wife's sister's husband		tcɛpθ tsolɛɬ
Sister's husband		
Parent-in-law of one's child / same, after child is dead	sqwalwas	sqwalwas nasxwam[123]

<u>Younger Generations</u>

	Saanich	Quamichan (Cowichan)
Son, daughter	mən•a	mən•a
Eldest child	latɬ	sant'le ?
Any middle child	anowiɬ	
Youngest child	sqɛ•q	sqɛ•q
Step-child	cniωɛ'ɛn	sɬmənən
Nephew or niece	stiuwan	stiwan
Son- or daughter-in-law	styutɛɬ	stutɛɬ
Grandchild	iωix	im•əθ
Great grandchild	okoxox ?	tsamox

---

[123] {Decedence, change of kin term at the death of a linking relative, is a feature of Salish kinship systems, thereby aunts and uncle are moved emotionally closer to niblings (nephews & nieces) at the death of their parents. jm}

Diamond Jenness
10 February 1886 – 29 November 1969

Child of the British Commonwealth, Diamond Jenness was born in Wellington, New Zealand, taking a BA (1907 Classics) and MA (1908) at Victoria University College of the University of New Zealand then a Diploma in Anthropology (1910), BA (1911), MA (1916) at Balliol College, University of Oxford, with fieldwork on D'Entrecasteaux Islands in eastern Papua New Guinea, where his brother in law was a missionary.

The turning point in his career came when he signed on as ethnologist with the Canadian Arctic Expedition from 1913 to 1916 under the leadership of both Vilhjalmur Stefansson and Dr Rudolph M Anderson, pursuing detailed studies of the Copper Inuit around Coronation Gulf (Akuliakattagmiut, Haneragmiut ~ Blond Eskimos, Kogluktogmiut, Pallirmiut, Puiplirmiut, Uallirgmiut ~ Kanianermiut bands), with Patsy Klengenberg, son of trader Christian Klengenberg, acting as interpreter. For two years he lived as an adopted son of a Puivik hunter named Ikpukhuak and his shaman wife Higalik ("Ice House"), hunting with his "family", sharing both their festivities and famine, and diagramming many string figures (cat's cradle) and recording hundreds of drum dance songs, poems, legends, and stories of wax phonographic cylinders.

Tragedy struck the expedition in the fall of 1913, when their ship Karluk became locked in the ice, pushed westward and crushed at Wrangel Island, where thirteen of the crew perished. Jenness was one of the six who had left the ship to hunt caribou for the crew. Survivors trekked to Barrow, Alaska to meet up with their two other expedition vessels. Jenness spent that winter at Harrison Bay, Alaska, where he learned to speak Inuit.

After graduation, he served as a WW I gunner with Canadian Expeditionary Force in Europe 1917-19. In 1920, Diamond married Frances Eilleen Bleakney Jenness and they had three sons: John L (Pete) Jenness, Stuart E Jenness, and Robert A (Bob) Jenness. Stuart edited and published his father's last works. But for his Canadian wife, Jenness would have accepted a generous offer to establish Anthropology at the University of Washington in the 1920 interim between Boasians Thomas T Waterman and Leslie Spier.

As major breakthroughs, he defined the foundational Dorset complex in Canada (in 1925) and Old Bering Sea complex in Alaska (in 1926), earning the title "Father of Eskimo Archaeology." The later Thule complex completed Arctic chronology.

In 1926, Jenness succeeded Canada's first Chief Anthropologist, Dr Edward Sapir, at the National Museum of Canada, struggling with politicians and meager budgets to expand exhibits, anthropological collections, and reputation. In 1937 he became president of the Society of American Archaeology, and in 1939 president of the American Anthropological Association. More personally, he sought to improve recognition, understanding, and living conditions of Canada's First Nations, Metis, Inuit, and native peoples.

During WW II, in 1941, Jenness was seconded to the Royal Canadian Air Force, serving until 1944 as civilian Deputy Director of Special Intelligence. In 1944 he became Chief of a newly established Inter-Services Topographic Department in the Canadian Department of National Defense, whose civilian branch in 1947 became the Geographic Bureau and subsequently the Geographic Branch in the Department of Mines and Resources. He retired in April 1948.

Between 1920 and 1970, Jenness authored more than 100 works on Canada's Inuit and First Nations people. Chief among these are his scholarly government report, *Life of the Copper Eskimos* (1922), his ever-popular account of two years with the Copper Inuit, *The People of the Twilight* (1928), his definitive and durable *The Indians of Canada* (1932, numerous reprints), and four scholarly reports on Eskimo Administration in Alaska, Canada, Labrador, and Greenland, plus a fifth report providing an analysis and overview of the four government systems (1962 - 1968). The year (1913 - 1914) he spent among the Inupiat of Northern Alaska, appears in *Dawn in Arctic Alaska* (1957, 1985). A year retired on Cyprus resulted in a study of that island economy, as a session at UBC encouraged the editing of his Katzie notes by Wilson Duff and Wayne Suttles.

Nansi Swayze published a brief popular account about Jenness' life in *The Man Hunters* (1960). Barnett Richling has, since 1989, published several scholarly articles on various aspects of Jenness' life, culminating with his *In Twilight and in Dawn: A Biography of Diamond Jenness* in 2012 by McGill-Queen's University Press. He continues to edit and publish Jenness's fieldnotes.

In 1953 Jenness was awarded a Guggenheim Fellowship, in 1962, the Massey Medal by the Royal Canadian Geographical Society, and in 1968 became a Companion of the Order of Canada. Between 1935 and 1968, he was awarded five honorary doctorate degrees (New Zealand, Waterloo, Carlton, Saskatchewan, McGill). In 1973 the Canadian government designated him a Person of National Historic Significance and the Diamond Jenness Secondary School in Hay River was named for him. In 1978 the Canadian Government named the middle peninsula on the west coast of Victoria Island for him, and in 2004 his name was used for a rock examined by the Mars exploration rover Opportunity.

After his field work on the Saanich Peninsula, the east coast of Vancouver Island, and the Fraser Valley in 1934 and 1935, Jenness began writing, completing nine of his sixteen planned chapters. Two volumes were projected. According to Chris Arnett in the Ormsby Review, Barnett Richling edited this Jenness text, adding material gleaned from his field notes, as *The WSANEC and Their Neighbours: Diamond Jenness on the Coast Salish of Vancouver Island, 1935*, carefully observing Jenness's twin penchants for favouring description over analysis and plain language over jargon. Divided into two parts: Part 1 reproduces the first nine chapters of the original manuscript, The Saanich Indians of Vancouver Island, with three final chapters prepared by Richling from the notes Jenness had arranged by subject matter. Part 2 consists of 45 narratives by Coast Salish elders from Saanich, Cowichan, and Katzie communities, including Origin Stories (*sxwi'em*) unknown outside oral traditions. His key sources ~ teachers were Old David at Saanich, Old Cyrus at Chilliwack, and Peter Pierre at Katzie (Richling 2012: 269-71).

Jenness was a traditional and perceptive anthropologist, using descriptive subject headings as well as probing ethno-ethnohistory – such as the nineteenth century Saanich warrior, *Kwalahunzit*, old religion, mythic eras, and cosmology. While a most welcome volume in the field of Coast Salish studies, *The WSANEC and Their Neighbours* also represents something of a lost opportunity because there is no attempt to engage with the descendant community, which is not surprising given that the editor, while an anthropologist, is not a Coast Salish specialist. Richling's purpose was instead to complete the manuscript Jenness left unfinished as a tribute.

He was aided by local academics, especially linguists Timothy Montler, Brent Galloway, and Donna Gerdts, along with tainted Brian Thom.

Richling's unfamiliarity with local sources is notable in the lack of reference to standard WSANEC publications such as Dave Elliott's *Salt Water People* (School District 63, 1990, edited by Janet Poth), or Earl Claxton Sr and John Elliott's *The Saanich Year* (Saanich School Board, 1993), and their *Reef Net Technology of the Salt Water People* (Saanich School Board, 1994). The distant relationship of the editor is also reflected in the absence of local geographical references in the index. Salt Spring Island is mentioned five times in the text but does not appear in the index. Simon Fraser gets a nod but not the Fraser River. Similarly, other landmarks (Point Roberts, Mayne Island, Pender Island, Tsartlip, Koksilah, Sooke, etc) and names – Albert Wesley, Jimmy Fraser, the various guardian spirits, etc. – while mentioned throughout the text, are not indexed. More familiarity or attention with the local cultural and historical context would have enhanced the work. Those familiar with Jenness's original 330 pages of notes will note the absence of historical and site-specific accounts of *stl'eluqum* (dangerous fierce, powerful beings) and famous Indigenous leaders such as *Tzouhalem*.

In 1936, Diamond Jenness visited the Fraser Valley community of Katzie where he interviewed Old Peter Pierre, a medicine man aged approximately 75 years, who shared details of the stories and legends of his people, eventually appearing as *The Faith of a Coast Salish Indian* (1955), edited by Wilson Duff. According to the Katzie First Nation in Pitt Meadows, Peter ("Old") Pierre had been chosen from age three from among generation to train from and carry a variety of traditional responsibilities; by eight, he began his training in the skills of a medicine-person and memory necessary to maintain the oral history of the Katzie people. His education began under the guidance of three elders that his mother hired. By fourteen, Peter Pierre was already a practicing medicine person. Throughout his life, he continued in his vocation, administering to the sick among the Coast Salish tribes, as far away as Cowichan. Peter's son Simon acted as an interpreter for his father in his work. Simon Pierre later served in London as interpreter for a delegation of chiefs eager to resolve land rights issues and he became prominent in efforts to repeal federal laws prohibiting the potlatch. By 1952, Simon Pierre allied with anthropologist Wayne Suttles, echoing the relationship that his father had had with Diamond Jenness, to generate a further written record of Katzie traditions and beliefs. Their collaboration, called *Katzie Ethnographic Notes*, was bound together with *The Faith of a Coast Salish Indian*, and remains in print.

LUSHOOTSEED & NORTHERN STRAITS LANGUAGES

Lushootseed has northern and southern dialect chains. Those of the north, with the larger population and proximity to the Coast Salish heartland on Boundary Bay and the Lower Fraser River, were Skagit (including the Sauk-Suiattle), Swinomish, and the Snohomish (including the Skykomish); while south of Whidbey Island, Whulshootseed dialects were Snoqualmi, Duwamish (including Muckleshoot), Puyallup, Nisqually, Steilacoom, and Sahewamish at the south, together with Suquamish on the west side (Suttles and Lane 1990). Important linguistic distinctions are respective accents on the first or second vowel of the basic root of a word, separate names for salmon species, some body parts, and some artifacts.

Culturally, the pattern number 4 (repetitions done four times) is used in the north but 5 in the south, as well as by Columbia River Chinooks and upriver Plateau tribes. Salishans of the inland, upriver, and southern Sound also held Plateau ideals of a kin-based society, while those of the coast emphasized class. "Southern Puget Sound culture emphasized spirit quests and had a lesser emphasis on inherited privileges than the Northerners" (Roberts 1975: 32, 35, 77).

Socially, the South Sound also stood apart because it had a smaller population, tribes without namesake rivers, less elaborated society, a large-mammal harpooner specialization, earlier European contact overland, more urbanization, and the innovative Indian Shaker Church.

While most Lushootseed "tribes" occupied a single river drainage, whose flow provided cohesion and identity to an otherwise diverse collection of communities and camps, three in the South Sound relied on passages – Duwamish, Sahewamish, and Suquamish.

The Duwamish once had a complex outlet like a letter H through the interconnecting Black River, since obliterated to build downtown Renton. The Sahewamish, merged with Squaxon Islanders, are named for the portage between the southern Sound and Hood Canal. Suquamish ancestral territory was the Kitsap Peninsula between the Sound and upper Hood Canal, without a major river.[124]

While all men hunted, career hunters were men with talents and powers to harpoon sea mammals or undertake the arduous task of hunting mountain goats. In the southern Sound, at least, these special hunters wore clothing and used equipment, such as quivers, made of cougar skin (Smith 1940: 309). Male career specializations included those of canoe maker, hunter, story teller, gambler, and harpooner carpenter, warrior, and ritualist (Smith 1940: 34, 49), while women excelled as midwives, weavers, and basketmakers (Collins 1974: 3).

Historically, Lushootseeds and Whulshootseeds raided each other for slaves. At least one prominent northern family maintained a fortified home in the South Sound at Quartermaster Harbor to take advantage of nearby Fort Nisqually, intermarry with Puyallup women, and raid Duwamish communities to take slaves. No southern colonies are known in the North Sound, though there was intermarriage among noble families in the past couple centuries. That

---

[124] By an irony of history, records at Fort Langley on the Fraser River noted the arrival of Suquamish with salmon in their canoe, which allowed US Federal Judge George Boldt (Finding of Fact #5, Order of 18 April 1975) to decree to their descendants such fishing rights in Canadian waters, though unenforceable. Acknowledging this one instance because it was written down denied all the others known to have occurred without documentation.

Whulsootseed kept NL slaves is illustrated by the life of Dr Simon, born a Snohomish, owned at Minter, and redeemed by William Tolmie at Ft Nisqually.

Native adzed-plank houses, bastions of communal life, were early targets of American authority. In 1871, Reverend Myron Eells, missionary and agent at Skokomish, had Klallam houses on the Port Townsend beach burned in a vain attempt to force a move to his reservation. About 1874, men desiring lands already improved, burned down the plank homes at Minter Creek on the Key Peninsula, and build their own cabins. Hostilities were averted because these landgrabbers deliberately kept away from the aboriginal Glen Cove fishery where this community rebuilt (Harmon 1995: 286).

Euro-American settlers established early hubs in the South Sound, preempting Fort Nisqually and Cowlitz Prairie founded by the Hudson Bay Company in 1833. Americans developed Olympia, which became the state capitol, Steilacoom, and Tacoma, which long delayed the eventually dominance of Seattle. Natives became dependent on manufactured trade goods, purchased by their trapped furs and labor. Logging became a source of funds for many native men, as cooking, housekeeping, and laundry did for native women. Some families soon became favorites of enterprising patrons, such as Ezra Meeker, who employed straw bosses to obtain and retain native workers for his hop fields.

Contrasts (55) of Northern (NL) and Southern (SL) Lushootseed

arm, wing əstabłaxad NL əsʔilaxad SL

bad saʔ NL qələb SL

basket (hard) spəču̓ʔ, yiq̓us NL syalt SL

black x̌ibə̓č NL x̌itu̓c SL

bow ča̓ʔsuč, q̓əčic NL ča̓cus SL

breast stabidgʷas NL sʔilidgʷas SL

canoe (middle) ʔudgʷił NL ʔacgʷił SL

child (any) čačas NL čačaš SL

child (own) bədaʔ NL bədəʔ SL

children stawix̌ʷəʔł, stawigʷəł NL wiw̓su SL

cradleboard skəkiʔi̓ʔł (NL) sx̌altəd (SL) [-iʔł *infant, child*]

dish (wood) qʷət̓ay̓ʔulč NL stə̓k̓ʷabulč SL

hand čaləs NL čaləš SL

hat šiqʷ NL sx̌ʷay̓ʔs SL

head -qid, sx̌əy̓us NL -ač, sx̌ay̓us SL

heart yədwas NL sc̓ali SL

how čal NL x̌id SL

hunt in forest šayil NL łəx̌ʷub SL

lost x̌ʷi̓l NL wix̌ʷ SL

meat biac NL bayac SL

mink bəščəb NL c̓bal̓qid SL

new, fresh x̌aw̓s NL ław̓t SL

nail something c̓is NL c̓əs SL

pick fruit c̓əbəb NL kʷil SL

red x̌ičə̓č NL x̌ik̓ʷiλ SL

rip sik̓ʷ NL x̌ʷət SL

rock č̓λa NL č̓əλəʔ SL

salmon sʔuladxʷ NL sčədadxʷ SL

    humpy hədú̓ʔ NL hə́jdu SL

    dog λx̌ʷay̓ʔ NL λ̓əx̌ʷay̓ʔ SL

    dried x̌ax̌yə̓λ, k̓ayayəʔ NL k̓ʷas SL

    fermented eggs sc̓əq NL duʔayus SL

    king yubə̓č NL sac̓əb SL

    sockeye sc̓uwad, sč̓iʔł, x̌ʷbadiʔ NL scəqiʔ SL

    silver sq̓ə̓čqs NL sac̓əb SL

        steelhead qiẇx̣ NL sk^wawəl̓ SL

see it šudx^w, šuɬ NL šudx^w SL
set nets jiq̓alad^zəd NL ɬiča?alik^w SL
shake d^zak^w NL d^zax^w SL
shell čawəy? NL čuwəy? SL with –ulč ending, a ceramic dish
shine g^wiličəbša NL šay SL
shirt pu?təd NL šx^wpiptx^w SL
six yəla?c NL d^zəlači SL
sleepy ?əx^ws?itutəb NL ?i?tut SL
spear pole čəsay? NL čəšay? SL
stand up kiis NL ɬx̣iɬč SL
star sčusad NL sčušad SL
ten ?uləx^w NL ?ulub SL
that one ti, tsi NL šə, sə SL
this ti?ə, tsi?ə NL ti, tsi ə SL
very cick̓^w NL cay SL
waterfowl bu?q^w NL əsq̓^waləš SL
wife čəg^was NL čəg^waš SL
women sɬəɬadəy? NL sɬadɬadəy? SL
year sd^zəlč̓ NL sd^zəladəb SL

d^zəg^wa? = professional, d^zəg^wə? = monster

x ə NL ə SL
x ə NL ə SL
x ə NL ə SL

Salish

~ SAANICH ~
~ SENĆOŦEN ~

e A   é Á   ə E   i I   ə Í   á O   u U   vowels

ṗ B   k C   č Ć   kʷ Ȼ   t' D   h H   consonants
q̇ K   q̇ʷ Ҡ   q K̲   qʷ K̇   l L   ł Ł
m M   n N   ŋ N̲   p P   k̇ʷ Q   s S
š Ś   t T   tᶿ Ṫ   ƛ̓ T̲   θ Ŧ   w W
xʷ W̲   x X   x̣ X̲   y Y   ,   ʔ   θ

Preferred alphabet all in Caps was developed by Dave Elliott of Tsartlip Reserve, 1970s, though it does not indicate stress, glottal stops, nor glottalized resonants. The full phonology is

p		t		č	kʷ	q	qʷ
ṗ	tᶿ’	t’	ƛ̓	č̌	k̇ʷ	q̇	q̇ʷ	ʔ ’
	θ	s	ł	š	xʷ	x̣	x̣ʷ	h
m		n	l	y	w	ŋ	
m’		n’	l’	y’	w’	ŋ’	

i	ə
e	a

FINALE

Sound and Straits branches of Coast Salish of the central Salish Sea shared many aspects of culture, as well as distinctive emphases. Puget Sound tribes were mostly distinguished by their own rivers, such as the Skagit, while Straights lived along coasts and islands, without major rivers. As a consequence their salmon catching gear are reef nets suspended between canoes in saltwater channels, especially for sockeye runs heading for the Fraser River.

On shore, Straits cultivate clam gardens to increase supplies, while Sounders rely on weirs and nets, adapted to local water conditions. On saltwater, society included more specialists, especially fierce warriors seeking fame and glory, including fortifying strategic locales newly claimed or annexed by them. Expansing to the south by Lekwiltok Kwagiuth with muskets, destabilized the region, increasing hostilities in historic times. Forts became deployed almost a thousand years ago with the spread of bow and arrows.

Usually overlooked are burial mounds along Canadian waters that were built a thousand years ago, presumable to further claim the land settled during the expansion of Coast Salish from the mouths of the Fraser River. Many survive on protected Canadian Forces lands near Victoria, as well as along the Lower Fraser.

Ritual Redeemings held by cooperating shamans characterized the Sound, along with the paired sg^{w}ǝdilich in five types (: 100), with a literal translation only in Lushootseed meaning "bent over to protect" to heal, cleanse, guard, and protect. By contrast, Straits had masks, usually s$\underline{x}$ays$\underline{x}$ay with protruding eyes and identifiable animal ~ bird heads that stick up like nose and ears, and a loop of scallop shells held in the hand as a rattle to punctuate dance steps. These protrusions include raven, owl, sawbill duck, beaver, spring salmon. To the north are Tal masks evoking Basket Ogress ~ D^{z}onok^{w}a, a Wild Woman spirit lurking in woods to steal children, who can escape by singing, which compels her to dance and forget. Special mt sheep horn rattles ~ sx^{y}elmǝx^{w}cǝs "round handheld" of mountain goat wool strands hanging from a golden turnover shape were family privileges, used singly and in multiple pairs, especially to cleanse lead-ins at the start of a naming, initiation, and, in the case of one Catholic priest, his ordination.

Both branches share Winter Spirit Dances by those possessed by guardian spirits, and indeed longhouses on both sides of the border also initiate US and BC residents, generally based on kinship ties if not ancestry to that smokehouse. Hostilities are past, at least intertribally, though some family feuds continue and will do so for decades. BC specialists at conducting and interpreting burnings for the dead have more prestige, especially in Washington State, and often will be hired for significant burnings, especially at the start of the Winter season and before important celebrations, such as Treaty Day.

Most obscure, deliberately so, for both branches is the genesis of named founders at specific places, well known for the matrilineal north, but overlooked for the Salish. Their importance is reflected in the repeating of many aspects from different frameworks or foci. Families pass on the names of these founders through their own leaders, who grow up with and into them. Announced by hosts at feasts, namings, funerals, they assert prestige for ancestors and, thereby, for themselves. Complex aspects of these names and namings have been explored here on both sides of the Salish Sea.

Censuses

Swinomish Robert Fay Coupeville 1857

Names	Age	Height	Description	No Wives	No Childs	Slaves	Wards	
Goliah	55	6 ft	Slim	1	1		16	
Sqay-quy	40	6	SubChief	4	7		5	
Charley	40	5-10%	SubChief	1			6	
Sto-dum-kaw	35	5-11		1	3			
Gen Kanen	31	5-9	SubChief	3	1	1	2	
Jack Hays	30	5-10		2	1	1	2	
Sqoo-li-koos-balt	45	5-9	SubChief	1	2			
Zake-de-dupe	50	6	SubChief	2				
Te-qua-be-hah	25	5-11		2	1		2	
Sque-wha-ude	35	5-9		1	1		1	
Stoduck	30	5-10		1			2	
Shoo-zal-at ka	40	5-10		1	3			
Tahk-Tal	60	5-8						
Su wah	35	5-8		1	4			
Ze-wha-lad-e	35	5-8		1	3			
Sa-watch-nas	30	5-8		1	2			
Docton	60	5-7		1	5			
See-uck	50	5-8		1	1		1	
Re Reton	21	5-8		1	1		1	
Lul-say-we	35	5-10			2			
Suh-hoo	23	5-11		1	3	1		
Shoo-lats-um	55	5-8		1	3	`		
Zla-uch	55	5-99						
Hads-ulk-tan	50	5-10			1		1	
Ipa-tit-soo	50	5-8		1	2			
Sdadze-alth	35	6-0		1	3			
Ko-ko-wal-ous	40	5-8		1				
Cla-ute	40	5-9		1	3			
Chut-Sale-a-bin	30	5-9		1			2	
Ei hi use	20	6-0		1	1			
E Whatte	35	5-8		1	4			
Sa-wha-use	19	5-7		1				
Ho-ka-lad-u	21	5-8		1	1			
Hud-Sa-canim	28	5-6						
Long John	38	6-		1				
totals	35			38	63	3	41	[2]
Zadts cum	22	5-7			1			
Pah-dah	18	5-6						
Hob-Say	21	5-10		2				

Hu-choh-hulton	38	5-6		1	4		
Tech-i-canum	20	5-8		1			
U-sta-ule	25	5-10		1	3		
Huch-quim-ton	40	5-7		2	2		
David	19	5-9		1		2	1
Zah-huse	30	5-9		1	1		
Geo Washington	32	5-6	SubChief	5	8		7
Ta-de-qul-ton	38	5-8		2	1		4
Bu quate-sah	50	5-10		1			
Samson	25	5-10		1			
Sal a ta use	18	5 6					
Qua Sum-kin	30	5-8		1	3		
So-o-nalth	17	5-6	Slim				
Sikes	20	5-10	Stout	1			
Patch a-canum	40	6-0		1	3		2
Chad nah	16	5-5	Slim				
Bets canum	23	5-7		1			
So-duck	16	5-1					
Shoo dah daous	18	5-5		1			
Gen Cap	24	5-6		1			1
Mis lah	25	5-7	Sick	1	1		
Ohe-coo-yah	17	5-4					
John Fay	23	5-5		1	1		1
Dab-it-Soo	20	5-6					
Cad-da	16	5-4					
Sda use	16	5 5	Slim				
Peter	20	5-7	Stout	1			
Ohd?-u-Shal	19	5-6		1			
Gov Stevens	30	5-7		2	5	1	2
S-dah-taloh	30	5-7		3			
Zads-sto-kum	30	5-9		1	1		
Soo goot-zah-kan	21	5-8			1		
totals	35			35	34	3	19 [3]
Ki quat soo	25	5-7		1			
Hoy yo	19	5-9					
Whey-ki use	22	5-8			1		
Se-i-a-qualth	18	5-5		1			
Ba-quats-at-ka	45	6-0		1			
Poo-pette	50	5-6		1	2		
Clah-ats ka	32	5-10		1	2		
Key-Sa-use	35	5-9		1	3		
Dook-Shame	40	5-11		1			
Pund shay	35	5-4		1			
	10			8	8		

	Age	Hgt		Wives	Children	Wards	Slaves
Swaut-het ute	50	5-5	Hair little guy	1	6		
Keds-ta-use	40	5-6		3			2
Ulth-Canum	35	5-2		1	1		1
Cub-by	25	5-7		2	3		1
Che-hay-calthle	30	5-7		1	2		1
Ste-Wah-hah	30	5-5		2	1		1
Gen Pierce	35	5-5	SubChief	1	7	3	2
Gen Scott	25	5-5	SubChief	4	2	1	3
Teb-a-hoot-soo	22	5-4		1	2		
Do-ho-bate-soot	60	5-0		1	3		4
To-kutch	28	5-4		4	2		
Swee-ta-uso	16	5-0					
Sliets-coe	25	5-6		1	3		
Ya-sa-hak	18	5-0	film on eyes				

Capt RC Fay IIA
Reports the death of Goliah Head Chief of the Scagits: the talks had with him & the wish expressed by Goliah that <u>Squi-Squi</u> should succeed him.

National Archives, Letters Received (Penn Cove) Fay to Superintendent Isaac Stevens + date 4 March 1857 M5 reel 10

* Biographies of Robert Colburn Fay (1820-1872) and Nathaniel Davis Hill (1824-1921) are in Pacific Plateau Portrayals ~ People, Places, Ponderings by Jay Miller (2017: 21, 22-26).

Snoqualmie columns on next page are age, hgt = height, wives, children = kids, wards ~ slaves, male = M, female = F

Census held in Hill Family papers box {MSS 12}, Jefferson County Historical Society, Port Townsend, WA

Snoqualmie

~ Snoqualmie 20 April 1856 Census ~
Nathaniel Hill Holmes Harbor

	Name	age	hgt	wives	kids	M	F		Remarks
1	Pat Kanam	38	5-4	4	6	2	2		Head Chief
2	SiHowie~Jim Kanam	32	5-7	3	1	1			brother to Pat paper
3	John Kanam	28	5-3	2	1				brother to Pat paper
4	Cush cush am	45	5-6	3	1	1	2		Second Chief
5	Hutty-a-Kanam	48	5-6	2	7		3	2	Sub Chief
6	Klemish-Kanam	34	5-9	3	5				Sub Chief
7	Yel-a-koose	18	5-7	0	0				son {inserted into list}
8	Nuque-a-Salt	26	5-7	1	1		3		Sub Chief "John"
9	Sah dah wah	43	5-8	2	6	1	2		Sub Chief
10	Wha ack	42	5-6	3	5				Sub Chief
11	Zul qua Kanum	26	5-8	1	1				Sub Chief "John"
12	Tah none a muck	38	5-6	2	2				Sub Chief, taken prisoner by Pat Kanam
13	William	18	5-3	0	0				son or ward Cush cush am, "Yay-a-let"
14	William	16	5-3	0	0				son of Hutty-a-Kanam
15	"Tom"	17	5-5	0	0				ward of Sah-da-wah *
16	"John"	18	5-4	0	0				son of Sah-da-wah *
17	Ayetsaka	33	5-5	1	1				Sub Chief, "Samuel"
18	Tow-ε-Pass	44	5-5	1	3				
19	Qua-lash-con	25	5-8	1	0				son in law Hutty-a-Kanam
20	Ash-hah-na-pow	44	5-5	1	2				taken prisoner by Pat – now ran off
21	O-hal-a-eck			1	4				taken prisoner by Pat – now ran off
22	Squi-que	45		1	0				taken prisoner by Pat – sent to see Owhi
23	Shmal-lo-wee	60		0	0	2			taken prisoner by Pat – sent to see Owhi
24	Kilose ~ "Tom"	24	5-5	1	0	0	0	0	I believe half slave to Pat
25	Quee lege	25	5-8	2	3	2			
26	Dui a oo Ko	19	5-4	1	1	1			"Charlie"
27	Cush sit	50	5-5	2	1				
28	Wah-wahs-at	25	5-7	1	1				son in law to Senocton
29	Sεnecton	46	5-6	0	2				
30	Cau sulk	16	5-3	0	0				son of Senocton
31	Swoot-Kanum	50	5-9	1	0		1		children all grown, Doctor or Tamanowas man
32	Sto-dock	24	5-7	1	0				half slave {word means 'slave'}
33	Tzalk-la-yuw p1/2	26	5-6	1	0				~~son of above doctor~~ half slave
34	Stick Kanem	45	5-9	1	0				relative of " "
35	Way tr cone	28	5-6	1	3	2	2		
36	She col ton	26							

#	Name	Age						Notes
37	Yep-pau-saa	28	5-8	1	2	2		
38	Mucklee	26	5-7	1	1			"John"
39	Twow-hock-sha	56	5-8	0	4			
40	Asi-how-et			2	2			son of above
41	Swud-shka	18	5-5	0	0			son of above
42	Sonuck-lu-ya	26	5-8	1	2			
43	Tosh-kate	44	5-8	1	2			
44	Swee-Rau	60	5-8	1	1			
45	Sill-a-qua	26	5-7	0	0			
46	Col-ta-gut	28	5-6	1	1	1	2	
47	Ka-pap-pa	18	5-6	0	0			"Charley"
48	Ass-how-oose	36	5-8	2	1		1 2	
49	Sos-hoi	18	5-5	0	0			Son of above
50	Whod-skate	18	5-4	0	0			all same as son
51	Ho-a-bill	22	5-4	1	2			
52	Sa-ba-hult	32	5-5	1	4			
53	Be-ya-Kanem	28	5-5	1	3			
54	La-ho-bit			1	2			"John" dead killed by Collins
55	Sa-whul-at	50		1	5			
56	Take-let	26	5-6	1	0			"George" used to live at Seattle
57	Zqua-but	24	5-4	1	0			"Tommy" used to live at Seattle
58	Tha-quilsh	35	5-8	1	3	1	1	dead killed by Collins
59	O-Ooh	22	5-6	0	0			"Dick" dead killed by Collins
60	Tgat-lop	56	5-5	0				
61	La ha buitch	30	5-6	1	1			son of Zat lop {~Tgat-lop}
62	Quait-la-huk	50	5-5	1	0			{shift to thin ink}
63	Sta-ba-luke	22	5-6	1	1			son of Cush cush am
64	So-ooke	24	5-9	1	1			relative of Cush cush am
65	Ska-op-ka	28	5-9	1	2	1		
66	Za-za-kuse	24	5-6	1	0			
67	Statch-lut	41	5-5	2	9			
68	Ya-ack-quilt	28	5-6	1	1			
69	Wah-chios	24	5-10	0	0			
70	Yo-ɛt-tun	50	5-5	1				
71	Why a Kanum	28	5-5	1	1			
72	Milleck-Kanum	50	5-6	1	0			
73	Hote lum cult	28	5-8	1	0			
74	Ka dah	33	5-6	1	11	2		"No Face"
75	Tug as Kanum	35	5-8	2	7			"sick"
76	Ky zon some	44	5-8	1	1	2		
77	Tzu zat lum cult	52	5-9					
78	Slock-kate	48	5-7	1	3			
79	Sde wah hud	18	5-5	0	0			
80	Whul-te-lat	25	5-6	2	1			

p2/3

#	Name	Age					Notes
81	Stah te qualt	40	5-7	1	2	1	
82	Clud Kanum	36	5-7	1	3	1	
83	Ya-ha-bult	54	5-8	0	0		
84	Elsh kate	34	5-7	0	1		
85	Elos Kanum	32	5-5	1	2		
86	Tgud-ɛ-w-kte	28	5-5	2	2		
87	Quot-cum	28	5-6	0	0		
88	Zat-lum-kin	33	5-5	1	3		"Chu Charco"
89	Qua-luck-bit	22	5-8	1	0		
90	Qui-ole-gult	40	5-9	1	4		
91	Ass-how-ɛɛs	33	5-6	1	2	4	
92	Ka showl gult	26	5-6	0			
93	Kae a ka zuse	16	5-4	0			
94	Ho-qua-salt	40	5-6	1	0	5	
95	Say-zuse	36	5-8	1	2		
96	Ya-huck		42	5-7	1	3	
97	Hus-sate	38	5-9	1	2		Left arm broken by a bear
98	Sla-hote	32	5-6	1	0		
99	Skla-use	33	5-9	3	2		"Daniel"
100	Klat-soot	28	5-8	1	2		
101	Pap-pa-shu	18	5-6	0	0	1	"Charley"
102	W-sunk	44	5-6	1	3		
103	Who-lat-at	26	5-8	1	1		
104	Stad da holt	26	5-8	1	3		
105	Ah-whel-use	17	5-5	0	0	3	
106	Tzop-Kanum	40	5-6	1	5		
107	La-ha-zuse	38	5-8	2	3	2	
108	Ad-ha-em	45	5-7	1	4		
109	Gu-si-zuse	25	5-10	0	0		"John"
110	Say-use-kum	33	5-7	1	1		"John"

p3/4

#	Name	Age					Notes
111	Squal-at-come	38	5-9	1	2		
112	Dɛ-da-da- use	18	5-6	0			son of the above
113	Hkah-be-a-cult	46	5-8	1	3		
114	Stick a may zuse	24		5-6	1	1	
115	Yo whay zuse	44	5-8	3	6		
116	La-wa-hut	24	5-6	1	1		
117	Chi-ya-use	30	5-8	1	1		
118	Ka-ba-oose	16	5-4	0	0		
119	Ny-es-Kanum	48	5-8	1	0		

Salishan Toponymy

Afable, Patricia, and Madison Beeler
 1996 Place Names. DC: Handbook of North American Indians, *Languages* 17: 185-199.

Bates, Dawn, Thom Hess, and Vi Hilbert
 1994 *Lushootseed Dictionary*. Seattle: University of Washington Press.

Bright, William
 2004 *Native American Placenames of the United States*. Norman: University of Oklahoma
    Press. 600pp.

Brooks, Pamela
 1997   John Peabody Harrington's Klallam and Chemakum Place Names.   Port Angeles:
    International Conference on Salish and Neighboring Languages 32: 144-188.

Bruseth, Nels
 1950 Indian Stories and Legends of the Stillaguamish, Sauks and Allied Tribes. Arlington
    (WA) Times Press. [1928]

Carlson, Keith Thor, ed.
 2001 *A Sto:lo Coast Salish Historical Atlas*. Halqemeylem Place Names in Sto:lō Territory by
    Sonny McHalsie: 134-153. Vancouver: Douglas & McIntyre, UW, Sto:lō Heritage Trust.

Castile, George, ed.
 1985 *The Indians of Puget Sound*. The Notebooks of Myron Eells. Walla Walla: University
    of Washington Press for Whitman College.

Collins, June
 1974 *Valley of the Spirits* ~ The Upper Skagit Indians of Western Washington.   Seattle:
    University of Washington Press.

Dailey, Tom
 2000 http://coastsalishmap.org

Eells, Myron
 1892 Aboriginal Geographic Names in the State of Washington. *American Anthropologist* V:
    27-35. [dreadful!]

Elliot, John

2005 Wsanec Place Name Map: 130-131 by Chris Paul. *Islands in the Salish Sea ~ A Community Atlas.* Sheila Harrington & Judi Stevenson, eds. Victoria: Touchwood Editions.

Elmendorf, William
1992 *The Structure of Twana Culture.* Geographical Sites: 29-55. Pullman: WSU Press. [1960]

Galloway, Brent, and Alan Richardson
1983 Nooksack Place Names: An Ethnohistorical and Linguistic Approach. Seattle: Working Papers of the International Conference on Salishan and Neighboring Languages 18: 133-196.

Gibbs, George
1853 Indian Nomenclature of Localities in Washington and Oregon Territories [West of the Cascades]. 14pp. ms # 714. [SI 248] DC: National Anthropological Archives.

Harrington, John Peabody
1981 The Papers of John Peabody Harrington in the Smithsonian Institution, 1907-1957. Elaine Mills, ed. 30 reels. Millwood, NY: Krause International Publications.

Hess, Thom
1976 *Dictionary of Puget Salish.* Seattle: University of Washington Press.

Hilbert, Vi, Jay Miller, and Zalmai Zahir
2001 *Puget Sound Geography* ~ sdaʔdaʔ gʷəl dibəl ləšucid ʔacaciltalbixʷ. A Draft Study of the Thomas Talbot Waterman Place Name Manuscript and Other Sources, Edited with Additional Material. Seattle: Lushootseed Press.

Hitchman, Robert
1985 *Place Names of Washington.* Tacoma: Washington State Historical Society.

Howell, Philip Hugh
1948 *Dictionary of Indian Geographical Names.* The Origin and Meaning of Indian Names. Everett: American Indian Historical Society.

Hunn, Eugene
1990 *Nch'i-Wana* "The Big River": Mid-Columbia Indians and Their Land. Seattle: University of Washington Press.
1994 Place-Names, Population Density, and the Magic Number 500. *Current Anthropology* 35: 81-85.
1996 Columbia Plateau Indian Place Names: What Can They Teach Us? *Journal of Linguistic Anthropology* 6 (1): 3-26.

Kennedy, Dorothy, and Randy Bouchard
  1983   Some Homalco Place Names 149, Some Klahoose Place Names 155, Some Sliamon
      Place Names 161, Some Island Comox Place Names 167 *Sliamon Life, Sliamon Lands*.
      Vancouver, BC: Talon Books.

Kinkade, Dale
  1991   *Upper Chehalis Dictionary*. University of Montana, Occasional Papers in Linguistics 7,
      Appendix A: 329-335.
  1997   Cowlitz (Salish) Place Names. Port Angeles: International Conference on Salish and
      Neighboring Languages 32: 249-264.
  2004 *Cowlitz Dictionary and Grammatical Sketch*. University of Montana, Occasional Papers
      in Linguistics 18, Appendix B: 327-335.
Kuipers, Aert H
  2002   *Salish Etymological Dictionary*.   University of Montana, Occasional Papers in
      Linguistics 16.

Lane, Robert, and Barbara Lane
  1977   Indians and Fisheries of the Skagit River System. Mid-Project Report. Skagit Salmon
      Study.

Lushootseed Press
  2001   *Puget Sound Geography* ~ sdaʔdaʔ gʷəɬ dibəɬ ləšučid ʔačačiɬtalbixʷ. Revising and
      Expanding the manuscript by TT Waterman. Vi Hilbert, Jay Miller, Zalmai Zahir, eds.
      Seattle: Lushootseed Research.

McArthur, Lewis
  1965 *Oregon Geographic Names*. Portland: Binford & Mort for Oregon Historical Society.

Montler, Timothy
  1991   Place Names: 85-91 #1763-1972. Saanich, North Strait Salish Classified Word List.
      Hull: Canadian Ethnlogy Service Paper #119 Mercury Series.

Nelson, Richard
  1994   The Embrace of Names: 14-21. *Northern Lights* ~ A Selection of New Writing from the
      American West. Deborah Clow & Donald Snow. Eds. Vintage Books, New York.

Onat, Astrida Blukis, and Jan Hollenbeck, eds.
  1981   Inventory of Native American Religious Use, Practices, Localities, and Resources. Study
      Area on the Mt. Baker - Snoqualmie National Forest, Washington State. Seattle: Institute
      of Cooperative Research.

Peter, Susie Sampson
  1995 x̌əčusədaʔ ʔə gʷəqʷulča ~ *The Wisdom of a Skagit Elder.* Transcribed by Vi Hilbert,
      Translated by Vi Hilbert and Jay Miller, Recorded by Leon Metcalf. Seattle: Lushootseed
      Press.

Powell, Jay V, William Penn, and Others
  1972 Place Names of the Quileute Indians. *Pacific Northwest Quarterly* 63 (3): 105-112.

Powell, Jay V, and Vickie Jensen
  1976 Quileute Place Names: 61-67. *Quileute* ~ An Introduction to the Indians of La Push.
      Seattle: University of Washington Press.

Reese, Gary Fuller
  1989 *Origins of Pierce County Place Names.* Tacoma R&M Press.

Richling, Barnett, ed.
  2016 Appendix D: Place Names: 181-183. The W̲SANEC and their Neighbors ~ Diamond
      Jenness on the Coast Salish on Vancouver Island, 1935. Oakville, ON: Rocks' Mills Press.

Rinker, Ann, and Maria Parker Pascua
  1989 Makah Place Names [updating TT Waterman: 1-12]. Olympia: Department of
      Community Development, Traditional Cultural Property Study.

Rozen, D.
  1985 Place Names of the Island Halkomelem Indian People. University of British Columbia,
      Sociology and Anthropology, MA Thesis.

Rundell, Hugh A
  1960 *Washington Names* ~ A Pronunciation Guide of Washington State Place Names.
      Pullman, Washington: KWSC at Washington State University.

Sampson, Martin
  1938 *The Swinomish Totem Pole, Tribal Legends.* Told to Rosalie Whitney. Bellingham,
      Washington: Union Printing Company.
  1972 *Indians of Skagit County.* Mount Vernon, Washington: Skagit County Historical
      Society, Series 2.

Seaburg, William
  1972 A Study of Selected Place Names of the Lummi Indians. Honolulu: University of
      Hawaii, Department of Linguistics, *Working Papers in Linguistics* 4 (3): 57-81.

Snyder, Sally
  50s Fieldnotes, place names, maps. Melville Jacobs Collection, UW SC.

Snyder, Warren
  1968 *Southern Puget Sound Salish*: Texts, Place Names, and Dictionary. Sacramento Anthropological Society Papers 8: 130-136.

Stewart , George
  1982 *Names on the Land.* A Historical Account of Placenaming in the United States. SF: Lexikos. [1945]

Suttles, Wayne
  2004 *Musqueam Reference Grammar.* Appendix 2, Names of Places and Peoples: 566-576. UBC Press.

Teit, James
  1908 Distribution of Tribes in Western Washington. Philadelphia: Boas Collection S 2a.2, American Philosophical Society.

Tweddell, Colin
  1950 The Snoqualmie-Duwamish Dialects of Puget Sound Salish. *University of Washington Publications in Anthropology* 12.
  1953 A Historical and Ethnological Study of the Snohomish Indian People. Docket 125, Indian Claims Commission. David Agee Horr, ed., *Coast Salish And Western Washington Indians v. Indian Claims Commission*, Findings. New York: Garland Publishing, Inc., 1974: 475-694.

Walbran, John
  1971 *British Columbia Coast Names, 1592-1906.* Vancouver: Douglas & McIntye. [1906]

Waterman, Thomas
  1922 The Geographical Names Used by the Indians of the Pacific Coast. *The Geographical Review* 12 (2): 175-194.

Wray, Jacilee, ed.
  2002 *Native Peoples of the Olympic Peninsula, Who We Are.* Norman: U of Oklahoma Press.

BIBLIOGRAPHY

Amoss, Pamela
 1978 *Coast Salish Spirit Dancing* ~ The Survival of an Ancestral Religion. Seattle: University of Washington Press.
 1982 Resurrection, Healing, and "the Shake": The Story of John and Mary Slocum. Journal of the American Academy of Religion, Thematic Studies XLVIII (3/4): 87-109.
 1990 The Indian Shaker Church. Handbook of North American Indians, *Northwest Coast*, Volume 7: 633-639.

Adams, John
 1973 *The Gitksan Potlatch*: Population Flux, Resource Ownership, and Reciprocity. Toronto: Holt, Rinehart and Winston of Canada.

Ballard, Arthur
 1927 Some Tales of the Southern Puget Sound Salish. University of Washington Publications in Anthropology 2 (3): 57-81.
 1929 Mythology of Southern Puget Sound. University of Washington Publications in Anthropology 6 (1): 31-150.

Barnett, Homer
 1955 *The Coast Salish of British Columbia*. Eugene: University of Oregon Press.
 1957 *Indian Shakers* ~ A Messianic Cult of the Pacific Northwest. Carbondale: Southern Illinois University Press.

Bates, Dawn, Thom Hess, and Vi Hilbert
 1994 *Lushootseed Dictionary*. Seattle: University of Washington Press.

Bean, Lowell and Thomas Blackburn
 1976 *Native Californians*: A Theoretical Perspective. Ramona, California: Ballena Press.

Bishop, Thomas.
 1916 Applications For Enrollment and Allotment, 1911-17. Records Relating to Enrollment of Washington Indians. Special Agent Charles E. Roblin. National Archives.

Boas, Franz
 1890 Sixth report of the committee on the northwest tribes of Canada, BAAS ~ British Association for the Advancement of Science.
 1891 Report of the 60th Meeting of the British Association for the Advancement of Science, London.
 1916 *Tsimshian Mythology*. Bureau of American Ethnology, Annual Report 31: 29-1037.

 1966 *Kwakiutl Ethnography*. Helen Codere, ed. University of Chicago Press.

Carlson, Barry, and Thom Hess.
  1971 Canoe Names in the Northwest, Areal Study. Anthropological Linguistics 12 (1): 17-24.

Collins, June
  1949 John Fornsby: The Personal Document of a Coast Salish Indian. Smith 1949: 287-341.
  1950a Growth of Class Distinctions and Political Authority among the Skagit Indians during the Contact Period. *American Anthropologist* 52 (3): 331-342.
  1950b The Indian Shaker Church. *Southwestern Journal of Anthropology* 6: 399-411.
  1952a An Interpretation of Skagit Intragroup Conflict during Acculturation. *American Anthropologist* 54: 347-355.
  1952b The Mythological Basis for Attitudes toward Animals among Salish-Speaking Indians. *Journal of American Folklore* 65 (258): 353-359.
  1966 Naming, Continuity, and Social Inheritance among the Coast Salish of Western Washington. *Papers of the Michigan Academy of Science, Arts, and Letters* 51: 425-36.
  1974 *Valley of the Spirits* ~ The Upper Skagit Indians of Western Washington. Seattle: University of Washington Press.
  1979 Multilineal Descent: A Coast Salish Strategy. *Currents in Anthropology*: 243-254. Robert Hinshaw, ed. The Hague: Mouton.

Cook, James
  1795 *A Voyage to the Pacific Ocean*, II, London, 2nd.

Corliss, Margaret M
  1972 The Snoqualmie Indians. *Fall City in the Valley of the Moon*: Chapter 12: 146-163. np.

Culin, Stewart
  1901 A Summer Trip Among The Western Indians (The Wanamaker Expdition). Bulletin of the Free Museum of Science and Art of the University of Pennsylvania. Chapter IV III (1): 143-164. January.

de Laguna, Frederica
  1972 *Under Mount Saint Elias*: The History and Culture of the Yakutat Tlingit. Washington: Smithsonian Institution Press. Three Volumes.

Dawson, George M
  1880 Report on the Queen Charlotte Islands, Geological Survey of Canada, Report of Progress, 1878-9, part B, Montreal.

Duff, Wilson
  1952 The Upper Stalo Indians of the Fraser River of British Columbia. Victoria: British Columbia Provincial Museum, *Anthropology in British Columbia*, Memoir # 1.

Dorsey, George
  1898 Accession 660: Salish of Puget Sound and Lake Washington. Chicago: Field Museum #55848 - 55960.
  1902 The Duwamish Spirit-Canoe and Its Use. Bulletin Free Museum of Science and Art, University of Pennsylvania 3 (4): 227-238.

Drucker, Philip
  1937 Diffusion in Northwest Coast Culture in the Light of Some Distributions. Ph.D. Dissertation, University of California at Berkeley: 1-156.

Dunn, John
  1976 Tsimshian Internal Relations Reconsidered: Southern Tsimshian. The Victoria Conference on Northwestern Languages: 62-82. British Columbia Provincial Museum.
  1978 *A Practical Dictionary of the Coast Tsimshian Language.* National Museum of Man, Mercury Series, Canadian Ethnology Service Paper 42: 1-145.
  1979 Inter-Ethnic Generation Skewing: Tsimshian, Tlingit, Haida. International Congress of Americanists, Vancouver, British Columbia.

Elmendorf, William, and Alfred Kroeber
  1960. *The Structure of Twana Culture* ~ With Comparative Notes of the Structure of Yurok Culture. Pullman: Washington State University Research Studies, Monographic Suppliment 2: 1-576.

Elmendorf, William
  1993 *Twana Narratives* ~ Native Historical Accounts of a Coast Salish People. Seattle: University of Washington Press.

Fogelson, Raymond, and Richard Adams
  1977 *The Anthropology of Power*: Ethnographic Studies from Asia, Oceania, and the New World. New York: Academic Press.

Frachtenberg, Leo
  1920 Eschatology of the Quileute Indians. *American Anthropology* 22: 330-340.
  1921 The Ceremonial Societies of the Quileute Indians. *American Anthropologist* 23: 320-352.

Garfield, Viola.
  1939 *Tsimshian Clan and Society.* University of Washington Publications in Anthropology 7 (3): 167-340.

Gibbs, George
  1877 Tribes of Western Washington and Northwestern Oregon. Washington, DC: Department of the Interior, United States Geographical and Geological Survey of the Rocky Mountain Region, Part II: 157-241.

1970 Dictionary of the Niskwalli (Nisqually) Indian Language – Western Washington. Extract from 1877 Contributions to North American Ethnology 1: 285-361. Seattle: The Shorey Book Store Facsimile Reproduction.

Gunther, Erna
1927 Klallam Ethnography. *University of Washington Publications in Anthropology* #1 (5).

Haeberlin, Hermann, and Erna Gunther
1930 The Indians of Puget Sound. *University of Washington Publications in Anthropology* #4 (1): 1-84.

Haeberlin, Hermann
1917 Puget Salish, 42 Notebooks. National Anthropological Archives #2965. 1337pp.
1918 SbEtEtda'q, A Shamanic Performance of the Coast Salish. American Anthropologist 20 (3): 249-257.
1924 Mythology of Puget Sound. Journal of American Folklore 37 (143-144): 371-438.

Hess, Thom
1976 *Dictionary of Puget Salish.* Seattle: University of Washington Press.
1977 Lushootseed Dialects. *Anthropological Linguistics* 19 (9): 403-419.

Hilbert, Vi, and Jay Miller
2004 That Salish Feeling… *Studies In Salish Linguistics in Honor of M Dale Kinkade.* Donna B Gerdts and Lisa Matthewson, eds. University of Montana, Occasional Papers in Linguistics #17: 197-210.

Hill-Tout, Charles Charles
1978 *The Salish People.* Ralph Maud, ed. I Thompson & Okanagan II Squamish (1897, 1900) & Lillooet III Mainland Halkomelem IV Sechelt & SE Vancouver Island. Vancouver, BC: Talon Books.

Hilton, Susanne and John Rath
1982 Objections to Franz Boas' Refering to Eating People in the Translation of the Kwakwala Terms of Baxubakwalanuxusiwe and Hamats!a: 98-106. Working Papers of the 17th International Conference on Salish and Neighboring Languages. Portland State University 9-11 May.

Hodge, Frederick
1907 *Handbook of American Indians North of Mexico.* Bureau of American Ethnology, Bulletin 30, Parts 1 and 2.

Holm, Bill and Bill Reid
1975 *Indian Art of the Northwest Coast* ~ A Dialogue on Craftsmanship and Aesthetics. Seattle: University of Washington Press.

Howay, FW
  1918 The Dog Hair Blankets of the Coast Salish. *Washington Historical Quarterly* 9 (3): 83-92.

Jenness, Diamond
  1955 The Faith of a Coast Salish Indian. Victoria: British Columbia Provincial Museum, *Anthropology in British Columbia* Memoir # 3.
  2016 The W̲SANEC and their Neighbors ~ Diamond Jenness on the Coast Salish on Vancouver Island, 1935. Barnett Richling, ed. Rocks' Mills Press, Oakville, ON.

Jewett, John R
  1924 The Adventures and Sufferings of John R Jewett. Edinburgh.

Jorgensen, Joseph
  1969 *Salish Language and Culture:* A Statistical Analysis of Internal Relationships, History, and Evolution. Bloomington: Indiana University Publications, Language Science Monographs 3.

Kane, Paul
  ?? Painting of the interior of a Songish house at Victoria, National Museum of Canada.

Keddie, Grant
  2003 *Songhees Pictorial*: A History of the Songhees People as Seen by Outsiders, 1790-1912, Royal BC Museum, Victoria, BC.

Kennedy, Dorothy, and Randy Bouchard
  1983 *Sliamon Life, Sliamon Lands*. Vancouver, BC: Talon Books.

Kinkade, Dale
  1983 Salish Evidence Against the Universality of 'Noun' And 'Verb'. Lingua 60: 25-60.
  1985 Letter of 19 July on Chehalis Terms.

Kissell, Mary Lois
  1916 A New Type of Spinning in North America. *American Anthropologist* 18: 204-270.
  1929 Organized Salish Blanket Pattern. *American Anthropologist* 31: 85-88.

Lane, Barbara
  1973 Political and Economic Aspects of Indian-White Culture Contact in Western Washington in the Mid-19th Century. May 10. United States v. Washington.

Levi-Strauss, Claude
  1982 *The Way of the Masks.* Sylvia Modelski, translator. Seattle: University of Washington Press.

McClellan, Catherine
  1975 *My Old People Say* ~ An Ethnographic Survey of Southern Yukon Territory. National Museums of Canada, Publications in Ethnology 6 (1, 2): 1-637.

Maclachlan, Morag, ed.
  1998 *The Fort Langley Journals, 1827-30.* Vancouver: University of British Columbia Press.

McIlwraith, Thomas
  1948 *The Bella Coola Indians.* Toronto: University of Toronto Press. 2 Volumes.

Menzies, Charles
  1923 Journal of Vancouver's Voyages, edited by CF Newcombe, Archives of BC, Memoir #V, Victoria BC.

Miller, Jay
  1976 The Northwest Coast Of What? Final Address at Conference on Northwest Coast Studies. Simon Fraser University and Canadian National Museum of Man, 12-16 May.
  1979a A Strucon Model of Delaware Culture and the Positioning of Mediators. *American Ethnologist* 6 (4): 791-802.
  1979b "Rock Art on the Amero-Canadian Plateau. Paper Read at New Directions in Native American Art History. October 24-26. Albuquerque, New Mexico.
  1980 High-Minded High Gods in North America. *Anthropos* 75: 916-919.
  1981 The Matter of the (Thoughtful) Heart: Centrality, Focality, or Overlap. *Journal of Anthropological Research* 36 (3): 338-342.
  1983 Numic Religion: An Overview of Power in the Great Basin of Native North America. *Anthropos* 78: 337-354.
  1997a Back to Basics ~ Chiefdoms in Puget Sound. *Ethnohistory* 44 (2): 375-387.
  1997b *Tsimshian Culture* ~ A Light Through the Ages. Lincoln: University of Nebraska Press.
  1998 Tsimshian Ethno-Ethnohistory: A "Real" Indigenous Chronology. *Ethnohistory* 45 (4): 657-674.
  1999 *Lushootseed Culture and the Shamanic Odyssey* ~ An Anchored Radiance. Lincoln: University of Nebraska Press.
  2000 Inflamed History: Violence Against Homesteading Indians in Washington Territory. *North Dakota Quarterly*, American Indian Issue, Summer/Fall, 67 (3/4): 162-173.
  2005 Dibble Cultivating Prairies to Beaches: The Real All Terrain Vehicle. *Journal of Anthropological Research.*

Miller, Jay, and Vi Hilbert
  1993 Caring for Control: A Pivot of Salishan Language and Culture. *American Indian Linguistics and Ethnography in Honor of Laurence C Thompson.* University of Montana, Occasional Papers in Linguistics 10: 237-239.

1996 Lushootseed Animal People: Mediation and Transformation from Myth to History. *Monsters, Tricksters, and Sacred Cows* ~ Animal Tales and American Identities: 138-156. A James Arnold, ed. New World Studies. Charlottesville: University of Virginia Press.

National Museum of Canada
 ?? Bulletin 65.

Ortiz, Alfonso
 1969 *The Tewa World* ~ Space, Time, Being, and Becoming in a Pueblo Society. University of Chicago Press.

Powell, JV, and Fred Woodruff
 1976 *Quileute Dictionary.* Northwest Anthropological Research Notes, Memoir 3.

Richling, Barnett
 2012 *In Twilight and in Dawn* ~ A Biography of Diamond Jenness, McGill-Queens University Press, Montreal.

Richling, Barnett, ed.
 2016 The W̲SANEC and their Neighbors ~ Diamond Jenness on the Coast Salish on Vancouver Island, 1935. Rocks' Mills Press, Oakville, ON.

Roberts, Natalie
 1975 A History of the Swinomish Tribal Community. University of Washington: Anthropology PhD Dissertation.

Roberts, Helen and Hermann Haeberlin
 1918 Some Songs of the Puget Sound Salish. *Journal of American Folklore* 31 (122): 496-520.

Roblin, Charles
 1919 January 31 Letter To Commissioner of Indian Affairs Summarizing Roll of Landless Indians of Western Washington State.

Sampson, Martin.
 1972 Indians of Skagit County. Mount Vernon, Washington: Skagit County Historical Society, Series 2.

Smith, Marian
 ms   Original Fieldnotes, MSS #2794, Royal Anthropological Archives, Microfilm, British Columbia Archives, MSS #2689.
 1940 *The Puyallup-Nisqually.* Columbia University Contributions to Anthropology 32.
 1941 The Coast Salish of Puget Sound. *American Anthropologist* 43: 197-211.

1949 *Indians of the Urban Northwest.*   Editor. Columbia University Contributions to Anthropology 36.

Snyder, Sally
1952-54 Typed Fieldnotes. Melville Jacobs Collection, Seattle: University of Washington Archives.
ms   Folktales of the Skagit. Copies at Lushootseed Research and University of Washington Archives.
1964 Skagit Society and Its Existential Basis: An Ethnofolkloristic Reconstruction. University of Washington: PhD Dissertation.
1975 Quest for the Sacred in Northern Puget Sound: An Interpretation of Potlatch. *Ethnology* 14 (2): 149-161.

Spier, Leslie
1935 The Prophet Dance of the Northwest and its Derivatives: The Source of the Ghost Dance. Mensha: General Series in Anthropology 1.

Stern, Bernhard
1934 The Lummi Indians of Northwest Washington. New York: Columbia University Contributions to Anthropology 17: 1-127.

Suttles, Wayne
1955 Katzie Ethnographic Notes, *Anthropology in British Columbia Memoir* # 2, Provincial Museum of British Columbia, Victoria.
1987 *Coast Salish Essays.* Seattle: University of Washington Press.

Underhill, Ruth.
1965 *Red Man's Religion* ~ Beliefs and Practices of the Indians North of Mexico. University of Chicago Press.

Vastokas, Joan, and Romas Vastokas
1973 *Sacred Art of the Algonkians* ~ A Study of the Peterborough Petroglyphs. Peterborough: Mansard Press.

Vance, Joseph A
1957 The Geology of the Sauk River area in the Northern Cascades of Washington. Seattle: UW PhD Dissertation.

Walkem, WW
1914 Stories of Early British Columbia. Vancouver.

Waterman, Thomas.
1930 The Paraphernalia of the Duwamish 'Spirit-Canoe' Ceremony. *Indian Notes* 7 (2): 129-148, 295-312, 535-561.

1973 Notes on the Ethnology of the Indians of Puget Sound. New York: Museum of the American Indian, Heye Foundation, *Indian Notes and Monographs*, Miscellaneous Series 59: 1-145.

Waterman, TT, and Geraldine Coffin
  1920 Types of Canoes on Puget Sound. New York: Museum of the American Indian, Heye Foundation, *Indian Notes and Monographs*, Miscellaneous Series 5: 1-43.

Waterman, TT, and Collaborators
  1921 Native Houses of Western North America. New York: Museum of the American Indian, Heye Foundation, *Indian Notes and Monographs*, Miscellaneous Series 11: 1-97.

Wike, Joyce
  1941 Modern Spirit Dancing of Northern Puget Sound. MA Thesis: University of Washington.
  1952 The Role of the Dead in Northwest Coast Culture. *Indian Tribes of Aboriginal America*: 97-103. Sol Tax, ed. Proceedings of the 29th International Congress of Americanists.

Wingert, Paul
  1949 *American Indian Sculpture* ~ A Study of the Northwest Coast. New York: JJ Augustin Publisher.

1

1855 Treaty War, 6, 52

A

Anderson, Charlie, 47
Arnett, Chris, 155

B

B to M, 1, 59 #24, 77 #37
Baby, 45, 75
Balliol College, 154
Barney Lake, 39, 57
Beacon Hill, BC, 89
Beecher Bay, BC, 90
bəloʔl, 43, 48
Bible, 76f, 82
Big Mission Creek, 8
Blaine, WA, 145
Boas, Franz, 72, 102, 112
Boundary Bay, 2, 105, 157
Breath, 21f, 45, 60, 72
Brentwood Bay, BC, 4, 88, 98, 105
Bruseth, Nels, 8, 41, 55

C

Campbell, Alice, 67
Canadian Arctic Expedition, 154
Canadian Expeditionary Force, 154
Captain Cook, 103
Cascades, 1, 8, 40, 54, 71, 86
čədəsqidəb, 1
Changers, 47, 71, 68, 86, 91
Chemainus, BC, 90, 92, 107
Chirouse, Fr Eugene, 52f
chisels, 106
clown ~ keenia, 139
coffins, 119, 133, 150
cohesion, 3, 6 13, 79, 112, 157
Columbia River, 3, 18, 44, 157
Comox, BC, 1, 88f, 112, 120f, 142
Concrete, WA, 31f, 67, 75, 85
Costanoans, 18

counters, 141
Cowichans, 1, 66, 84, 88, 92, 99, 104, 120f, 130, 142, 152f
Cowlitz Prairie, 3, 158
Creek Woman ~ Haida, 14

D

Dalles, WA, 34, 53
Dawn, 62
Day Creek, WA, 32, 40, 55
Decedence, 153 #123
dentalium, 111
Diablo Dam, 55
Diaper Boy, 49f, 75, 86
dice, 141
dicta, 8, 71f, 85f
dogs, 48, 56, 69, 93, 100, 159
dog, sun, 142
dog, woolly, 93, 109
Dorset complex, 154
Dugualla Bay, WA, 48, 68
dukʷibəł, 46, 54
Dungeness, WA, 51, 66, 84

E

eclipse, 50, 142
Eells, Rev Myron, 3, 158
epidemics, 6, 43, 58, 120

F

Fornsby, John, 44, 47, 51, 65 83
Fort Nisqually, 3, 51, 65, 83, 157

G

Galloway, Brent, 156
ghost, 22f, 44, 48, 53, 61f, 71, 73, 86, 133, 143, 150
Gibbs, George, 15f, 24f, 55, 65
Glacier Peak, 86
Glen Cove, 4, 158
Goliah, 43, 48, 52, 65, 68, 83, 85
Granny's Hill, 1

H

Halalt, BC, 4, 90
Hill-Tout, Charles, 72
Hockey, 140
House, 57, 112f, 154
Howard, Mary Carolyn, 178
Hudson's Bay Company, 3, 9, 82, 102, 158
Hwanam ~ 1st Man, 115

I

Ikpukhuak Inuit, 154
Indien, 1 #1
Iroquois, 84

J

Joe, Andrew Span, 43, 48, 69, 87

K

k̓waagʷaɬx̌ʷ grass, 71
Kane, Paul, 66, 84, 104
Kanim, Jerry, 44, 64
k̓ək̓ədəb 1st Man, 43, 67
kʷəskadəb, 43, 51, 65f, 75
kindred, nodal & stem, 80
Kitsap Peninsula, 6, 8, 157
Klengenberg, Patsy, 154
Knife, 46, 75, 86
Komiakin, BC, 130
Kwakiutls, 44, 66, 70, 88, 102, 119
Kwalahunzit ~ war lord, 119f
Kʷaskadub, 82f

L

Lake Chelan, 8, 53
Latasse, David, 4, 124
lehal game, 120, 140f
Lekwiltok, 66, 162
ləx̌albid, 43, 48, 51, 69, 75
Little Earths, 21, 59, 63f
log jam, 8, 30
loincloths, 109
Lone Tree Point, 48
ɬuqali Wolves, 44

M

masks ~ swaysway, 46, 139, 162
Masonics, 3
Matecom,~ King Philip, 87
Mayne Islanders, 92, 116, 120, 156
McLeod, Annie, 457
Meeker, Ezra, 3, 158
Milky Way, 23, 50, 142
Mill Bay, BC, 4, 88, 90
mind ~ shalli, 144
minmints kindred, 73
Minter Creek, 4, 158
Mosquitos, 62
mountain goat, 3, 6, 46, 58, 69, 74, 86, 95, 157, 162
Mukilteo, 65, 83

N

Nanaimo, BC, 4, 66, 88, 90, 100, 119, 146f
Neetlum, 66, 84
nettles, 7, 83, 96f, 105, 112, 147, 56
Newcombe, W.A, 105
nɬəʔkəpmxʷ ~ Thompsons, 54 See Steetaths
North Cascades, 86
Nusmatta, 73f

O

Oak Harbor, WA, 43, 68, 85
Old Bering Sea complex, 154
Orcas island, 7

P

paq̓ʷ, 57
Patricia Bay, BC, 4, 89
Penn Cove, WA, 68, 83
pətiyus, 52
Pierre, Peter, 4, 71f, 155
Pilling, Arnold, 18
pits, deer, 93
Point Roberts, WA, 72, 91, 99, 100, 121
ponchos, 109
Port Townsend, WA, 3, 96 #51, 158
Portage, WA, 37f, 46f, 54f, 75
potatoes, 6, 9, 54, 82, 108f, 131

Potlatch ~ Give-Away, 14, 51, 66, 74, 114, 136f

priest ~ *θiθa*, 93

Pull and Be Damned Road, 48, 69, 86

Q

qʷəłʔits ~ weir net, 70

Qomoqwa, 73

Quartermaster Harbor, 3, 83, 157

R

Rainbow Bridge, 45

ramages, 80

red ochre, 93, 101, 109, 125, 134f, 145f

Robe Boy, 47f, 69, 75, 86f

S

sadᶻəhəbixʷ slaver, 83

sakoblk̓əd 1ˢᵗ Son, 68

sakʷats grass, 93

Salish Sea, 1, 4, 162

salmon, 3, 6f, 16, 51, 70f, 81, 91f, 99, 128, 146f, 159

Saltspring Island, BC, 92, 128 #104

Sampson, Alfonso, 45

Sampson, Martin, 18, 25, 44, 46, 49, 52f, 57, 71, 75

Sapir, Edward, 154

sditləb ~ Sneatlum, 83

šəbəd ~ trawl net, 53, 70f

sept, 77f, 80f

sexual equality, 20

sgʷədiləč, 44, 46, 58, 75

sgʷigʷi invite 15

shadow, 72f, 143f

Shaker Church, 3, 20, 75, 86, 157

Shield, 44, 58, 68, 86

Skagit, 4f, 14, 24f, 43f, 83f, 157, 162

Skagits, Upper & Lower, 38, 43, 55f

Skʷanaylets ~ Fish Lord, 97f

slaves ~ skwaias, 116

sƛ̓əbibtəkəd, 52f

Slocums, 3, 20, 75, 82, 87

smətnaq ~ Redeeming, 59

Smith, Marian, 9, 70, 76, 79

Smokehouse, 76, 82

Sneatlam, 51, 65f, 84f; effigy 83

Sneatlum Point, 43, 67f, 83f

sniƛəb, 66 See Neetlum ~ Sneatlum

Snyder, Sally, 24f, 43f

Snyder, Warren, 15

sockeye, 11, 72, 91, 99f, 123, 135, 146, 159, 162

Sooke, BC, 88, 90, 101, 115, 121, 156

sorcery, 10 #12, 21, 134

souls, 9, 22, 45, 50, 55, 61f, 70f, 94, 119, 124, 133f, 142f

spəltədaq ~ Redeeming, 59 #24

spinner, 98

sqəlalitut, 11

Star Child, 24, 50

status, 9f, 16f, 44, 70, 81, 115f, 137, 148

Stefansson, Vilhjalmur, 154

Stellar's jay, 48

stitał, 54

Sullivan Flats, 43

Sullivan Slough, 44, 69, 86

Sumas Lake, BC, 95f #50

Swaal, 2 #2

Swadabsh, 43, 51, 68f, 75, 85

Swaneset, 72f

sx̱ʷalo ~ sgʷala, reef net, 70, 99, 145

T

Tahuya River, 8

tattooing, 73, 111f

Thomas, Jennie, 43

Thunderbird, 128

tiyułəbaxʷəd, 55

Tolt, WA, 21

tools, 9, 11, 46, 50, 61, 73, 106, 128, 133f

Transformers, 47, 78

Tulalip, WA, 4, 52

tumpline, 93

tuxʷiqədəb, 48, 69

V

Victoria, BC, 88, 90, 102f, 130, 162
vine maple, 46, 58

W

wapato, 6
Wealth power, 66f, 85
Westholme, BC ~ Halalt, 4, 93f, 133, 146f, 152
Whidbey Island, 3, 27, 43, 51f, 65, 83, 157
Wike, Joyce, 45, 76
Worm ~ slave woman, 116 #93

X

x̣aʔx̣a ~ x̱a'x̱a, 11, 71, 75, 78f
x̌ʷatsʔalʔal, ~ High House, 57
X-ray sight, 21

Y

ẏagʷałiẇ ~ ẏagʷało, 53
yarrow, 133

Please Help Eliminate Typo Gnomes

Jay Miller's books & E-books @ Amazon.com

ACCULTURATING AMELIA ~ Round Valley 1937 California
ALASKA EDGE ISLAND ~ Siberian Yupiks of St Lawrence Island
ALLIED MOUNDS ~ Touching the Earth, Modeling the World, Reaching the Sky
ANIMAL PEOPLE ADVENTURES ~ Native North American Tribal Stories
AT BAY ~ Cultures Converging through Southwest Washington   > 5
BALLARD BULWARK ~
CHACO ECHOES ~ Pervasive Keresan Priesthoods
CHACOKIA ~ Chaco, Cahokia, Cities & Ceremonies ~ Bundles & Blood Lines Centuries Ago
CHINOOK CONCERNS ~ Emma Millett Luscier, Isabella Bertrand, Verne Ray
CIRCLING FOUR CORNERS ~ Re-Viewing Native American Indiens   > 10
CROSSING ~ LINES: An Educational Memoir of Native North America
DEL-AWARE ~ Lenape Legacies
DELAWARE INTEGRITY ~ Rituals, Removals, Reforms by Lenape Indiens
DISCLAIMING TREATIES I ~ Puget Tribes 1927 Testimonies
DISCLAIMING TREATIES II ~ Puget Tribes 1927 Testimonies   > 15
ELDERS' DIALOG ~ Ed Davis & Vi Hilbert Discuss Native Puget Sound Language, Culture, & Heritage
EVERGREEN ETHNOGRAPHIES ~ Hoh, Chehalis, Suquamish, and Snoqualmi of Western Washington
FEDERAL FISH FILES ~ Swindell 1942 Treaty Rights Report
GEORGE GIBBS NORTHWEST ARRAY ~ Full Reports, Place Names, Word List, Artifact Names, and Guide
GRASSROOTS JANET ~ Advancing Salish and Traditional Cultures   > 20
HERMAN HAEBERLIN REGAINED ~ Anthropology and Artifacts of Puget Sound 1916-17
HERSTORY NW ~ Women Upholding Native Traditions
INDIEN ~ ETHNOGRAPHY: Cultural Traditions of Native North America
INDIEN ~ ETHNOLOGY: Grounded, Gendered, Meaningful Cultural Traditions
LESCHI IN LOVE ~ A Novel of Native Puget Sound > x2   > 25
MARCO MUCK MASKS ~ Frank Cushing on Marshes and Mounds
MINTER BAY ~ Land, Lore, Loss, and Lucre in the South Salish Sea
NATIVE MET HOW ~ Improving Posterity
OLD LUKH ~ A Novel of Native Puget Sound Daily Life, Places, and Stories
OVER THE FALLS ~ Sdoqwalbixw Survivance Surrounding Seattle   > 30
PACIFIC PLATEAU PORTRAYALS ~ People Places Ponderings
RAY'S ARRAY ~ Raymond D Fogelson's Works
RIGHTING NATIVE PLACES ~ Adventures in Northwest Geography
SAHAPTINS STUDIES ~ Columbia River Plateau, Cora Du Bois, Homer Garner Barnett, Gerald Raymond Desmond
SDOQWALBIXW   > 35
SOUND SALISH STRAITS ~ Central Salish Sea Cultures
UNSETTLING SEATTLE ~ Arresting Local Talent and Academic Illiteracy
WRITING WORDS IN WARY WORLDS ~ World Wide Improved Spellings of Native America Languages > 38

JONA Memoirs

RESCUES, RANTS, & RESEARCHES ~ A Re-View of Jay Miller's Writings on Northwest Indien Cultures ~ #9
TRIBAL TRIO of the Northwest Coast by Kenneth D Tollefson ~ #10
INTERWEAVING COAST SALISH CULTURAL SYSTEMS ~ Collected Works of Pamela Thorsen Amoss ~ #14

University of Nebraska Press

ANCESTRAL MOUNDS ~ Vitality and Volatility Crossing Native North America 2015
HONNE ~ The Spirit of the Chehalis 2015

190